A Guide to the
Project Management Body of Knowledge
(PMBOK® Guide)

an American National Standard
ANSI/PMI 99-001-2000

A Guide to the
Project Management Body of Knowledge
(PMBOK® Guide)

2000 Edition

Project Management Institute

Newtown Square, Pennsylvania USA

Library of Congress Cataloging-in-Publication Data

A guide to the project management body of knowledge (PMBOK® guide).--2000 ed.
       p.   cm.
   Includes bibliographical references and index.
   ISBN 1-880410-22-2 (alk. paper)--ISBN 1-880410-23-0 (pbk. : alk. paper)
   1. Industrial project management. I. Title: PMBOK® guide. II. Project Management
Institute.
HD69.P75 G845   2001
658.4'04—dc21   00-051727
                                                       CIP

ISBN: 1-880410-23-0 (paperback)
ISBN: 1-880410-22-2 (hardcover)
ISBN: 1-880410-25-7 (CD-ROM)

Published by: Project Management Institute, Inc.
              Four Campus Boulevard
              Newtown Square, Pennsylvania 19073-3299 USA
              Phone: 610-356-4600 or Visit our website: www.pmi.org
              E-mail: pmihq@pmi.org

PMI Publishing Division welcomes corrections and comments on its documents. In addition to comments directed to PMI about the substance of *A Guide to the Project Management Body of Knowledge*, please feel free to send comments on typographical, formatting, or other errors. Simply make a copy of the relevant page of the *PMBOK® Guide*, mark the error, and send it to: Book Editor, PMI Publishing, Four Campus Boulevard, Newtown Square, Pennsylvania 19073-3299 USA, phone: 610/356-4600, fax: 610/356-4647, e-mail: booked@pmi.org.

"PMI" and the PMI logo are service and trademarks registered in the United States and other nations; "PMP" and the PMP logo are certification marks registered in the United States and other nations; "PMBOK", "PM Network", and "PMI Today" are trademarks registered in the United States and other nations; and "Project Management Journal" and "Building professionalism in project management." are trademarks of the Project Management Institute, Inc.

PMI® books are available at special quantity discounts to use as premiums and sales promotions, or for use in corporate training programs, as well as other educational programs. For more information, please write to the Bookstore Administrator, PMI Publishing, Four Campus Boulevard, Newtown Square, Pennsylvania 19073-3299 USA. Or contact your local bookstore.

Printed in the United States of America. No part of this work may be reproduced or transmitted in any form or by any means, electronic, manual, photocopying, recording, or by any information storage and retrieval system, without prior written permission of the publisher.

The paper used in this book complies with the Permanent Paper Standard issued by the National Information Standards Organization (Z39.48—1984).

Printed and bound by Automated Graphic Systems, White Plains, Maryland, USA.

10   9   8   7   6   5   4   3   2

Contents

List of Figures

A Guide to the Project Management Body of Knowledge (PMBOK® Guide) 2000 Edition
©2000 Project Management Institute, Four Campus Boulevard, Newtown Square, PA 19073-3299 USA

Preface to the 2000 Edition

This document supersedes the Project Management Institute's (PMI®) *A Guide to the Project Management Body of Knowledge (PMBOK® Guide)*, published in 1996.

The scope of the project to update the 1996 publication was to:

■ Add new material reflecting the growth of the knowledge and practices in the field of project management by capturing those practices, tools, techniques, and other relevant items that have become generally accepted. (*Generally accepted* means being applicable to most projects most of the time and having widespread consensus about their value and usefulness.)

■ Add clarification to text and figures to make this document more beneficial to users.

■ Correct existing errors in the predecessor document.

To assist users of this document, who may be familiar with its predecessor, we have summarized the major differences here.

1. *Throughout the document, we clarified that projects manage to requirements, which emerge from needs, wants, and expectations.*

2. *We strengthened linkages to organizational strategy throughout the document.*

3. *We provided more emphasis on progressive elaboration in Section 1.2.3.*

4. *We acknowledged the role of the Project Office in Section 2.3.4.*

5. *We added references to project management involving developing economies, as well as social, economic, and environmental impacts, in Section 2.5.4.*

6. *We added expanded treatment of Earned Value Management in Chapter 4 (Project Integration Management), Chapter 7 (Project Cost Management), and Chapter 10 (Project Communications Management).*

7. *We rewrote Chapter 11 (Project Risk Management). The chapter now contains six processes instead of the previous four processes. The six processes are Risk Management Planning, Risk Identification, Qualitative Risk Analysis, Quantitative Risk Analysis, Risk Response Planning, and Risk Monitoring and Control.*

8. *We moved scope verification from an executing process to a controlling process.*

9. *We changed the name of Process 4.3 from Overall Change Control to Integrated Change Control to emphasize the importance of change control throughout the entirety of the project.*

10. *We added a chart that maps the thirty-nine Project Management processes against the five Project Management Process Groups and the nine Project Management Knowlege Areas in Figure 3-9.*

11. *We standardized terminology throughout the document from "supplier" to "seller."*

12. *We added several Tools and Techniques*:

■ *Chapter 4 (Project Integration Management)*
  ◆ *Earned Value Management (EVM)*
  ◆ *Preventive Action*

- *Chapter 5 (Project Scope Management)*
  - ◆ *Scope Statement Updates*
  - ◆ *Project Plan*
  - ◆ *Adjusted Baseline*
- *Chapter 6 (Project Time Management)*
  - ◆ *Quantitatively Based Durations*
  - ◆ *Reserve Time (contingency)*
  - ◆ *Coding Structure*
  - ◆ *Variance Analysis*
  - ◆ *Milestones*
  - ◆ *Activity Attributes*
  - ◆ *Computerized Tools*
- *Chapter 7 (Project Cost Management)*
  - ◆ *Estimating Publications*
  - ◆ *Earned Value Measurement*
- *Chapter 8 (Project Quality Management)*
  - ◆ *Cost of Quality*
- *Chapter 10 (Project Communications Management)*
  - ◆ *Project Reports*
  - ◆ *Project Presentations*
  - ◆ *Project Closure*
- *Chapter 11 (Project Risk Management— this chapter is rewritten)*

The body of knowledge of the project management profession continues to grow, and PMI intends to update the *PMBOK® Guide* on a periodic basis. Therefore, if you have any comments about this document or suggestions about how this document can be improved, please send them to:

PMI Project Management Standards Program
Project Management Institute
Four Campus Boulevard
Newtown Square, PA 19073-3299 USA
Phone: +610-356-4600
Fax: +610-356-4647
Email: pmihq@pmi.org
Internet: http://www.pmi.org

A Guide to the Project Management Body of Knowledge (PMBOK® Guide) 2000 Edition
©2000 Project Management Institute, Four Campus Boulevard, Newtown Square, PA 19073-3299 USA

SECTION I

THE PROJECT MANAGEMENT FRAMEWORK

Chapter 1

Introduction

The *Project Management Body of Knowledge* (PMBOK®) is an inclusive term that describes the sum of knowledge within the profession of project management. As with other professions such as law, medicine, and accounting, the body of knowledge rests with the practitioners and academics that apply and advance it. The full project management body of knowledge includes knowledge of proven traditional practices that are widely applied, as well as knowledge of innovative and advanced practices that have seen more limited use, and includes both published and unpublished material.

This chapter defines and explains several key terms and provides an overview of the rest of the document. It includes the following major sections:

1.1 Purpose of This Guide
1.2 What Is a Project?
1.3 What Is Project Management?
1.4 Relationship to Other Management Disciplines
1.5 Related Endeavors

1.1 PURPOSE OF THIS GUIDE

Project management is an emerging profession. The primary purpose of this document is to identify and describe that subset of the PMBOK® that is generally accepted. *Generally accepted* means that the knowledge and practices described are applicable to most projects most of the time, and that there is widespread consensus about their value and usefulness. Generally accepted does not mean that the knowledge and practices described are or should be applied uniformly on all projects; the project management team is always responsible for determining what is appropriate for any given project.

This document is also intended to provide a common lexicon within the profession and practice for talking and writing about project management. Project management is a relatively young profession, and while there is substantial commonality around what is done, there is relatively little commonality in the terms used.

This document provides a basic reference for anyone interested in the profession of project management. This includes, but is not limited to:

- Senior executives.
- Managers of project managers.
- Project managers and other project team members.
- Project customers and other project stakeholders.
- Functional managers with employees assigned to project teams.
- Educators teaching project management and related subjects.
- Consultants and other specialists in project management and related fields.
- Trainers developing project management educational programs.

As a basic reference, this document is neither comprehensive nor all inclusive. Appendix E discusses application area extensions while Appendix F lists sources of further information on project management.

This document is also used by the Project Management Institute as a basic reference about project management knowledge and practices for its professional development programs including:

- Certification of Project Management Professionals (PMP®).
- Accreditation of educational programs in project management.

1.2 WHAT IS A PROJECT?

Organizations perform work. Work generally involves either operations or projects, although the two may overlap. Operations and projects share many characteristics; for example, they are:

- Performed by people.
- Constrained by limited resources.
- Planned, executed, and controlled.

Projects are often implemented as a means of achieving an organization's strategic plan. Operations and projects differ primarily in that operations are ongoing and repetitive while projects are temporary and unique. A project can thus be defined in terms of its distinctive characteristics—*a project is a temporary endeavor undertaken to create a unique product or service. Temporary* means that every project has a definite beginning and a definite end. *Unique* means that the product or service is different in some distinguishing way from all other products or services. For many organizations, projects are a means to respond to those requests that cannot be addressed within the organization's normal operational limits.

Projects are undertaken at all levels of the organization. They may involve a single person or many thousands. Their duration ranges from a few weeks to more than five years. Projects may involve a single unit of one organization or may cross organizational boundaries, as in joint ventures and partnering. Projects are critical to the realization of the performing organization's business strategy because projects are a means by which strategy is implemented. Examples of projects include:

- Developing a new product or service.
- Effecting a change in structure, staffing, or style of an organization.
- Designing a new transportation vehicle.
- Developing or acquiring a new or modified information system.
- Constructing a building or facility.
- Building a water system for a community in a developing country.
- Running a campaign for political office.
- Implementing a new business procedure or process.

A Guide to the Project Management Body of Knowledge (PMBOK® Guide) 2000 Edition
©2000 Project Management Institute, Four Campus Boulevard, Newtown Square, PA 19073-3299 USA

1.2.1 Temporary

Temporary means that every project has a definite beginning and a definite end. The end is reached when the project's objectives have been achieved, or when it becomes clear that the project objectives will not or cannot be met, or the need for the project no longer exists and the project is terminated. Temporary does not necessarily mean short in duration; many projects last for several years. In every case, however, the duration of a project is finite; projects are not ongoing efforts.

In addition, temporary does not generally apply to the product or service created by the project. Projects may often have intended and unintended social, economic, and environmental impacts that far outlast the projects themselves. Most projects are undertaken to create a lasting result. For example, a project to erect a national monument will create a result expected to last centuries. A series of projects and/or complementary projects in parallel may be required to achieve a strategic objective.

The objectives of projects and operations are fundamentally different. The objective of a project is to attain the objective and close the project. The objective of an ongoing nonprojectized operation is normally to sustain the business. Projects are fundamentally different because the project ceases when its declared objectives have been attained, while nonproject undertakings adopt a new set of objectives and continue to work.

The temporary nature of projects may apply to other aspects of the endeavor as well:

- The opportunity or market window is usually temporary—most projects have a limited time frame in which to produce their product or service.
- The project team, as a team, seldom outlives the project—most projects are performed by a team created for the sole purpose of performing the project, and the team is disbanded when the project is complete.

1.2.2 Unique Product, Service, or Result

Projects involve doing something that has not been done before and which is, therefore, *unique*. A product or service may be unique even if the category to which it belongs is large. For example, many thousands of office buildings have been developed, but each individual facility is unique—different owner, different design, different location, different contractors, and so on. The presence of repetitive elements does not change the fundamental uniqueness of the project work. For example:

- A project to develop a new commercial airliner may require multiple prototypes.
- A project to bring a new drug to market may require thousands of doses of the drug to support clinical trials.
- A real estate development project may include hundreds of individual units.
- A development project (e.g., water and sanitation) may be implemented in five geographic areas.

1.2.3 Progressive Elaboration

Progressive elaboration is a characteristic of projects that integrates the concepts of temporary and unique. Because the product of each project is unique, the characteristics that distinguish the product or service must be progressively elaborated. *Progressively* means "proceeding in steps; continuing steadily by increments," while *elaborated* means "worked out with care and detail; developed thoroughly" (1). These distinguishing characteristics will be broadly defined early in the project, and will be made more explicit and detailed as the project team develops a better and more complete understanding of the product.

Progressive elaboration of product characteristics must be carefully coordinated with proper project scope definition, particularly if the project is performed under contract. When properly defined, the scope of the project—the work to be done—should remain constant even as the product characteristics are progressively elaborated. The relationship between product scope and project scope is discussed further in the introduction to Chapter 5.

The following two examples illustrate progressive elaboration in two different application areas.

Example 1. Development of a chemical processing plant begins with process engineering to define the characteristics of the process. These characteristics are used to design the major processing units. This information becomes the basis for engineering design, which defines both the detail plant layout and the mechanical characteristics of the process units and ancillary facilities. All of these result in design drawings that are elaborated to produce fabrication drawings (construction isometrics). During construction, interpretations and adaptations are made as needed and subject to proper approval. This further elaboration of the characteristics is captured by *as-built* drawings. During test and turnover, further elaboration of the characteristics is often made in the form of final operating adjustments.

Example 2. The product of an economic development project may initially be defined as: "Improve the quality of life of the lowest income residents of community X." As the project proceeds, the products may be described more specifically as, for example: "Provide access to food and water to 500 low income residents in community X." The next round of progressive elaboration might focus exclusively on increasing agriculture production and marketing, with provision of water deemed to be secondary priority to be initiated once the agriculture component is well under way.

1.3 WHAT IS PROJECT MANAGEMENT?

Project management is the application of knowledge, skills, tools, and techniques to project activities to meet project requirements. Project management is accomplished through the use of the processes such as: initiating, planning, executing, controlling, and closing. The project team manages the work of the projects, and the work typically involves:

■ Competing demands for: scope, time, cost, risk, and quality.
■ Stakeholders with differing needs and expectations.
■ Identified requirements.

It is important to note that many of the processes within project management are iterative in nature. This is in part due to the existence of and the necessity for progressive elaboration in a project throughout the project life cycle; i.e., the more you know about your project, the better you are able to manage it.

The term *project management* is sometimes used to describe an organizational approach to the management of ongoing operations. This approach, more properly called *management by projects*, treats many aspects of ongoing operations as projects to apply project management techniques to them. Although an

A Guide to the Project Management Body of Knowledge (PMBOK® Guide) 2000 Edition
©2000 Project Management Institute, Four Campus Boulevard, Newtown Square, PA 19073-3299 USA

understanding of project management is critical to an organization that is managing by projects, a detailed discussion of the approach itself is outside the scope of this document.

Knowledge about project management can be organized in many ways. This document has two major sections and twelve chapters, as described below.

1.3.1   The Project Management Framework

Section I, The Project Management Framework, provides a basic structure for understanding project management.

Chapter 1, **Introduction**, defines key terms and provides an overview of the rest of the document.

Chapter 2, **The Project Management Context**, describes the environment in which projects operate. The project management team must understand this broader context—managing the day-to-day activities of the project is necessary for success but not sufficient.

Chapter 3, **Project Management Processes**, describes a generalized view of how the various project management processes commonly interact. Understanding these interactions is essential to understanding the material presented in Chapters 4 through 12.

1.3.2   The Project Management Knowledge Areas

Section II, The Project Management Knowledge Areas, describes project management knowledge and practice in terms of their component processes. These processes have been organized into nine knowledge areas, as described below and as illustrated in **Figure 1-1**.

Chapter 4, **Project Integration Management**, describes the processes required to ensure that the various elements of the project are properly coordinated. It consists of project plan development, project plan execution, and integrated change control.

Chapter 5, **Project Scope Management**, describes the processes required to ensure that the project includes all the work required, and only the work required, to complete the project successfully. It consists of initiation, scope planning, scope definition, scope verification, and scope change control.

Chapter 6, **Project Time Management**, describes the processes required to ensure timely completion of the project. It consists of activity definition, activity sequencing, activity duration estimating, schedule development, and schedule control.

Chapter 7, **Project Cost Management**, describes the processes required to ensure that the project is completed within the approved budget. It consists of resource planning, cost estimating, cost budgeting, and cost control.

Chapter 8, **Project Quality Management**, describes the processes required to ensure that the project will satisfy the needs for which it was undertaken. It consists of quality planning, quality assurance, and quality control.

Chapter 9, **Project Human Resource Management**, describes the processes required to make the most effective use of the people involved with the project. It consists of organizational planning, staff acquisition, and team development.

Chapter 10, **Project Communications Management**, describes the processes required to ensure timely and appropriate generation, collection, dissemination,

Figure 1–1 | 1.4

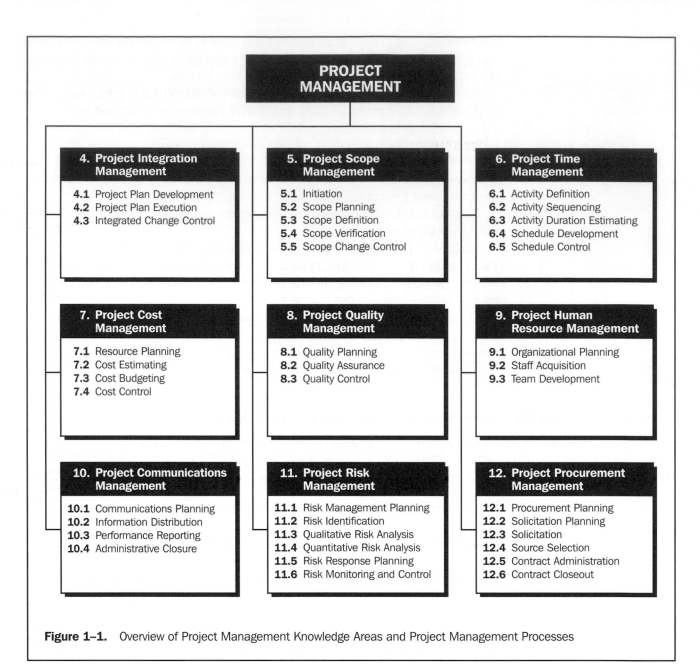

Figure 1–1. Overview of Project Management Knowledge Areas and Project Management Processes

storage, and ultimate disposition of project information. It consists of communications planning, information distribution, performance reporting, and administrative closure.

Chapter 11, **Project Risk Management**, describes the processes concerned with identifying, analyzing, and responding to project risk. It consists of risk management planning, risk identification, qualitative risk analysis, quantitative risk analysis, risk response planning, and risk monitoring and control.

Chapter 12, **Project Procurement Management**, describes the processes required to acquire goods and services from outside the performing organization. It consists of procurement planning, solicitation planning, solicitation, source selection, contract administration, and contract closeout.

A Guide to the Project Management Body of Knowledge (PMBOK® Guide) 2000 Edition
©2000 Project Management Institute, Four Campus Boulevard, Newtown Square, PA 19073-3299 USA

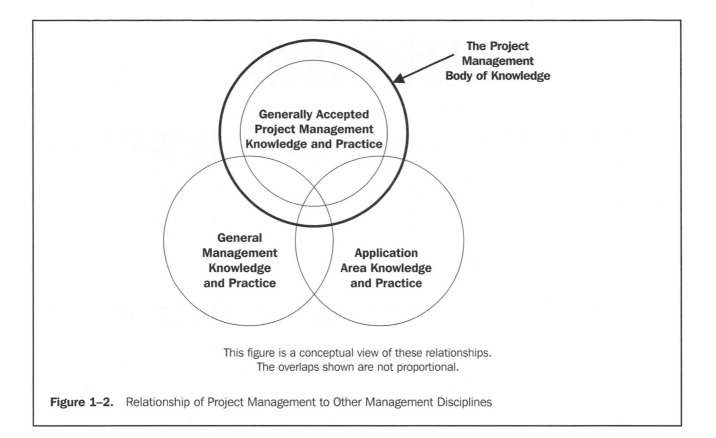

This figure is a conceptual view of these relationships.
The overlaps shown are not proportional.

Figure 1–2. Relationship of Project Management to Other Management Disciplines

1.4 RELATIONSHIP TO OTHER MANAGEMENT DISCIPLINES

Much of the knowledge needed to manage projects is unique to project management (e.g., critical path analysis and work breakdown structures). However, the PMBOK® does overlap other management disciplines, as illustrated in **Figure 1-2**.

General management encompasses planning, organizing, staffing, executing, and controlling the operations of an ongoing enterprise. General management also includes supporting disciplines such as law, strategic planning, logistics, and human resources management. The PMBOK® overlaps or modifies general management in many areas—organizational behavior, financial forecasting, and planning techniques, to name just a few. Section 2.4 provides a more detailed discussion of general management.

Application areas are categories of projects that have common elements significant in such projects, but are not needed or present in all projects. Application areas are usually defined in terms of:

- Functional departments and supporting disciplines, such as legal, production and inventory management, marketing, logistics and personnel.
- Technical elements, such as software development, pharmaceuticals, water and sanitation engineering, or construction engineering.
- Management specializations, such as government contracting, community development, or new product development.
- Industry groups, such as automotive, chemicals, agriculture, or financial services.
  Appendix E includes a more detailed discussion of project management application areas.

1.5 RELATED ENDEAVORS

Certain types of endeavors are closely related to projects. There is often a hierarchy of strategic plan, program, project, and subproject, in which a program consisting of several associated projects will contribute to the achievement of a strategic plan. These related undertakings are described below.

Programs. A *program* is a group of projects managed in a coordinated way to obtain benefits not available from managing them individually (2). Many programs also include elements of ongoing operations. For example:

■ The "XYZ airplane program" includes both the project or projects to design and develop the aircraft, as well as the ongoing manufacturing and support of that craft in the field.

■ Many electronics firms have *program managers* who are responsible for both individual product releases (projects) and the coordination of multiple releases over time (an ongoing operation).

Programs may also involve a series of repetitive or cyclical undertakings; for example:

■ Utilities often speak of an annual "construction program," a regular, ongoing operation that involves many projects.

■ Many nonprofit organizations have a "fundraising program," an ongoing effort to obtain financial support that often involves a series of discrete projects, such as a membership drive or an auction.

■ Publishing a newspaper or magazine is also a program—the periodical itself is an ongoing effort, but each individual issue is a project.

In some application areas, program management and project management are treated as synonyms; in others, project management is a subset of program management. This diversity of meaning makes it imperative that any discussion of *program* management versus *project* management be preceded by agreement on a clear and consistent definition of each term.

Subprojects. Projects are frequently divided into more manageable components or subprojects. *Subprojects* are often contracted to an external enterprise or to another functional unit in the performing organization. Examples include:

■ Subprojects based on the project process, such as a single phase.

■ Subprojects according to human resource skill requirements, such as the installation of plumbing or electrical fixtures on a construction project.

■ Subprojects involving technology, such as automated testing of computer programs on a software development project.

Subprojects are typically referred to as projects and managed as such.

Project Portfolio Management. Project portfolio management refers to the selection and support of projects or program investments. These investments in projects and programs are guided by the organization's strategic plan and available resources.

A Guide to the Project Management Body of Knowledge (PMBOK® Guide) 2000 Edition
©2000 Project Management Institute, Four Campus Boulevard, Newtown Square, PA 19073-3299 USA

Chapter 2

The Project Management Context

Projects and project management operate in an environment broader than that of the project itself. The project management team must understand this broader context—managing the day-to-day activities of the project is necessary for success but not sufficient. This chapter describes key aspects of the project management context not covered elsewhere in this document. The topics included here are:

2.1 Project Phases and the Project Life Cycle
2.2 Project Stakeholders
2.3 Organizational Influences
2.4 Key General Management Skills
2.5 Social-Economic-Environmental Influences

2.1 PROJECT PHASES AND THE PROJECT LIFE CYCLE

Because projects are unique undertakings, they involve a degree of uncertainty. Organizations performing projects will usually divide each project into several *project phases* to improve management control and provide for links to the ongoing operations of the performing organization. Collectively, the project phases are known as the *project life cycle*.

2.1.1 Characteristics of Project Phases

Each project phase is marked by completion of one or more deliverables. A *deliverable* is a tangible, verifiable work product such as a feasibility study, a detail design, or a working prototype. The deliverables, and hence the phases, are part of a generally sequential logic designed to ensure proper definition of the product of the project.

The conclusion of a project phase is generally marked by a review of both key deliverables and project performance to date, to a) determine if the project should continue into its next phase and b) detect and correct errors cost effectively. These phase-end reviews are often called *phase exits*, *stage gates*, or *kill points*.

Each project phase normally includes a set of defined deliverables designed to establish the desired level of management control. The majority of these items are related to the primary phase deliverable, and the phases typically take their names from these items: requirements, design, build, test, startup, turnover, and others, as appropriate. Several representative project life cycles are described in Section 2.1.3.

2.1.2 Characteristics of the Project Life Cycle

The project life cycle serves to define the beginning and the end of a project. For example, when an organization identifies an opportunity to which it would like to respond, it will often authorize a needs assessment and/or a feasibility study to decide if it should undertake a project. The project life-cycle definition will determine whether the feasibility study is treated as the first project phase or as a separate, standalone project.

The project life-cycle definition will also determine which transitional actions at the beginning and the end of the project are included and which are not. In this manner, the project life-cycle definition can be used to link the project to the ongoing operations of the performing organization.

The phase sequence defined by most project life cycles generally involves some form of technology transfer or handoff such as requirements to design, construction to operations, or design to manufacturing. Deliverables from the preceding phase are usually approved before work starts on the next phase. However, a subsequent phase is sometimes begun prior to approval of the previous phase deliverables when the risks involved are deemed acceptable. This practice of overlapping phases is often called *fast tracking*.

Project life cycles generally define:
- What technical work should be done in each phase (e.g., is the work of the architect part of the definition phase or part of the execution phase?).
- Who should be involved in each phase (e.g., implementers who need to be involved with requirements and design).

Project life-cycle descriptions may be very general or very detailed. Highly detailed descriptions may have numerous forms, charts, and checklists to provide structure and consistency. Such detailed approaches are often called *project management methodologies*.

Most project life-cycle descriptions share a number of common characteristics:
- Cost and staffing levels are low at the start, higher toward the end, and drop rapidly as the project draws to a conclusion. This pattern is illustrated in **Figure 2-1**.
- The probability of successfully completing the project is lowest, and hence risk and uncertainty are highest, at the start of the project. The probability of successful completion generally gets progressively higher as the project continues.
- The ability of the stakeholders to influence the final characteristics of the project's product and the final cost of the project is highest at the start and gets progressively lower as the project continues. A major contributor to this phenomenon is that the cost of changes and error correction generally increases as the project continues.

Care should be taken to distinguish the *project* life cycle from the *product* life cycle. For example, a project undertaken to bring a new desktop computer to market is but one phase or stage of the product life cycle.

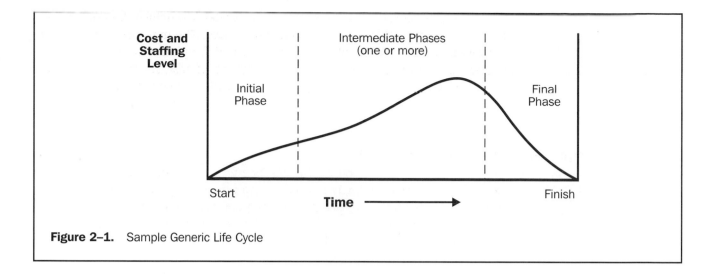

Figure 2–1. Sample Generic Life Cycle

Although many project life cycles have similar phase names with similar deliverables required, few are identical. Most have four or five phases, but some have nine or more. Even within a single application area, there can be significant variations—one organization's software development life cycle may have a single design phase while another's has separate phases for functional and detail design.

Subprojects within projects may also have distinct project life cycles. For example, an architectural firm hired to design a new office building is first involved in the owner's definition phase when doing the design, and in the owner's implementation phase when supporting the construction effort. The architect's design project, however, will have its own series of phases from conceptual development through definition and implementation to closure. The architect may even treat designing the facility and supporting the construction as separate projects with their own distinct phases.

2.1.3 Representative Project Life Cycles

The following project life cycles have been chosen to illustrate the diversity of approaches in use. The examples shown are typical; they are neither recommended nor preferred. In each case, the phase names and major deliverables are those described by the author for each of the figures.

Defense acquisition. The United States Department of Defense Instruction 5000.2 in Final Coordination Draft, April 2000, describes a series of acquisition milestones and phases as illustrated in **Figure 2-2**.

■ Concept and technology development—paper studies of alternative concepts for meeting a mission need; development of subsystems/components and concept/technology demonstration of new system concepts. Ends with selection of a system architecture and a mature technology to be used.

■ System development and demonstration—system integration; risk reduction; demonstration of engineering development models; development and early operational test and evaluation. Ends with system demonstration in an operational environment.

■ Production and deployment—low rate initial production (LRIP); complete development of manufacturing capability; phase overlaps with ongoing operations and support.

Figure 2–2 | Figure 2–3

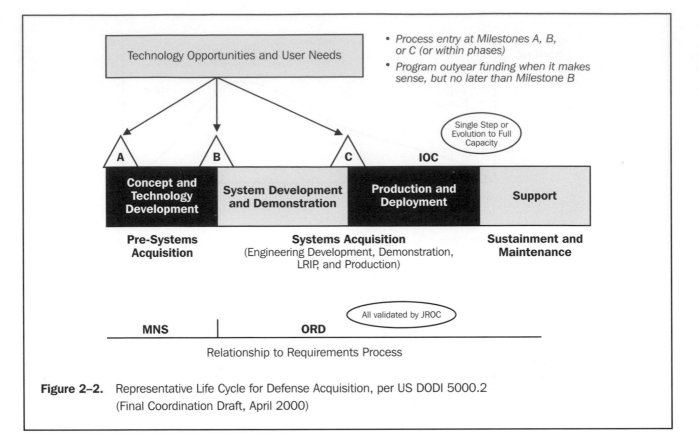

Figure 2–2. Representative Life Cycle for Defense Acquisition, per US DODI 5000.2 (Final Coordination Draft, April 2000)

■ Support—this phase is part of the *product* life cycle, but is really ongoing management. Various *projects* may be conducted during this phase to improve capability, correct defects, etc.

Construction. Adapted from Morris (1), describes a construction project life cycle, as illustrated in **Figure 2-3**.

■ Feasibility—project formulation, feasibility studies, and strategy design and approval. A go/no-go decision is made at the end of this phase.

■ Planning and design—base design, cost and schedule, contract terms and conditions, and detailed planning. Major contracts are let at the end of this phase.

■ Construction—manufacturing, delivery, civil works, installation, and testing. The facility is substantially complete at the end of this phase.

■ Turnover and startup—final testing and maintenance. The facility is in full operation at the end of this phase.

Pharmaceuticals. Murphy (2) describes a project life cycle for pharmaceutical new product development in the United States, as illustrated in **Figure 2-4**.

■ Discovery and screening—includes basic and applied research to identify candidates for preclinical testing.

■ Preclinical development—includes laboratory and animal testing to determine safety and efficacy, as well as preparation and filing of an Investigational New Drug (IND) application.

■ Registration(s) workup—includes Clinical Phase I, II, and III tests, as well as preparation and filing of a New Drug Application (NDA).

■ Postsubmission activity—includes additional work as required to support Food and Drug Administration review of the NDA.

A Guide to the Project Management Body of Knowledge (PMBOK® Guide) 2000 Edition
©2000 Project Management Institute, Four Campus Boulevard, Newtown Square, PA 19073-3299 USA

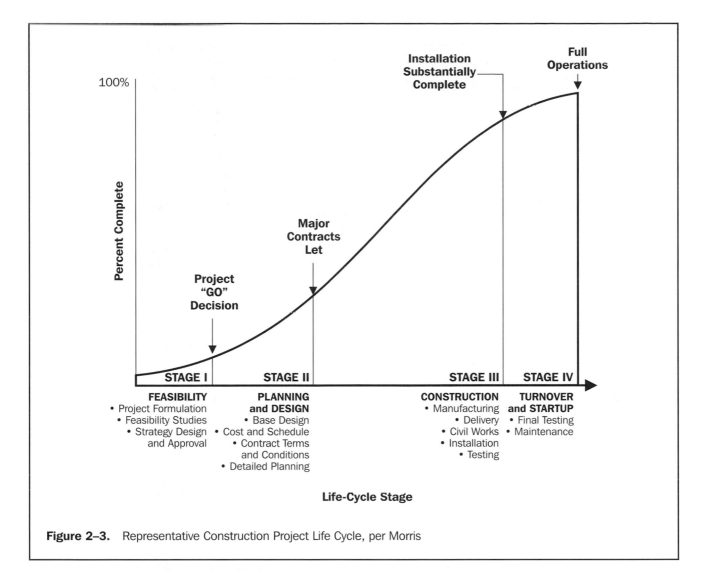

Figure 2–3. Representative Construction Project Life Cycle, per Morris

Software development. There are a number of software life-cycle models in use such as the waterfall model. Muench, et al. (3) describe a spiral model for software development with four cycles and four quadrants, as illustrated in **Figure 2-5**.

- Proof-of-concept cycle—capture business requirements, define goals for proof of concept, produce conceptual system design and logic design, and construct the proof of concept, produce acceptance test plans, conduct risk analysis, and make recommendations.
- First-build cycle—derive system requirements, define goals for first build, produce logical system design, design and construct the first build, produce system test plans, evaluate the first build, and make recommendations.
- Second-build cycle—derive subsystem requirements, define goals for second build, produce physical design, construct the second build, produce subsystem test plans, evaluate the second build, and make recommendations.
- Final cycle—complete unit requirements and final design, construct final build, and perform unit, subsystem, system, and acceptance tests.

Figure 2–4 | Figure 2–5

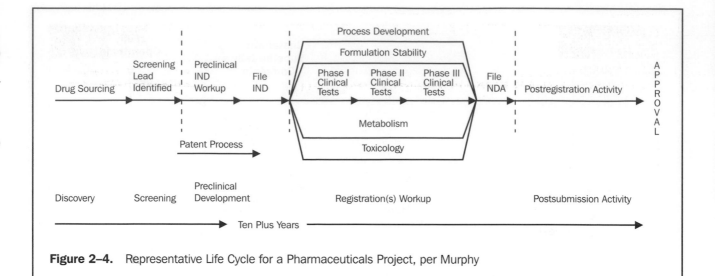

Figure 2–4. Representative Life Cycle for a Pharmaceuticals Project, per Murphy

2.2 PROJECT STAKEHOLDERS

Project stakeholders are individuals and organizations that are actively involved in the project, or whose interests may be positively or negatively affected as a result of project execution or project completion; they may also exert influence over the project and its results. The project management team must identify the stakeholders, determine their requirements, and then manage and influence those requirements to ensure a successful project. Stakeholder identification is often especially difficult. For example, is an assembly-line worker whose future employment depends on the outcome of a new product-design project a stakeholder?

Key stakeholders on every project include:

■ Project manager—the individual responsible for managing the project.

■ Customer—the individual or organization that will use the project's product. There may be multiple layers of customers. For example, the customers for a new pharmaceutical product may include the doctors who prescribe it, the patients who take it, and the insurers who pay for it. In some application areas, *customer* and *user* are synonymous, while in others customer refers to the entity purchasing the project's results and users are those who will directly use the project's product.

■ Performing organization—the enterprise whose employees are most directly involved in doing the work of the project.

■ Project team members—the group that is performing the work of the project.

■ Sponsor—the individual or group within or external to the performing organization that provides the financial resources, in cash or in kind, for the project.

In addition to these, there are many different names and categories of project stakeholders—internal and external, owners and funders, sellers and contractors, team members and their families, government agencies and media outlets, individual citizens, temporary or permanent lobbying organizations, and society at large. The naming or grouping of stakeholders is primarily an aid to identifying which individuals and organizations view themselves as stakeholders. Stakeholder roles and responsibilities may overlap, as when an engineering firm provides financing for a plant that it is designing.

A Guide to the Project Management Body of Knowledge (PMBOK® Guide) 2000 Edition

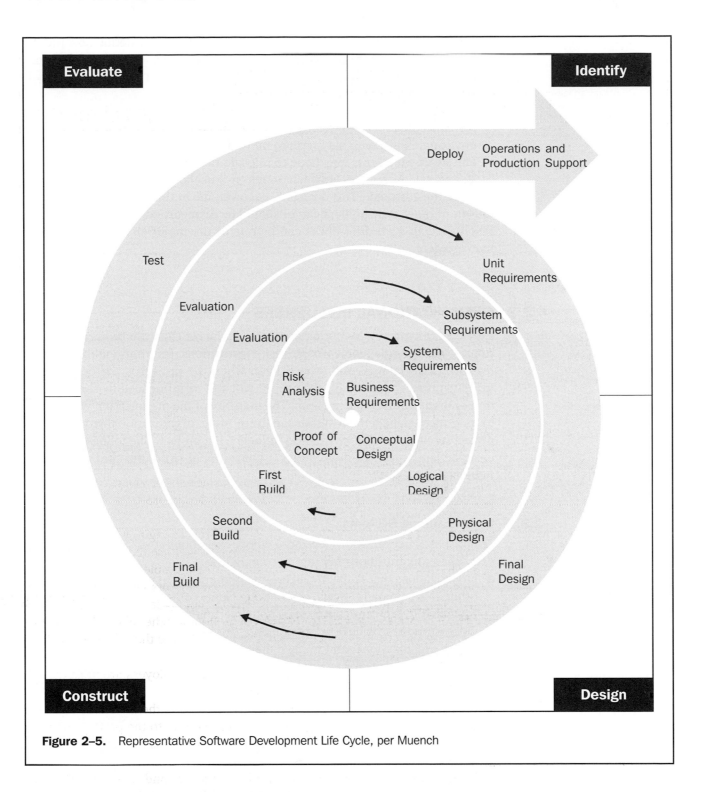

Figure 2–5. Representative Software Development Life Cycle, per Muench

Managing stakeholder expectations may be difficult because stakeholders often have very different objectives that may come into conflict. For example:

■ The manager of a department that has requested a new management information system may desire low cost, the system architect may emphasize technical excellence, and the programming contractor may be most interested in maximizing its profit.

- The vice president of research at an electronics firm may define new product success as state-of-the-art technology, the vice president of manufacturing may define it as world-class practices, and the vice president of marketing may be primarily concerned with the number of new features.
- The owner of a real estate development project may be focused on timely performance, the local governing body may desire to maximize tax revenue, an environmental group may wish to minimize adverse environmental impacts, and nearby residents may hope to relocate the project.

In general, differences between or among stakeholders should be resolved in favor of the customer. This does not, however, mean that the needs and expectations of other stakeholders can or should be disregarded. Finding appropriate resolutions to such differences can be one of the major challenges of project management.

2.3 ORGANIZATIONAL INFLUENCES

Projects are typically part of an organization larger than the project—corporations, government agencies, health-care institutions, international bodies, professional associations, and others. Even when the project is the organization (joint ventures, partnering), the project will still be influenced by the organization or organizations that set it up. The maturity of the organization with respect to its project management systems, culture, style, organizational structure, and project management office can also influence the project. The following sections describe key aspects of these larger organizational structures that are likely to influence the project.

2.3.1 Organizational Systems

Project-based organizations are those whose operations consist primarily of projects. These organizations fall into two categories:

- Organizations that derive their revenue primarily from performing projects for others—architectural firms, engineering firms, consultants, construction contractors, government contractors, nongovernmental organizations, etc.
- Organizations that have adopted *management by projects* (see Section 1.3).

These organizations tend to have management systems in place to facilitate project management. For example, their financial systems are often specifically designed for accounting, tracking, and reporting on multiple simultaneous projects.

Nonproject-based organizations often lack management systems designed to support project needs efficiently and effectively. The absence of project-oriented systems usually makes project management more difficult. In some cases, nonproject-based organizations will have departments or other subunits that operate as project-based organizations with systems to match.

The project management team should be acutely aware of how the organization's systems affect the project. For example, if the organization rewards its functional managers for charging staff time to projects, then the project management team may need to implement controls to ensure that assigned staff members are being used effectively on the project.

Organization Structure / Project Characteristics	Functional	Matrix			Projectized
		Weak Matrix	Balanced Matrix	Strong Matrix	
Project Manager's Authority	Little or None	Limited	Low to Moderate	Moderate to High	High to Almost Total
Percent of Performing Organization's Personnel Assigned Full Time to Project Work	Virtually None	0–25%	15–60%	50–95%	85–100%
Project Manager's Role	Part-time	Part-time	Full-time	Full-time	Full-time
Common Titles for Project Manager's Role	Project Coordinator/ Project Leader	Project Coordinator/ Project Leader	Project Manager/ Project Officer	Project Manager/ Program Manager	Project Manager/ Program Manager
Project Management Administrative Staff	Part-time	Part-time	Part-time	Full-time	Full-time

Figure 2–6. Organizational Structure Influences on Projects

2.3.2 Organizational Cultures and Styles

Most organizations have developed unique and describable cultures. These cultures are reflected in their shared values, norms, beliefs, and expectations; in their policies and procedures; in their view of authority relationships; and in numerous other factors. Organizational cultures often have a direct influence on the project. For example:

- A team proposing an unusual or high-risk approach is more likely to secure approval in an aggressive or entrepreneurial organization.
- A project manager with a highly participative style is apt to encounter problems in a rigidly hierarchical organization, while a project manager with an authoritarian style will be equally challenged in a participative organization.

2.3.3 Organizational Structure

The structure of the performing organization often constrains the availability of or terms under which resources become available to the project. Organizational structures can be characterized as spanning a spectrum from *functional* to *projectized*, with a variety of matrix structures in between. **Figure 2-6** shows key project-related characteristics of the major types of enterprise organizational structures. Project organization is discussed in Section 9.1, Organizational Planning.

The classic *functional organization*, shown in **Figure 2-7**, is a hierarchy where each employee has one clear superior. Staff members are grouped by specialty, such as production, marketing, engineering, and accounting at the top level, with engineering further subdivided into functional organizations that support the business of the larger organization (e.g., mechanical and electrical). Functional organizations still have projects, but the perceived scope of the project is limited to the boundaries of the function: the engineering department in a functional organization will do its work independent of the manufacturing or marketing departments.

Figure 2–7 | 2.4

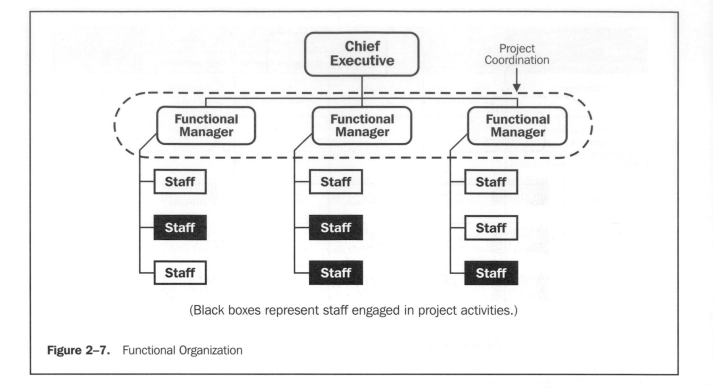

(Black boxes represent staff engaged in project activities.)

Figure 2–7. Functional Organization

For example, when a new product development is undertaken in a purely functional organization, the design phase is often called a *design project* and includes only engineering department staff. If questions about manufacturing arise, they are passed up the hierarchy to the department head, who consults with the head of the manufacturing department. The engineering department head then passes the answer back down the hierarchy to the engineering project manager.

At the opposite end of the spectrum is the *projectized organization*, shown in **Figure 2-8**. In a projectized organization, team members are often collocated. Most of the organization's resources are involved in project work, and project managers have a great deal of independence and authority. Projectized organizations often have organizational units called departments, but these groups either report directly to the project manager or provide support services to the various projects.

Matrix organizations, as shown in **Figures 2-9** through **2-11**, are a blend of functional and projectized characteristics. Weak matrices maintain many of the characteristics of a functional organization, and the project manager role is more that of a coordinator or expediter than that of a manager. In similar fashion, strong matrices have many of the characteristics of the projectized organization—full-time project managers with considerable authority and full-time project administrative staff.

Most modern organizations involve all these structures at various levels, as shown in **Figure 2-12**. For example, even a fundamentally functional organization may create a special project team to handle a critical project. Such a team may have many of the characteristics of a project in a projectized organization. The team may include full-time staff from different functional departments, it may develop its own set of operating procedures, and it may operate outside the standard, formalized reporting structure.

A Guide to the Project Management Body of Knowledge (PMBOK® Guide) 2000 Edition
©2000 Project Management Institute, Four Campus Boulevard, Newtown Square, PA 19073-3299 USA

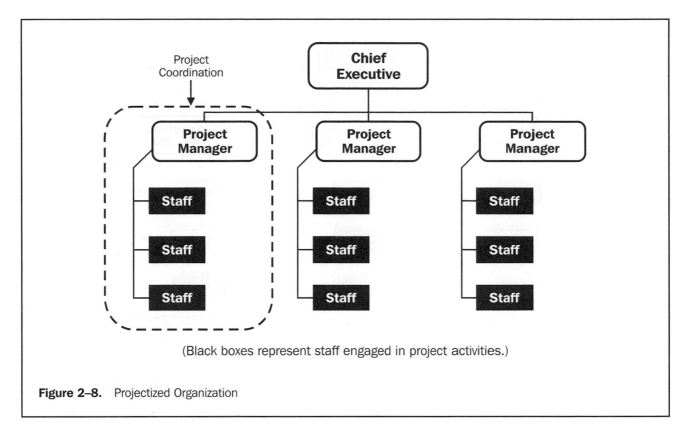

(Black boxes represent staff engaged in project activities.)

Figure 2–8. Projectized Organization

2.3.4 Project Office

There is a range of uses for what constitutes a project office. A project office may operate on a continuum from providing support functions to project managers in the form of training, software, templates, etc. to actually being responsible for the results of the project.

2.4 KEY GENERAL MANAGEMENT SKILLS

General management is a broad subject dealing with every aspect of managing an ongoing enterprise. Among other topics, it includes:

■ Finance and accounting, sales and marketing, research and development, and manufacturing and distribution.

■ Strategic planning, tactical planning, and operational planning.

■ Organizational structures, organizational behavior, personnel administration, compensation, benefits, and career paths.

■ Managing work relationships through motivation, delegation, supervision, team building, conflict management, and other techniques.

■ Managing oneself through personal time management, stress management, and other techniques.

General management skills provide much of the foundation for building project management skills. They are often essential for the project manager. On any given project, skill in any number of general management areas may be required. This section describes key general management skills that are *highly likely to affect most projects* and that are not covered elsewhere in this document.

Figure 2–9 | Figure 2–12

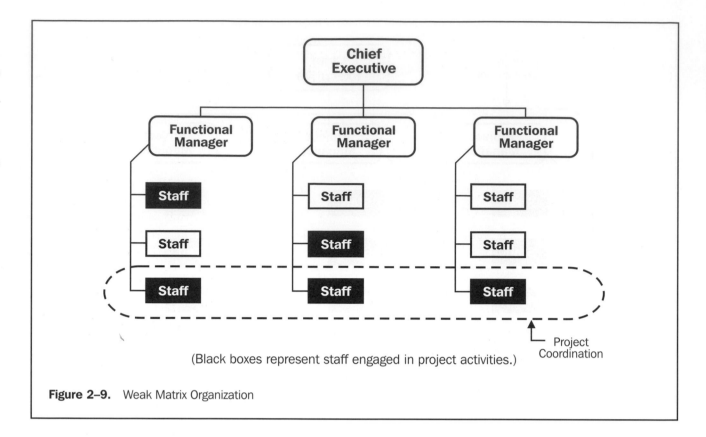

(Black boxes represent staff engaged in project activities.)

Figure 2–9. Weak Matrix Organization

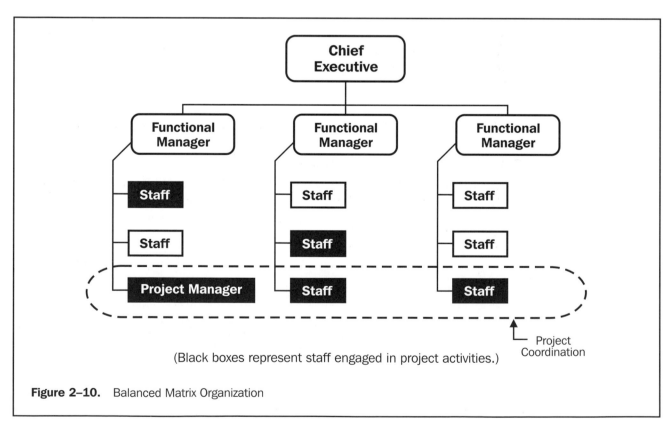

(Black boxes represent staff engaged in project activities.)

Figure 2–10. Balanced Matrix Organization

A Guide to the Project Management Body of Knowledge (PMBOK® Guide) 2000 Edition
©2000 Project Management Institute, Four Campus Boulevard, Newtown Square, PA 19073-3299 USA

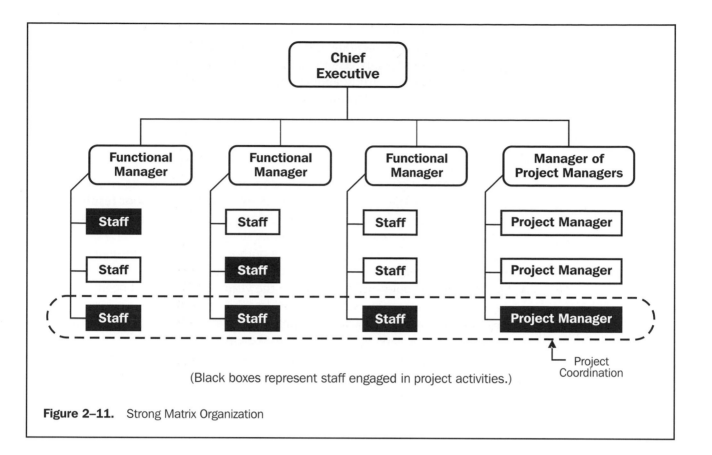

(Black boxes represent staff engaged in project activities.)

Figure 2–11. Strong Matrix Organization

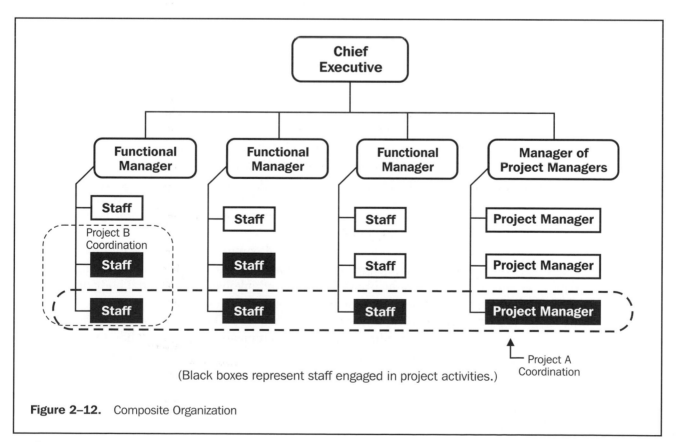

(Black boxes represent staff engaged in project activities.)

Figure 2–12. Composite Organization

These skills are well documented in the general management literature, and their application is fundamentally the same on a project.

There are also many general management skills that are relevant only on certain projects or in certain application areas. For example, team member safety is critical on virtually all construction projects and of little concern on most software development projects.

2.4.1 Leading

Kotter (4) distinguishes between *leading* and *managing* while emphasizing the need for both: one without the other is likely to produce poor results. He says that managing is primarily concerned with "consistently producing key results expected by stakeholders," while leading involves:

- Establishing direction—developing both a vision of the future and strategies for producing the changes needed to achieve that vision.
- Aligning people—communicating the vision by words and deeds to all those whose cooperation may be needed to achieve the vision.
- Motivating and inspiring—helping people energize themselves to overcome political, bureaucratic, and resource barriers to change.

On a project, particularly a larger project, the project manager is generally expected to be the project's leader as well. Leadership is not, however, limited to the project manager: it may be demonstrated by many different individuals at many different times during the project. Leadership must be demonstrated at all levels of the project (project leadership, technical leadership, and team leadership).

2.4.2 Communicating

Communicating involves the exchange of information. The sender is responsible for making the information clear, unambiguous, and complete so that the receiver can receive it correctly. The receiver is responsible for making sure that the information is received in its entirety and understood correctly. Communicating has many dimensions:

- Written and oral, listening and speaking.
- Internal (within the project) and external (to the customer, the media, the public, etc.).
- Formal (reports, briefings, etc.) and informal (memos, ad hoc conversations, etc.).
- Vertical (up and down the organization) and horizontal (with peers and partner organization).

The general management skill of communicating is related to, but not the same as, Project Communications Management (described in Chapter 10). Communicating is the broader subject and involves a substantial body of knowledge that is not unique to the project context, for example:

- Sender-receiver models—feedback loops, barriers to communications, etc.
- Choice of media—when to communicate in writing, when to communicate orally, when to write an informal memo, when to write a formal report, etc.

A Guide to the Project Management Body of Knowledge (PMBOK® Guide) 2000 Edition
©2000 Project Management Institute, Four Campus Boulevard, Newtown Square, PA 19073-3299 USA

■ Writing style—active versus passive voice, sentence structure, word choice, etc.
■ Presentation techniques—body language, design of visual aids, etc.
■ Meeting management techniques—preparing an agenda, dealing with conflict, etc.

Project Communications Management is the application of these broad concepts to the specific needs of a project—for example, deciding how, when, in what form, and to whom to report project performance.

2.4.3 Negotiating

Negotiating involves conferring with others to come to terms with them or reach an agreement. Agreements may be negotiated directly or with assistance; mediation and arbitration are two types of assisted negotiation.

Negotiations occur around many issues, at many times, and at many levels of the project. During the course of a typical project, project staff is likely to negotiate for any or all of the following:

■ Scope, cost, and schedule objectives.
■ Changes to scope, cost, or schedule.
■ Contract terms and conditions.
■ Assignments.
■ Resources.

2.4.4 Problem Solving

Problem solving involves a combination of problem definition and decision-making.

Problem definition requires distinguishing between causes and symptoms. Problems may be internal (a key employee is reassigned to another project) or external (a permit required to begin work is delayed). Problems may be technical (differences of opinion about the best way to design a product), managerial (a functional group is not producing according to plan), or interpersonal (personality or style clashes).

Decision-making includes analyzing the problem to identify viable solutions, and then making a choice from among them. Decisions can be made or obtained (from the customer, from the team, or from a functional manager). Once made, decisions must be implemented. Decisions also have a time element to them—the "right" decision may not be the "best" decision if it is made too early or too late.

2.4.5 Influencing the Organization

Influencing the organization involves the ability to "get things done." It requires an understanding of both the formal and informal structures of all the organizations involved—the performing organization, customer, partners, contractors, and numerous others, as appropriate. Influencing the organization also requires an understanding of the mechanics of power and politics.

Both power and politics are used here in their positive senses. Pfeffer (5) defines power as "the potential ability to influence behavior, to change the course of events, to overcome resistance, and to get people to do things that they would not otherwise do." In similar fashion, Eccles et al. (6) say that "politics is about getting collective action from a group of people who may have quite different interests. It is about being willing to use conflict and disorder creatively. The negative sense, of course, derives from the fact that attempts to reconcile these interests result in power struggles and organizational games that can sometimes take on a thoroughly unproductive life of their own."

2.5 SOCIAL-ECONOMIC-ENVIRONMENTAL INFLUENCES

Like general management, *socioeconomic influences* include a wide range of topics and issues. The project management team must understand that current conditions and trends in this area may have a major effect on its project: a small change here can translate, usually with a time lag, into cataclysmic upheavals in the project itself. Of the many potential socioeconomic influences, several major categories that frequently affect projects are described briefly below.

2.5.1 Standards and Regulations

The International Organization for Standardization (ISO) differentiates between standards and regulations as follows (7):

- A *standard* is a "document approved by a recognized body, that provides, for common and repeated use, rules, guidelines, or characteristics for products, processes or services with which compliance is not mandatory." There are numerous standards in use covering everything from thermal stability of hydraulic fluids to the size of computer diskettes.
- A *regulation* is a "document, which lays down product, process or service characteristics, including the applicable administrative provisions, with which compliance is mandatory." Building codes are an example of regulations.

Care must be used in discussing standards and regulations since there is a vast gray area between the two; for example:

- Standards often begin as guidelines that describe a preferred approach, and later, with widespread adoption, become *de facto* regulations (e.g., the use of the Critical Path Method for scheduling major construction projects).
- Compliance may be mandated at different levels (e.g., by a government agency, by the management of the performing organization, or by the project management team).

For many projects, standards and regulations (by whatever definition) are well known, and project plans can reflect their effects. In other cases, the influence is unknown or uncertain and must be considered under Project Risk Management (described in Chapter 11).

A Guide to the Project Management Body of Knowledge (PMBOK® Guide) 2000 Edition
©2000 Project Management Institute, Four Campus Boulevard, Newtown Square, PA 19073-3299 USA

2.5.2 Internationalization

As more and more organizations engage in work that spans national boundaries, more and more projects span national boundaries as well. In addition to the traditional concerns of scope, cost, time, and quality, the project management team must also consider the effect of time-zone differences, national and regional holidays, travel requirements for face-to-face meetings, the logistics of teleconferencing, and often volatile political differences.

2.5.3 Cultural Influences

Culture is the "totality of socially transmitted behavior patterns, arts, beliefs, institutions, and all other products of human work and thought" (8). Every project must operate within a context of one or more cultural norms. This area of influence includes political, economic, demographic, educational, ethical, ethnic, religious, and other areas of practice, belief, and attitudes that affect the way that people and organizations interact.

2.5.4 Social-Economic-Environmental Sustainability

Virtually all projects are planned and implemented in a social, economic, and environmental context, and have intended and unintended positive and/or negative impacts. Organizations are increasingly accountable for impacts resulting from a project (e.g., accidental destruction of archeological sites in a road construction project), as well as for the effects of a project on people, the economy, and the environment long after it has been completed (e.g., a roadway can facilitate the access to and destruction of a once pristine environment).

Chapter 3

Project Management Processes

Project management is an integrative endeavor—an action, or failure to take action, in one area will usually affect other areas. The interactions may be straightforward and well understood, or they may be subtle and uncertain. For example, a scope change will almost always affect project cost, but it may or may not affect team morale or product quality.

These interactions often require tradeoffs among project objectives—performance in one area may be enhanced only by sacrificing performance in another. The specific performance tradeoffs may vary from project to project and organization to organization. Successful project management requires actively managing these interactions. Many project management practitioners refer to the project triple constraint as a framework for evaluating competing demands. The project triple constraint is often depicted as a triangle where either the sides or corners represent one of the parameters being managed by the project team.

To help in understanding the integrative nature of project management, and to emphasize the importance of integration, this document describes project management in terms of its component processes and their interactions. This chapter provides an introduction to the concept of project management as a number of interlinked processes, and thus provides an essential foundation for understanding the process descriptions in Chapters 4 through 12. It includes the following major sections:

3.1 Project Processes
3.2 Process Groups
3.3 Process Interactions
3.4 Customizing Process Interactions
3.5 Mapping of Project Management Processes

3.1 PROJECT PROCESSES

Projects are composed of processes. A *process* is "a series of actions bringing about a result" (1). Project processes are performed by people and generally fall into one of two major categories:

Figure 3–3 | 3.2

- *Project management processes* describe, organize, and complete the work of the project. The project management processes that are applicable to most projects, most of the time, are described briefly in this chapter and in detail in Chapters 4 through 12.
- *Product-oriented processes* specify and create the project's product. Product-oriented processes are typically defined by the project life cycle (discussed in Section 2.1) and vary by application area (discussed in Appendix E).

Project management processes and product-oriented processes overlap and interact throughout the project. For example, the scope of the project cannot be defined in the absence of some basic understanding of how to create the product.

3.2 PROCESS GROUPS

Project management processes can be organized into five groups of one or more processes each:

- Initiating processes—authorizing the project or phase.
- Planning processes—defining and refining objectives and selecting the best of the alternative courses of action to attain the objectives that the project was undertaken to address.
- Executing processes—coordinating people and other resources to carry out the plan.
- Controlling processes—ensuring that project objectives are met by monitoring and measuring progress regularly to identify variances from plan so that corrective action can be taken when necessary.
- Closing processes—formalizing acceptance of the project or phase and bringing it to an orderly end.

The process groups are linked by the results they produce—the result or outcome of one often becomes an input to another. Among the central process groups, the links are iterated—planning provides executing with a documented project plan early on, and then provides documented updates to the plan as the project progresses. These connections are illustrated in **Figure 3-1**. In addition, the project management process groups are not discrete, one-time events; they are overlapping activities that occur at varying levels of intensity throughout each phase of the project. **Figure 3-2** illustrates how the process groups overlap and vary within a phase.

Finally, the process group interactions also cross phases such that closing one phase provides an input to initiating the next. For example, closing a design phase requires customer acceptance of the design document. Simultaneously, the design document defines the product description for the ensuing implementation phase. This interaction is illustrated in **Figure 3-3**.

Repeating the initiation processes at the start of each phase helps to keep the project focused on the business need that it was undertaken to address. It should also help ensure that the project is halted if the business need no longer exists, or if the project is unlikely to satisfy that need. Business needs are discussed in more detail in the introduction to Section 5.1, Initiation.

It is important to note that the actual inputs and outputs of the processes depend upon the phase in which they are carried out. Although **Figure 3-3** is drawn with discrete phases and discrete processes, in an actual project there will be many overlaps. The planning process, for example, must not only provide

A Guide to the Project Management Body of Knowledge (PMBOK® Guide) 2000 Edition
©2000 Project Management Institute, Four Campus Boulevard, Newtown Square, PA 19073-3299 USA

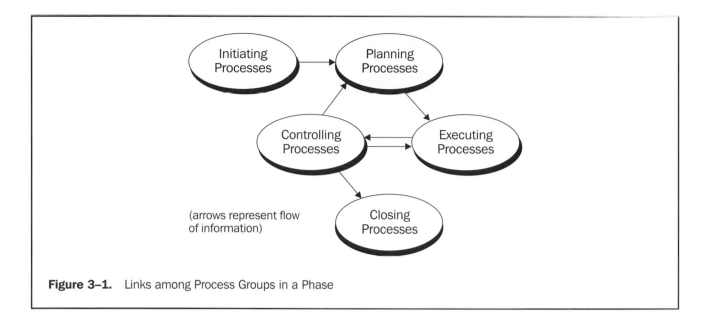

Figure 3–1. Links among Process Groups in a Phase

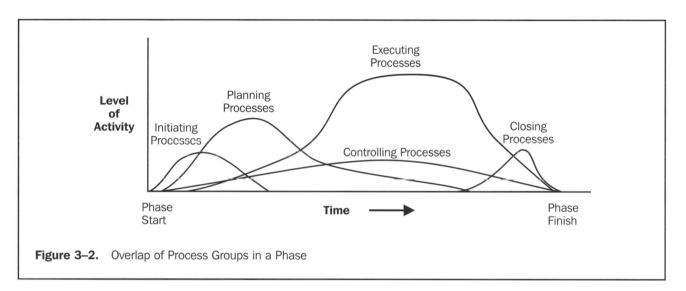

Figure 3–2. Overlap of Process Groups in a Phase

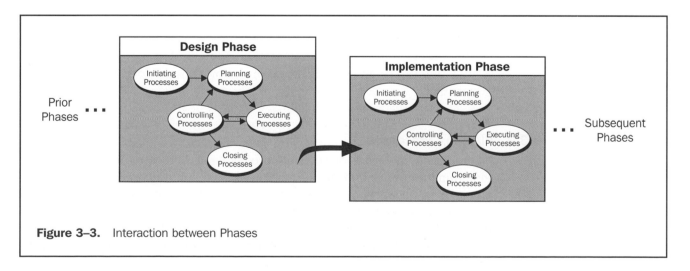

Figure 3–3. Interaction between Phases

Figure 3-4 | Figure 3-5

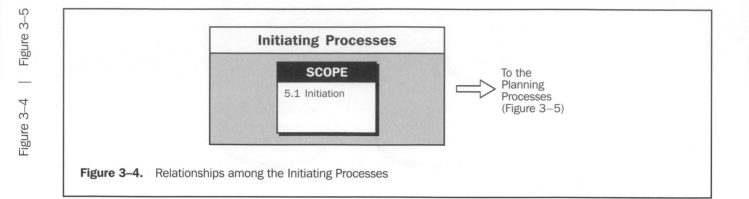

Figure 3–4. Relationships among the Initiating Processes

details of the work to be done to bring the current phase of the project to successful completion, but must also provide some preliminary description of work to be done in later phases. This progressive detailing of the project plan is often called *rolling wave planning, indicating that planning is an iterative and ongoing process*.

Involving stakeholders in the project phases generally improves the probability of satisfying customer requirements and realizes the *buy-in* or shared ownership of the project by the stakeholders, which is often critical to project success.

3.3 PROCESS INTERACTIONS

Within each process group, the individual processes are linked by their inputs and outputs. By focusing on these links, we can describe each process in terms of its:
- Inputs—documents or documentable items that will be acted upon.
- Tools and techniques—mechanisms applied to the inputs to create the outputs.
- Outputs—documents or documentable items that are a result of the process.

The project management processes common to most projects in most application areas are listed here and described in detail in Chapters 4 through 12. The numbers in parentheses after the process names identify the chapter and section where each is described. The process interactions illustrated here are also typical of most projects in most application areas. Section 3.4 discusses customizing both process descriptions and interactions.

3.3.1 Initiating Processes

Figure 3-4 illustrates the single process in this process group.
- Initiation (5.1)—authorizing the project or phase is part of project scope management.

3.3.2 Planning Processes

Planning is of major importance to a project because the project involves doing something that has not been done before. As a result, there are relatively more processes in this section. However, the number of processes does not mean that project management is primarily planning—the amount of planning performed should be commensurate with the scope of the project and the usefulness of the information developed. Planning is an ongoing effort throughout the life of the project.

A Guide to the Project Management Body of Knowledge (PMBOK® Guide) 2000 Edition
©2000 Project Management Institute, Four Campus Boulevard, Newtown Square, PA 19073-3299 USA

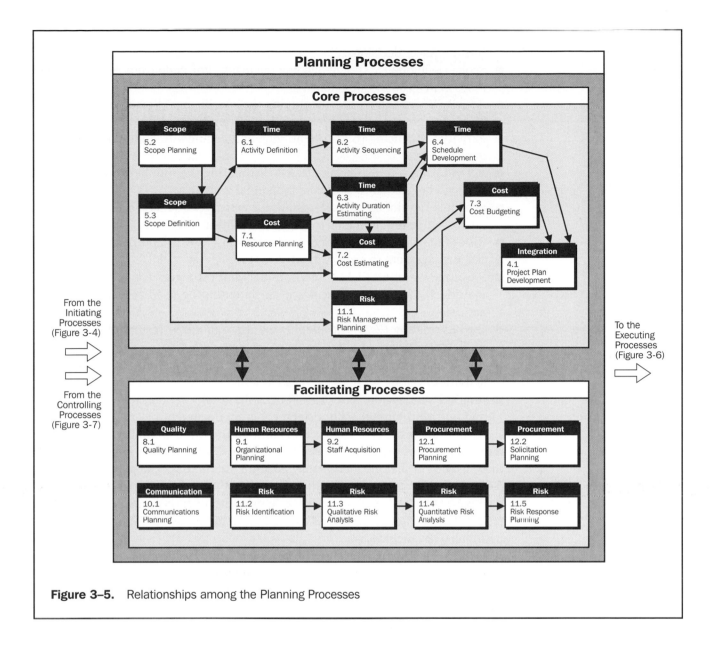

Figure 3–5. Relationships among the Planning Processes

The relationships among the project planning processes are shown in **Figure 3-5** (this chart is an explosion of the ellipse labeled "Planning Processes" in **Figure 3-1**). These processes are subject to frequent iterations prior to completing the project plan. For example, if the initial completion date is unacceptable, project resources, cost, or even scope may need to be redefined. In addition, planning is not an exact science—two different teams could generate very different plans for the same project.

Core processes. Some planning processes have clear dependencies that require them to be performed in essentially the same order on most projects. For example, activities must be defined before they can be scheduled or costed. These *core planning processes* may be iterated several times during any one phase of a project. They include:

- Scope Planning (5.2)—developing a written scope statement as the basis for future project decisions.
- Scope Definition (5.3)—subdividing the major project deliverables into smaller, more manageable components.
- Activity Definition (6.1)—identifying the specific activities that must be performed to produce the various project deliverables.
- Activity Sequencing (6.2)—identifying and documenting interactivity dependencies.
- Activity Duration Estimating (6.3)—estimating the number of work periods that will be needed to complete individual activities.
- Schedule Development (6.4)—analyzing activity sequences, activity durations, and resource requirements to create the project schedule.
- Risk Management Planning (11.1)—deciding how to approach and plan for risk management in a project.
- Resource Planning (7.1)—determining what resources (people, equipment, materials) and what quantities of each should be used to perform project activities.
- Cost Estimating (7.2)—developing an approximation (estimate) of the costs of the resources required to complete project activities.
- Cost Budgeting (7.3)—allocating the overall cost estimate to individual work activities.
- Project Plan Development (4.1)—taking the results of other planning processes and putting them into a consistent, coherent document.

Facilitating processes. Interactions among the other planning processes are more dependent on the nature of the project. For example, on some projects, there may be little or no identifiable risk until after most of the planning has been done and the team recognizes that the cost and schedule targets are extremely aggressive and thus involve considerable risk. Although these *facilitating processes* are performed intermittently and as needed during project planning, they are not optional. They include:

- Quality Planning (8.1)—identifying which quality standards are relevant to the project and determining how to satisfy them.
- Organizational Planning (9.1)—identifying, documenting, and assigning project roles, responsibilities, and reporting relationships.
- Staff Acquisition (9.2)—getting the human resources needed assigned to and working on the project.
- Communications Planning (10.1)—determining the information and communications needs of the stakeholders: who needs what information, when will they need it, and how will it be given to them.
- Risk Identification (11.2)—determining which risks might affect the project and documenting their characteristics.
- Qualitative Risk Analysis (11.3)—performing a qualitative analysis of risks and conditions to prioritize their effects on project objectives.
- Quantitative Risk Analysis (11.4)—measuring the probability and impact of risks and estimating their implications for project objectives.
- Risk Response Planning (11.5)—developing procedures and techniques to enhance opportunities and to reduce threats to the project's objectives from risk.

A Guide to the Project Management Body of Knowledge (PMBOK® Guide) 2000 Edition
©2000 Project Management Institute, Four Campus Boulevard, Newtown Square, PA 19073-3299 USA

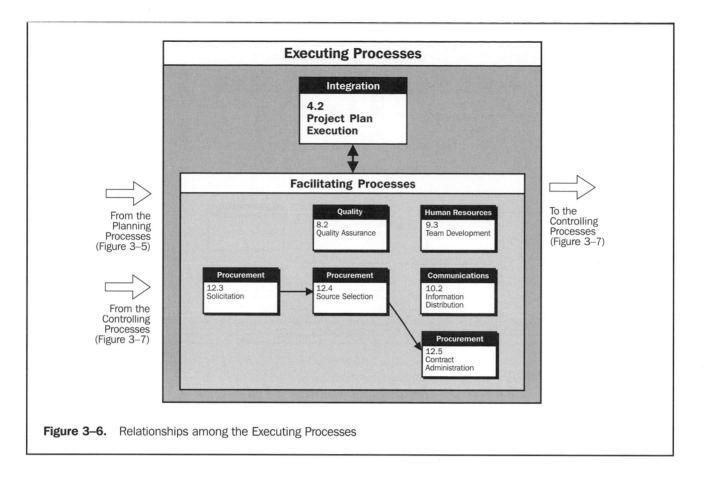

Figure 3–6. Relationships among the Executing Processes

- Procurement Planning (12.1)—determining what to procure, how much to procure, and when.
- Solicitation Planning (12.2)—documenting product requirements and identifying potential sources.

3.3.3 Executing Processes

The executing processes include core processes and facilitating processes. **Figure 3-6** illustrates how the following core and facilitating processes interact:

- Project Plan Execution (4.2)—carrying out the project plan by performing the activities included therein.
- Quality Assurance (8.2)—evaluating overall project performance on a regular basis to provide confidence that the project will satisfy the relevant quality standards.
- Team Development (9.3)—developing individual and group competencies to enhance project performance.
- Information Distribution (10.2)—making needed information available to project stakeholders in a timely manner.
- Solicitation (12.3)—obtaining quotations, bids, offers, or proposals as appropriate.
- Source Selection (12.4)—choosing from among potential sellers.
- Contract Administration (12.5)—managing the relationship with the seller.

Figure 3–7 | 3.4

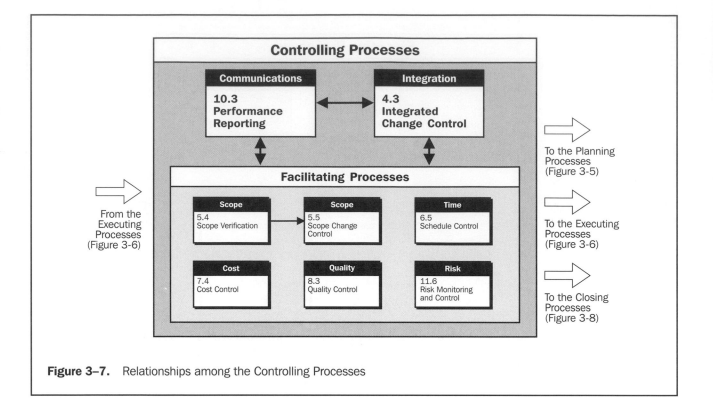

Figure 3–7. Relationships among the Controlling Processes

3.3.4 Controlling Processes

Project performance must be monitored and measured regularly to identify variances from the plan. Variances are fed into the control processes in the various knowledge areas. To the extent that significant variances are observed (i.e., those that jeopardize the project objectives), adjustments to the plan are made by repeating the appropriate project planning processes. For example, a missed activity finish date may require adjustments to the current staffing plan, reliance on overtime, or tradeoffs between budget and schedule objectives. Controlling also includes taking preventive action in anticipation of possible problems.

The controlling process group contains core processes and facilitating processes. **Figure 3-7** illustrates how the following core and facilitating processes interact:

- Integrated Change Control (4.3)—coordinating changes across the entire project.
- Scope Verification (5.4)—formalizing acceptance of the project scope.
- Scope Change Control (5.5)—controlling changes to project scope.
- Schedule Control (6.5)—controlling changes to the project schedule.
- Cost Control (7.4)—controlling changes to the project budget.
- Quality Control (8.3)—monitoring specific project results to determine if they comply with relevant quality standards and identifying ways to eliminate causes of unsatisfactory performance.
- Performance Reporting (10.3)—collecting and disseminating performance information. This includes status reporting, progress measurement, and forecasting.
- Risk Monitoring and Control (11.6)—keeping track of identified risks, monitoring residual risks and identifying new risks, ensuring the execution of risk plans, and evaluating their effectiveness in reducing risk.

A Guide to the Project Management Body of Knowledge (PMBOK® Guide) 2000 Edition

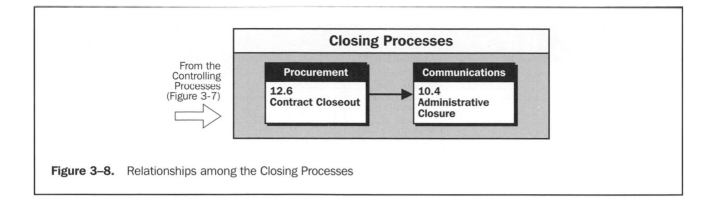

Figure 3–8. Relationships among the Closing Processes

3.3.5 Closing Processes

Figure 3-8 illustrates how the following core processes interact:

■ Contract Closeout (12.6)—completion and settlement of the contract, including resolution of any open items.

■ Administrative Closure (10.4)—generating, gathering, and disseminating information to formalize phase or project completion, including evaluating the project and compiling lessons learned for use in planning future projects or phases.

3.4 CUSTOMIZING PROCESS INTERACTIONS

The processes and interactions in Section 3.3 meet the test of general acceptance—they apply to most projects most of the time. However, not all of the processes will be needed on all projects, and not all of the interactions will apply to all projects. For example:

■ An organization that makes extensive use of contractors may explicitly describe where in the planning process each procurement process occurs.

■ The absence of a process does not mean that it should not be performed. The project management team should identify and manage all the processes that are needed to ensure a successful project.

■ Projects that are dependent on unique resources (commercial software development, biopharmaceuticals, etc.) may define roles and responsibilities prior to scope definition, since what can be done may be a function of who will be available to do it.

■ Some process outputs may be predefined as constraints. For example, management may specify a target completion date, rather than allowing it to be determined by the planning process. An imposed completion date may increase project risk, add cost, and compromise quality.

■ Larger projects may need relatively more detail. For example, risk identification might be further subdivided to focus separately on identifying cost risks, schedule risks, technical risks, and quality risks.

■ On subprojects and smaller projects, relatively little effort will be spent on processes whose outputs have been defined at the project level (e.g., a subcontractor may ignore risks explicitly assumed by the prime contractor), or on processes that provide only marginal utility (e.g., there may be no formal communications plan on a four-person project).

Figure 3–9 | Section II

Process Groups / Knowledge Area	Initiating	Planning	Executing	Controlling	Closing
4. Project Integration Management		4.1 Project Plan Development	4.2 Project Plan Execution	4.3 Integrated Change Control	
5. Project Scope Management	5.1 Initiation	5.2 Scope Planning 5.3 Scope Definition		5.4 Scope Verification 5.5 Scope Change Control	
6. Project Time Management		6.1 Activity Definition 6.2 Activity Sequencing 6.3 Activity Duration Estimating 6.4 Schedule Development		6.5 Schedule Control	
7. Project Cost Management		7.1 Resource Planning 7.2 Cost Estimating 7.3 Cost Budgeting		7.4 Cost Control	
8. Project Quality Management		8.1 Quality Planning	8.2 Quality Assurance	8.3 Quality Control	
9. Project Human Resource Management		9.1 Organizational Planning 9.2 Staff Acquisition	9.3 Team Development		
10. Project Communications Management		10.1 Communications Planning	10.2 Information Distribution	10.3 Performance Reporting	10.4 Administrative Closure
11. Project Risk Management		11.1 Risk Management Planning 11.2 Risk Identification 11.3 Qualitative Risk Analysis 11.4 Quantitative Risk Analysis 11.5 Risk Response Planning		11.6 Risk Monitoring and Control	
12. Project Procurement Management		12.1 Procurement Planning 12.2 Solicitation Planning	12.3 Solicitation 12.4 Source Selection 12.5 Contract Administration		12.6 Contract Closeout

Figure 3–9. Mapping of Project Management Processes to the Process Groups and Knowledge Areas

3.5 MAPPING OF PROJECT MANAGEMENT PROCESSES

Figure 3-9 reflects the mapping of the thirty-nine project management processes to the five project management process groups of initiating, planning, executing, controlling, and closing and the nine project management knowledge areas in Chapters 4–12.

This diagram is not meant to be exclusive, but to indicate generally where the project management processes fit into both the project management process groups and the project management knowledge areas.

A Guide to the Project Management Body of Knowledge (PMBOK® Guide) 2000 Edition
©2000 Project Management Institute, Four Campus Boulevard, Newtown Square, PA 19073-3299 USA

SECTION II

THE PROJECT MANAGEMENT KNOWLEDGE AREAS

4. Project Integration Management

5. Project Scope Management

6. Project Time Management

7. Project Cost Management

8. Project Quality Management

9. Project Human Resource Management

10. Project Communications Management

11. Project Risk Management

12. Project Procurement Management

Chapter 4

Project Integration Management

Project Integration Management includes the processes required to ensure that the various elements of the project are properly coordinated. It involves making tradeoffs among competing objectives and alternatives to meet or exceed stakeholder needs and expectations. While all project management processes are integrative to some extent, the processes described in this chapter are *primarily* integrative. **Figure 4-1** provides an overview of the following major processes:

4.1 **Project Plan Development**—integrating and coordinating all project plans to create a consistent, coherent document.

4.2 **Project Plan Execution**—carrying out the project plan by performing the activities included therein.

4.3 **Integrated Change Control**—coordinating changes across the entire project.

These processes interact with each other and with the processes in the other knowledge areas as well. Each process may involve effort from one or more individuals or groups of individuals, based on the needs of the project. Each process generally occurs at least once in every project phase.

Although the processes are presented here as discrete elements with well-defined interfaces, in practice they may overlap and interact in ways not detailed here. Process interactions are discussed in detail in Chapter 3.

The processes, tools, and techniques used to integrate *project management* processes are the focus of this chapter. For example, project integration management comes into play when a cost estimate is needed for a contingency plan, or when risks associated with various staffing alternatives must be identified. However, for a project to be completed successfully, integration must also occur in a number of other areas as well. For example:

■ The work of the project must be integrated with the ongoing operations of the performing organization.

■ Product scope and project scope must be integrated (the difference between product and project scope is discussed in the introduction to Chapter 5).

One of the techniques used to both integrate the various processes and to measure the performance of the project as it moves from initiation through to completion is Earned Value Management (EVM). EVM will be discussed in this chapter as a project integrating methodology, while earned value (EV), the technique, will

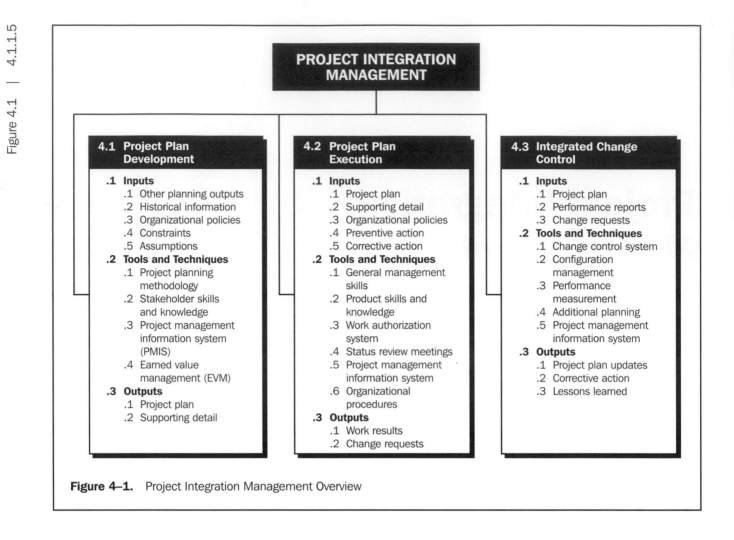

Figure 4–1. Project Integration Management Overview

be discussed in other chapters as a tool to measure performance against the project plan.

Project management software is a tool that aids integration within a project. And it may span all project management processes.

4.1 PROJECT PLAN DEVELOPMENT

Project plan development uses the outputs of the other planning processes, including strategic planning, to create a consistent, coherent document that can be used to guide both project execution and project control. This process is almost always iterated several times. For example, the initial draft may include generic resource requirements and an undated sequence of activities while the subsequent versions of the plan will include specific resources and explicit dates. The project scope of work is an iterative process that is generally done by the project team with the use of a Work Breakdown Structure (WBS), allowing the team to capture and then decompose all of the work of the project. All of the defined work must be planned, estimated and scheduled, and authorized with the use of detailed integrated management control plans sometimes called *Control Account Plans,* or CAPs, in the EVM process. The sum of all the integrated management control plans will constitute the total project scope.

A Guide to the Project Management Body of Knowledge (PMBOK® Guide) 2000 Edition
©2000 Project Management Institute, Four Campus Boulevard, Newtown Square, PA 19073-3299 USA

The project plan is used to:
- Guide project execution.
- Document project planning assumptions.
- Document project planning decisions regarding alternatives chosen.
- Facilitate communication among stakeholders.
- Define key management reviews as to content, extent, and timing.
- Provide a baseline for progress measurement and project control.

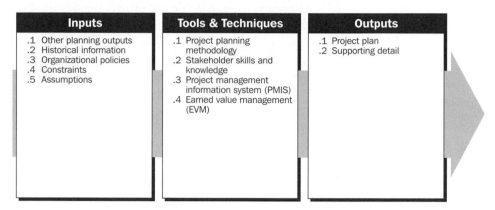

Inputs	Tools & Techniques	Outputs
.1 Other planning outputs .2 Historical information .3 Organizational policies .4 Constraints .5 Assumptions	.1 Project planning methodology .2 Stakeholder skills and knowledge .3 Project management information system (PMIS) .4 Earned value management (EVM)	.1 Project plan .2 Supporting detail

4.1.1 Inputs to Project Plan Development

.1 *Other planning outputs.* All of the outputs of the planning processes in the other knowledge areas (Section 3.3 provides a summary of these project planning processes) are inputs to developing the project plan. Other planning outputs include both base documents, such as the WBS, and the supporting detail. Many projects will also require application area-specific inputs (e.g., most major projects will require a cash-flow forecast).

.2 *Historical information.* The available historical information (e.g., estimating databases, records of past project performance) should have been consulted during the other project planning processes. This information should also be available during project plan development to assist with verifying assumptions and assessing alternatives that are identified as part of this process.

.3 *Organizational policies.* Any and all of the organizations involved in the project may have formal and informal policies whose effects must be considered. Organizational policies that typically must be considered include, but are not limited to:
- Quality management—process audits, continuous improvement targets.
- Personnel administration—hiring and firing guidelines, employee performance reviews.
- Financial controls—time reporting, required expenditure and disbursement reviews, accounting codes, standard contract provisions.

.4 *Constraints.* A constraint is an applicable restriction that will affect the performance of the project. For example, a predefined budget is a constraint that is highly likely to limit the team's options regarding scope, staffing, and schedule. When a project is performed under contract, contractual provisions will generally be constraints.

.5 *Assumptions.* Assumptions are factors that, for planning purposes, are considered to be true, real, or certain. Assumptions affect all aspects of project planning, and are part of the progressive elaboration of the project. Project teams frequently identify, document, and validate assumptions as part of their planning process.

For example, if the date that a key person will become available is uncertain, the team may assume a specific start date. Assumptions generally involve a degree of risk.

4.1.2 Tools and Techniques for Project Plan Development

.1 *Project planning methodology.* A project planning methodology is any structured approach used to guide the project team during development of the project plan. It may be as simple as standard forms and templates (whether paper or electronic, formal or informal) or as complex as a series of required simulations (e.g., Monte Carlo analysis of schedule risk). Most project planning methodologies make use of a combination of "hard" tools, such as project management software, and "soft" tools, such as facilitated startup meetings.

.2 *Stakeholder skills and knowledge.* Every stakeholder has skills and knowledge that may be useful in developing the project plan. The project management team must create an environment in which the stakeholders can contribute appropriately (see also Section 9.3, Team Development). Who contributes, what they contribute, and when they contribute will vary. For example:

- On a construction project being done under a lump-sum contract, the professional cost engineer will make a major contribution to the profitability objective during proposal preparation when the contract amount is being determined.

- On a project where staffing is defined in advance, the individual contributors may contribute significantly to meeting cost and schedule objectives by reviewing duration and effort estimates for reasonableness.

.3 *Project management information system (PMIS).* A PMIS consists of the tools and techniques used to gather, integrate, and disseminate the outputs of project management processes. It is used to support all aspects of the project from initiating through closing, and can include both manual and automated systems.

.4 *Earned value management (EVM).* A technique used to integrate the project's scope, schedule, and resources and to measure and report project performance from initiation to closeout. Further discussions on EVM can be found in Section 7.4.2.3.

4.1.3 Outputs from Project Plan Development

.1 *Project plan.* The project plan is a formal, approved document used to manage project execution. The project schedule lists planned dates for performing activities and meeting milestones identified in the project plan (see Section 6.4.3.1). The project plan and schedule should be distributed as defined in the communications management plan (e.g., management of the performing organization may require broad coverage with little detail, while a contractor may require complete details on a single subject). In some application areas, the term *integrated project plan* is used to refer to this document.

A clear distinction should be made between the project plan and the project performance measurement baselines. The project plan is a document or collection of documents that should be expected to change over time as more information becomes available about the project. The performance measurement baselines will usually change only intermittently, and then generally only in response to an approved scope of work or deliverable change.

A Guide to the Project Management Body of Knowledge (PMBOK® Guide) 2000 Edition
©2000 Project Management Institute, Four Campus Boulevard, Newtown Square, PA 19073-3299 USA

There are many ways to organize and present the project plan, but it commonly includes all of the following (these items are described in more detail elsewhere):

- Project charter.
- A description of the project management approach or strategy (a summary of the individual management plans from the other knowledge areas).
- Scope statement, which includes the project objectives and the project deliverables.
- WBS to the level at which control will be exercised, as a baseline scope document.
- Cost estimates, scheduled start and finish dates (schedule), and responsibility assignments for each deliverable within the WBS to the level at which control will be exercised.
- Performance measurement baselines for technical scope, schedule, and cost—i.e., the schedule baseline (project schedule) and the cost baseline (time-phased project budget).
- Major milestones and target dates for each.
- Key or required staff and their expected cost and/or effort.
- Risk management plan, including: key risks, including constraints and assumptions, and planned responses and contingencies (where appropriate) for each.
- Subsidiary management plans, namely:
  - ◆ Scope management plan (Section 5.2.3.3).
  - ◆ Schedule management plan (Section 6.4.3.3).
  - ◆ Cost management plan (Section 7.2.3.3).
  - ◆ Quality management plan (Section 8.1.3.1).
  - ◆ Staffing management plan (Section 9.1.3.2).
  - ◆ Communications management plan (Section 10.1.3.1).
  - ◆ Risk response plan (Section 11.5.3.1).
  - ◆ Procurement management plan (Section 12.1.3.1).
      Each of these plans could be included if needed and with detail to the extent required for each specific project.
- Open issues and pending decisions.

Other project planning outputs should be included in the formal plan, based upon the needs of the individual project. For example, the project plan for a large project will generally include a project organization chart.

.2 *Supporting detail.* Supporting detail for the project plan includes:

- Outputs from other planning processes that are not included in the project plan.
- Additional information or documentation generated during development of the project plan (e.g., constraints and assumptions that were not previously known).
- Technical documentation; such as, a history of all requirements, specifications, and conceptual designs.
- Documentation of relevant standards.
- Specifications from early project development planning.

This material should be organized as needed to facilitate its use during project plan execution.

4.2 PROJECT PLAN EXECUTION

Project plan execution is the primary process for carrying out the project plan—the vast majority of the project's budget will be expended in performing this process. In this process, the project manager and the project management team must coordinate and direct the various technical and organizational interfaces that exist in the project. It is the project process that is most directly affected by the project application area in that the product of the project is actually created here. Performance against the project baseline must be continuously monitored so that corrective actions can be taken based on actual performance against the project plan. Periodic forecasts of the final cost and schedule results will be made to support the analysis.

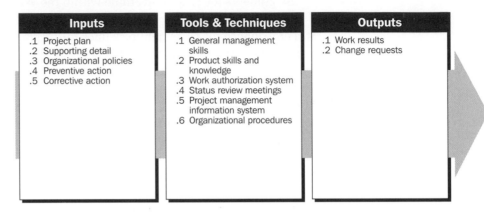

Inputs	Tools & Techniques	Outputs
.1 Project plan .2 Supporting detail .3 Organizational policies .4 Preventive action .5 Corrective action	.1 General management skills .2 Product skills and knowledge .3 Work authorization system .4 Status review meetings .5 Project management information system .6 Organizational procedures	.1 Work results .2 Change requests

4.2.1 Inputs to Project Plan Execution

.1 Project plan. The project plan is described in Section 4.1.3.1. The subsidiary management plans (scope management plan, risk management plan, procurement management plan, configuration management plan, etc.) and the performance measurement baselines are key inputs to project plan execution.

.2 Supporting detail. Supporting detail is described in Section 4.1.3.2.

.3 Organizational policies. Organizational policies are described in Section 4.1.1.3. Any and all of the organizations involved in the project may have formal and informal policies that may affect project plan execution.

.4 Preventive action. Preventive action is anything that reduces the probability of potential consequences of project risk events.

.5 Corrective action. Corrective action is anything done to bring expected future project performance in line with the project plan. Corrective action is an output of the various control processes—as an input here it completes the feedback loop needed to ensure effective project management.

4.2.2 Tools and Techniques for Project Plan Execution

.1 General management skills. General management skills such as leadership, communicating, and negotiating are essential to effective project plan execution. General management skills are described in Section 2.4.

.2 Product skills and knowledge. The project team must have access to an appropriate set of skills and knowledge about the project's product. The necessary skills are defined as part of planning (especially in resource planning, Section 7.1) and are provided through the staff acquisition process (described in Section 9.2).

A Guide to the Project Management Body of Knowledge (PMBOK® Guide) 2000 Edition
©2000 Project Management Institute, Four Campus Boulevard, Newtown Square, PA 19073-3299 USA

.3 *Work authorization system.* A work authorization system is a formal procedure for sanctioning project work to ensure that work is done at the right time and in the proper sequence. The primary mechanism is typically a written authorization to begin work on a specific activity or work package.

The design of a work authorization system should balance the value of the control provided with the cost of that control. For example, on many smaller projects, verbal authorizations will be adequate.

.4 *Status review meetings.* Status review meetings are regularly scheduled meetings held to exchange information about the project. On most projects, status review meetings will be held at various frequencies and on different levels (e.g., the project management team may meet weekly by itself and monthly with the customer).

.5 *Project management information system.* The PMIS is described in Section 4.1.2.3.

.6 *Organizational procedures.* Any and all of the organizations involved in the project may have formal and informal procedures that are useful during project execution.

4.2.3 Outputs from Project Plan Execution

.1 *Work results.* Work results are the outcomes of the activities performed to accomplish the project. Information on work results—which deliverables have been completed and which have not, to what extent quality standards are being met, what costs have been incurred or committed, etc.—is collected as part of project plan execution and fed into the performance reporting process (see Section 10.3 for a more detailed discussion of performance reporting). It should be noted that although outcomes are frequently tangible deliverables such as buildings, roads, etc., they are also often intangibles such as people trained who can effectively apply that training.

.2 *Change requests.* Change requests (e.g., to expand or contract project scope, to modify cost [budgets], or schedule estimates [dates, etc.]) are often identified while the work of the project is being done.

4.3 INTEGRATED CHANGE CONTROL

Integrated change control is concerned with a) influencing the factors that create changes to ensure that changes are agreed upon , b) determining that a change has occurred, and c) managing the actual changes when and as they occur. The original defined project scope and the integrated performance baseline must be maintained by continuously managing changes to the baseline, either by rejecting new changes or by approving changes and incorporating them into a revised project baseline. Integrated change control requires:

- Maintaining the integrity of the performance measurement baselines.
- Ensuring that changes to the product scope are reflected in the definition of the project scope. (The difference between product and project scope is discussed in the introduction to Chapter 5.)
- Coordinating changes across knowledge areas, as illustrated in **Figure 4-2**. For example, a proposed schedule change will often affect cost, risk, quality, and staffing.

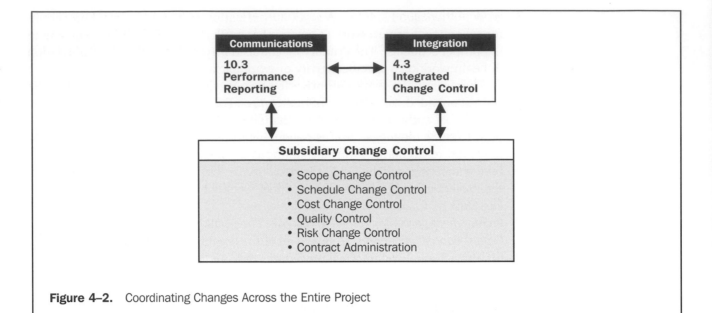

Figure 4–2. Coordinating Changes Across the Entire Project

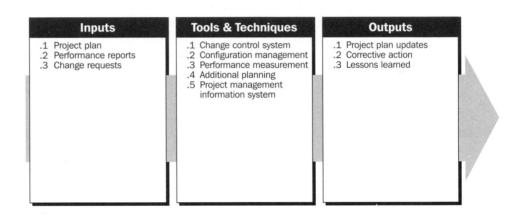

4.3.1 Inputs to Integrated Change Control

.1 Project plan. The project plan provides the baseline against which changes will be controlled (see Section 4.1.3.1).

.2 Performance reports. Performance reports (described in Section 10.3) provide information on project performance. Performance reports may also alert the project team to issues that may cause problems in the future.

.3 Change requests. Change requests may occur in many forms—oral or written, direct or indirect, externally or internally initiated, and legally mandated or optional.

4.3.2 Tools and Techniques for Integrated Change Control

.1 Change control system. A change control system is a collection of formal, documented procedures that defines how project performance will be monitored and evaluated, and includes the steps by which official project documents may be changed. It includes the paperwork, tracking systems, processes, and approval levels necessary for authorizing changes.

A Guide to the Project Management Body of Knowledge (PMBOK® Guide) 2000 Edition
©2000 Project Management Institute, Four Campus Boulevard, Newtown Square, PA 19073-3299 USA

In many cases, the performing organization will have a change control system that can be adopted "as is" for use by the project. However, if an appropriate system is not available, the project management team will need to develop one as part of the project.

Many change control systems include a group responsible for approving or rejecting proposed changes. The roles and responsibilities of these groups are clearly defined within the change control system and agreed upon by all key stakeholders. Organizations vary by the definition of the board; however, some common occurrences are Change Control Board (CCB), Engineering Review Board (ERB), Technical Review Board (TRB), Technical Assessment Board (TAB), and a variety of others. The change control system must also include procedures to handle changes that may be approved without prior review, for example, as the result of emergencies. Typically, a change control system will allow for "automatic" approval of defined categories of changes. These changes must still be documented and captured so that the evolution of the baseline can be documented.

.2 *Configuration management.* Configuration management is any documented procedure used to apply technical and administrative direction and surveillance to:

- Identify and document the functional and physical characteristics of an item or system.
- Control any changes to such characteristics.
- Record and report the change and its implementation status.
- Audit the items and system to verify conformance to requirements.

In many application areas, configuration management is a subset of the change control system and is used to ensure that the description of the project's product is correct and complete. In other application areas, change control refers to any systematic effort to manage project change.

.3 *Performance measurement.* Performance measurement techniques such as EV (described in Section 10.3.2.4) help to assess whether variances from the plan require corrective action.

.4 *Additional planning.* Projects seldom run exactly according to plan. Prospective changes may require new or revised cost estimates, modified activity sequences, schedules, resource requirements, analysis of risk response alternatives, or other adjustments to the project plan.

.5 *Project management information system.* PMIS is described in Section 4.1.2.3.

4.3.3 Outputs from Integrated Change Control

.1 *Project plan updates.* Project plan updates are any modification to the contents of the project plan or the supporting detail (described in Sections 4.1.3.1 and 4.1.3.2, respectively). Appropriate stakeholders must be notified as needed.

.2 *Corrective action.* Corrective action is described in Section 4.2.1.5.

.3 *Lessons learned.* The causes of variances, the reasoning behind the corrective action chosen, and other types of lessons learned should be documented so that they become part of the historical database for both this project and other projects of the performing organization. The database is also the basis for knowledge management.

Chapter 5

Project Scope Management

Project Scope Management includes the processes required to ensure that the project includes all the work required, and only the work required, to complete the project successfully (1). It is primarily concerned with defining and controlling what is or is not included in the project. **Figure 5-1** provides an overview of the major project scope management processes:

5.1 **Initiation**—authorizing the project or phase.

5.2 **Scope Planning**—developing a written scope statement as the basis for future project decisions.

5.3 **Scope Definition**—subdividing the major project deliverables into smaller, more manageable components.

5.4 **Scope Verification**—formalizing acceptance of the project scope.

5.5 **Scope Change Control**—controlling changes to project scope.

These processes interact with each other and with the processes in the other knowledge areas as well. Each process may involve effort from one or more individuals or groups of individuals, based on the needs of the project. Each process generally occurs at least once in every project phase.

Although the processes are presented here as discrete components with well-defined interfaces, in practice they may overlap and interact in ways not detailed here. Process interactions are discussed in detail in Chapter 3.

In the project context, the term *scope* may refer to:

■ Product scope—the features and functions that characterize a product or service.

■ Project scope—the work that must be done to deliver a product with the specified features and functions.

The processes, tools, and techniques used to manage *project* scope are the focus of this chapter. The processes, tools, and techniques used to manage *product* scope vary by application area and are usually defined as part of the project life cycle (the project life cycle is discussed in Section 2.1).

A project generally results in a single product, but that product may include subsidiary components, each with its own separate but interdependent product scopes. For example, a new telephone system would generally include four subsidiary components—hardware, software, training, and implementation.

Completion of the project scope is measured against the project plan, but completion of the product scope is measured against the product requirements. Both types of scope management must be well integrated to ensure that the work of the project will result in delivery of the specified product.

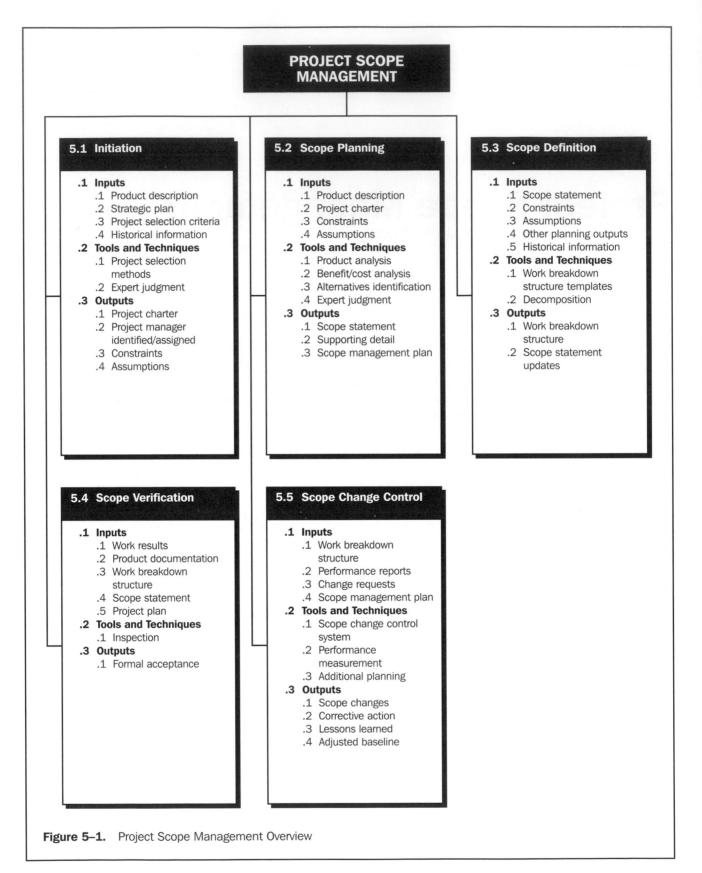

PROJECT SCOPE MANAGEMENT

5.1 Initiation

.1 Inputs
.1 Product description
.2 Strategic plan
.3 Project selection criteria
.4 Historical information
.2 Tools and Techniques
.1 Project selection methods
.2 Expert judgment
.3 Outputs
.1 Project charter
.2 Project manager identified/assigned
.3 Constraints
.4 Assumptions

5.2 Scope Planning

.1 Inputs
.1 Product description
.2 Project charter
.3 Constraints
.4 Assumptions
.2 Tools and Techniques
.1 Product analysis
.2 Benefit/cost analysis
.3 Alternatives identification
.4 Expert judgment
.3 Outputs
.1 Scope statement
.2 Supporting detail
.3 Scope management plan

5.3 Scope Definition

.1 Inputs
.1 Scope statement
.2 Constraints
.3 Assumptions
.4 Other planning outputs
.5 Historical information
.2 Tools and Techniques
.1 Work breakdown structure templates
.2 Decomposition
.3 Outputs
.1 Work breakdown structure
.2 Scope statement updates

5.4 Scope Verification

.1 Inputs
.1 Work results
.2 Product documentation
.3 Work breakdown structure
.4 Scope statement
.5 Project plan
.2 Tools and Techniques
.1 Inspection
.3 Outputs
.1 Formal acceptance

5.5 Scope Change Control

.1 Inputs
.1 Work breakdown structure
.2 Performance reports
.3 Change requests
.4 Scope management plan
.2 Tools and Techniques
.1 Scope change control system
.2 Performance measurement
.3 Additional planning
.3 Outputs
.1 Scope changes
.2 Corrective action
.3 Lessons learned
.4 Adjusted baseline

Figure 5–1. Project Scope Management Overview

A Guide to the Project Management Body of Knowledge (PMBOK® Guide) 2000 Edition
©2000 Project Management Institute, Four Campus Boulevard, Newtown Square, PA 19073-3299 USA

5.1 INITIATION

Initiation is the process of formally authorizing a new project or that an existing project should continue into its next phase (see Section 2.1 for a more detailed discussion of project phases). This formal initiation links the project to the ongoing work of the performing organization. In some organizations, a project is not formally initiated until after completion of a needs assessment, a feasibility study, a preliminary plan, or some other equivalent form of analysis that was itself separately initiated. Some types of projects, especially internal service projects and new product development projects, are initiated informally, and some limited amount of work is done to secure the approvals needed for formal initiation. Projects are typically authorized as a result of one or more of the following:

- A market demand (e.g., a car company authorizes a project to build more fuel-efficient cars in response to gasoline shortages).
- A business need (e.g., a training company authorizes a project to create a new course to increase its revenues).
- A customer request (e.g., an electric utility authorizes a project to build a new substation to serve a new industrial park).
- A technological advance (e.g., an electronics firm authorizes a new project to develop a video game player after advances in computer memory).
- A legal requirement (e.g., a paint manufacturer authorizes a project to establish guidelines for the handling of toxic materials).
- A social need (e.g., a nongovernmental organization in a developing country authorizes a project to provide potable water systems, latrines, and sanitation education to low-income communities suffering from high rates of cholera).

These stimuli may also be called problems, opportunities, or business requirements. The central theme of all these terms is that management generally must make a decision about how to respond.

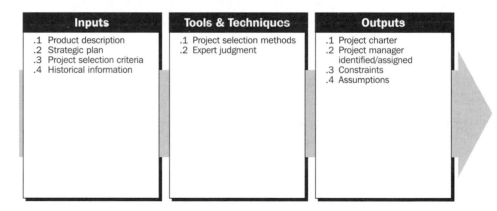

Inputs	Tools & Techniques	Outputs
.1 Product description	.1 Project selection methods	.1 Project charter
.2 Strategic plan	.2 Expert judgment	.2 Project manager identified/assigned
.3 Project selection criteria		.3 Constraints
.4 Historical information		.4 Assumptions

5.1.1 Inputs to Initiation

.1 *Product description.* The product description documents the characteristics of the product or service that the project was undertaken to create. The product description will generally have less detail in early phases and more detail in later ones as the product characteristics are progressively elaborated.

The product description should also document the relationship between the product or service being created and the business need or other stimulus that gave rise to the project (see the list in Section 5.1). While the form and substance of the product description will vary, it should always be detailed enough to support later project planning.

Many projects involve one organization (the seller) doing work under contract to another (the buyer). In such circumstances, the initial product description is usually provided by the buyer.

.2 *Strategic plan.* All projects should be supportive of the performing organization's strategic goals—the strategic plan of the performing organization should be considered as a factor in project selection decisions.

.3 *Project selection criteria.* Project selection criteria are typically defined in terms of the merits of the product of the project and can cover the full range of possible management concerns (financial return, market share, public perceptions, etc.).

.4 *Historical information.* Historical information about both the results of previous project selection decisions and previous project performance should be considered to the extent that it is available. When initiation involves approval for the next phase of a project, information about the results of previous phases is often critical.

5.1.2 Tools and Techniques for Initiation

.1 *Project selection methods.* Project selection methods involve measuring value or attractiveness to the project owner. Project selection methods include considering the decision criterion (multiple criteria, if used, should be combined into a single value function) and a means to calculate value under uncertainty. These are known as the *decision model* and *calculation method*. Project selection also applies to choosing the alternative ways of doing the project. Optimization tools can be used to search for the optimal combination of decision variables. Project selection methods generally fall into one of two broad categories (2):

- Benefit measurement methods—comparative approaches, scoring models, benefit contribution, or economic models.
- Constrained optimization methods—mathematical models using linear, non-linear, dynamic, integer, and multi-objective programming algorithms.

These methods are often referred to as *decision models*. Decision models include generalized techniques (Decision Trees, Forced Choice, and others), as well as specialized ones (Analytic Hierarchy Process, Logical Framework Analysis, and others). Applying complex project selection criteria in a sophisticated model is often treated as a separate project phase.

.2 *Expert judgment.* Expert judgment will often be required to assess the inputs to this process. Such expertise may be provided by any group or individual with specialized knowledge or training, and is available from many sources, including:

- Other units within the performing organization.
- Consultants.
- Stakeholders, including customers.
- Professional and technical associations.
- Industry groups.

5.1.3 Outputs from Initiation

.1 *Project charter.* A project charter is a document that formally authorizes a project. It should include, either directly or by reference to other documents:

- The business need that the project was undertaken to address.
- The product description (described in Section 5.1.1.1).

The project charter should be issued by a manager external to the project, and at a level appropriate to the needs of the project. It provides the project manager with the authority to apply organizational resources to project activities.

A Guide to the Project Management Body of Knowledge (PMBOK® Guide) 2000 Edition
©2000 Project Management Institute, Four Campus Boulevard, Newtown Square, PA 19073-3299 USA

When a project is performed under contract, the signed contract will generally serve as the project charter for the seller.

.2 *Project manager identified/assigned.* In general, the project manager should be identified and assigned as early in the project as is feasible. The project manager should always be assigned prior to the start of project plan execution (described in Section 4.2) and preferably before much project planning has been done (the project planning processes are described in Section 3.3.2).

.3 *Constraints.* Constraints are factors that will limit the project management team's options. For example, a predefined budget is a constraint that is highly likely to limit the team's options regarding scope, staffing, and schedule.

When a project is performed under contract, contractual provisions will generally be constraints. Another example is a requirement that the product of the project be socially, economically, and environmentally sustainable, which will also have an effect on the project's scope, staffing, and schedule.

.4 *Assumptions.* See Section 4.1.1.5.

5.2 SCOPE PLANNING

Scope planning is the process of progressively elaborating and documenting the project work (project scope) that produces the product of the project. Project scope planning starts with the initial inputs of product description, the project charter, and the initial definition of constraints and assumptions. Note that the product description incorporates product requirements that reflect agreed-upon customer needs and the product design that meets the product requirements. The outputs of scope planning are the scope statement and scope management plan, with the supporting detail. The scope statement forms the basis for an agreement between the project and the project customer by identifying both the project objectives and the project deliverables. Project teams develop multiple scope statements that are appropriate for the level of project work decomposition.

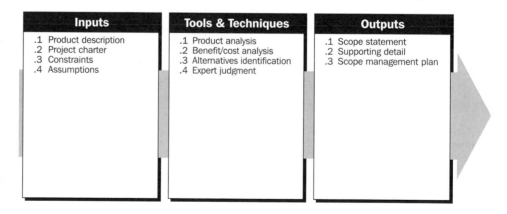

Inputs	Tools & Techniques	Outputs
.1 Product description .2 Project charter .3 Constraints .4 Assumptions	.1 Product analysis .2 Benefit/cost analysis .3 Alternatives identification .4 Expert judgment	.1 Scope statement .2 Supporting detail .3 Scope management plan

5.2.1 Inputs to Scope Planning

.1 *Product description.* The product description is discussed in Section 5.1.1.1.

.2 *Project charter.* The project charter is described in Section 5.1.3.1.

.3 *Constraints.* Constraints are described in Section 5.1.3.3.

.4 *Assumptions.* Assumptions are described in Section 4.1.1.5.

5.2.2 Tools and Techniques for Scope Planning

.1 *Product analysis.* Product analysis involves developing a better understanding of the product of the project. It includes techniques such as product breakdown analysis, systems engineering, value engineering, value analysis, function analysis, and quality function deployment.

.2 *Benefit/cost analysis.* Benefit/cost analysis involves estimating tangible and intangible costs (outlays) and benefits (returns) of various project and product alternatives, and then using financial measures, such as return on investment or payback period, to assess the relative desirability of the identified alternatives.

.3 *Alternatives identification.* This is a general term for any technique used to generate different approaches to the project. There is a variety of general management techniques often used here, the most common of which are brainstorming and lateral thinking.

.4 *Expert judgment.* Expert judgment is described in Section 5.1.2.2.

5.2.3 Outputs from Scope Planning

.1 *Scope statement.* The scope statement provides a documented basis for making future project decisions and for confirming or developing common understanding of project scope among the stakeholders. As the project progresses, the scope statement may need to be revised or refined to reflect approved changes to the scope of the project. The scope statement should include, either directly or by reference to other documents:

- Project justification—the business need that the project was undertaken to address. The project justification provides the basis for evaluating future tradeoffs.
- Project's product—a brief summary of the product description (the product description is discussed in Section 5.1.1.1).
- Project deliverables—a list of the summary-level subproducts whose full and satisfactory delivery marks completion of the project. For example, the major deliverables for a software development project might include the working computer code, a user manual, and an interactive tutorial. When known, exclusions should be identified, but anything not explicitly included is implicitly excluded.
- Project objectives—the quantifiable criteria that must be met for the project to be considered successful. Project objectives must include at least cost, schedule, and quality measures. Project objectives should have an attribute (e.g., cost), a metric (e.g., United States [U.S.] dollars), and an absolute or relative value (e.g., less than 1.5 million). Unquantified objectives (e.g., "customer satisfaction") entail high risk to successful accomplishment.

.2 *Supporting detail.* Supporting detail for the scope statement should be documented and organized as needed to facilitate its use by other project management processes. Supporting detail should always include documentation of all identified assumptions and constraints. The amount of additional detail may vary by application area.

.3 *Scope management plan.* This document describes how project scope will be managed and how scope changes will be integrated into the project. It should also include an assessment of the expected stability of the project scope (i.e., how likely is it to change, how frequently, and by how much). The scope management plan should also include a clear description of how scope changes will be identified and classified. (This is particularly difficult—and therefore absolutely essential—when the product characteristics are still being elaborated.)

A Guide to the Project Management Body of Knowledge (PMBOK® Guide) 2000 Edition
©2000 Project Management Institute, Four Campus Boulevard, Newtown Square, PA 19073-3299 USA

A scope management plan may be formal or informal, highly detailed or broadly framed, based on the needs of the project. It is a subsidiary component of the project plan (described in Section 4.1.3.1).

5.3 SCOPE DEFINITION

Scope definition involves subdividing the major project deliverables (as identified in the scope statement as defined in Section 5.2.3.1) into smaller, more manageable components to:

- Improve the accuracy of cost, duration, and resource estimates.
- Define a baseline for performance measurement and control.
- Facilitate clear responsibility assignments.

Proper scope definition is critical to project success. "When there is poor scope definition, final project costs can be expected to be higher because of the inevitable changes which disrupt project rhythm, cause rework, increase project time, and lower the productivity and morale of the workforce" (3).

Inputs	Tools & Techniques	Outputs
.1 Scope statement .2 Constraints .3 Assumptions .4 Other planning outputs .5 Historical information	.1 Work breakdown structure templates .2 Decomposition	.1 Work breakdown structure .2 Scope statement updates

5.3.1 Inputs to Scope Definition

.1 Scope statement. The scope statement is described in Section 5.2.3.1.

.2 Constraints. Constraints are described in Section 5.1.3.3. When a project is done under contract, the constraints defined by contractual provisions are often important considerations during scope definition.

.3 Assumptions. Assumptions are described in Section 4.1.1.5.

.4 Other planning outputs. The outputs of the processes in other knowledge areas should be reviewed for possible impact on project scope definition.

.5 Historical information. Historical information about previous projects should be considered during scope definition. Information about errors and omissions on previous projects should be especially useful.

5.3.2 Tools and Techniques for Scope Definition

.1 Work breakdown structure templates. A WBS (described in Section 5.3.3.1) from a previous project can often be used as a template for a new project. Although each project is unique, WBSs can often be "reused" since most projects will resemble another project to some extent. For example, most projects within a given organization will have the same or similar project life cycles, and will thus have the same or similar deliverables required from each phase.

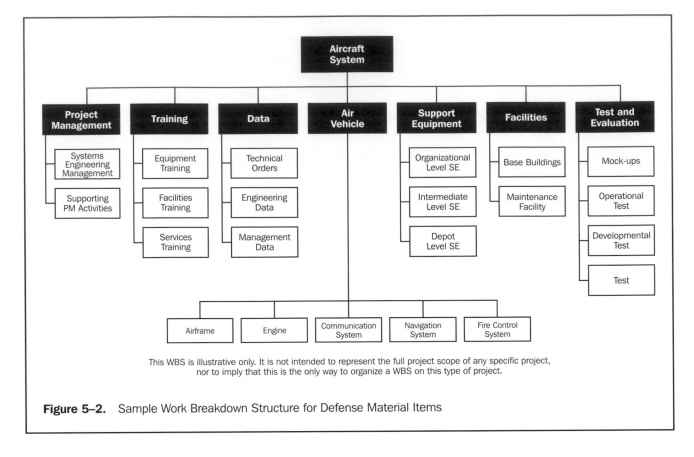

This WBS is illustrative only. It is not intended to represent the full project scope of any specific project, nor to imply that this is the only way to organize a WBS on this type of project.

Figure 5–2. Sample Work Breakdown Structure for Defense Material Items

Many application areas or performing organizations have standard or semi-standard WBSs that can be used as templates. For example, the U.S. Department of Defense has recommended standards WBSs for Defense Material Items (MIL-HDBK-881). A portion of one of these templates is shown as **Figure 5-2**.

.2 *Decomposition.* Decomposition involves subdividing the major project deliverables or subdeliverables into smaller, more manageable components until the deliverables are defined in sufficient detail to support development of project activities (planning, executing, controlling, and closing). Decomposition involves the following major steps:

(1) Identify the major deliverables of the project, including project management. The major deliverables should always be defined in terms of how the project will actually be organized. For example:

■ The phases of the project life cycle may be used as the first level of decomposition with the project deliverables repeated at the second level, as illustrated in **Figure 5-3**.

■ The organizing principle within each branch of the WBS may vary, as illustrated in **Figure 5-4**.

(2) Decide if adequate cost and duration estimates can be developed at this level of detail for each deliverable. The meaning of *adequate* may change over the course of the project—decomposition of a deliverable that will be produced far in the future may not be possible. For each deliverable, proceed to Step 4 if there is adequate detail, to Step 3 if there is not—this means that different deliverables may have differing levels of decomposition.

A Guide to the Project Management Body of Knowledge (PMBOK® Guide) 2000 Edition
©2000 Project Management Institute, Four Campus Boulevard, Newtown Square, PA 19073-3299 USA

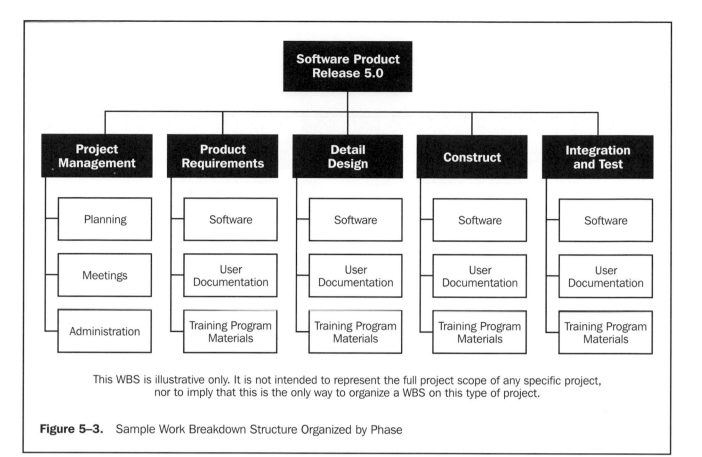

This WBS is illustrative only. It is not intended to represent the full project scope of any specific project, nor to imply that this is the only way to organize a WBS on this type of project.

Figure 5–3. Sample Work Breakdown Structure Organized by Phase

(3) Identify constituent components of the deliverable. Constituent components should be described in terms of tangible, verifiable results to facilitate performance measurement. As with the major components, the constituent components should be defined in terms of how the work of the project will actually be organized and the work of the project accomplished. Tangible, verifiable results can include services as well as products (e.g., *status reporting* could be described as *weekly status reports*; for a manufactured item, constituent components might include several individual components plus *final assembly*). Repeat Step 2 on each constituent component.

(4) Verify the correctness of the decomposition:

■ Are the lower-level items both necessary and sufficient for completion of the decomposed item? If not, the constituent components must be modified (added to, deleted from, or redefined).

■ Is each item clearly and completely defined? If not, the descriptions must be revised or expanded.

■ Can each item be appropriately scheduled? Budgeted? Assigned to a specific organizational unit (e.g., department, team, or person) who will accept responsibility for satisfactory completion of the item? If not, revisions are needed to provide adequate management control.

5.3.3 Outputs from Scope Definition

.1 Work breakdown structure. A WBS is a deliverable-oriented grouping of project components that organizes and defines the total scope of the project; work not

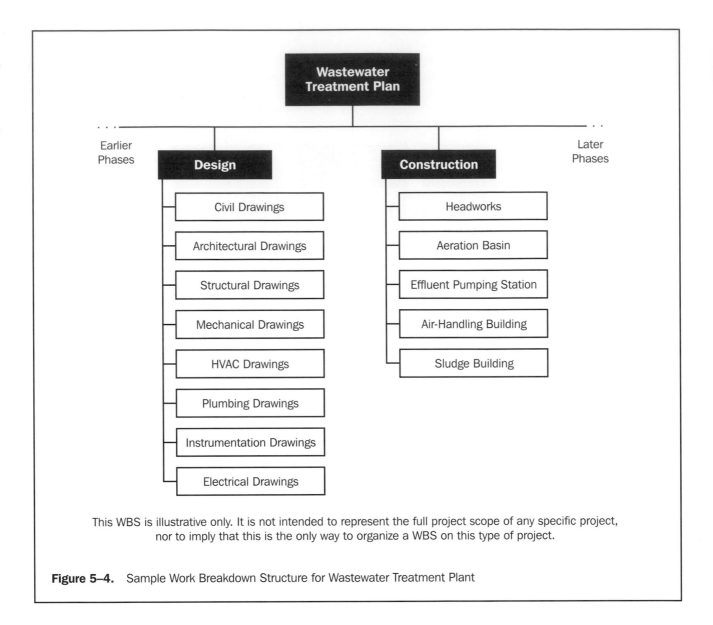

This WBS is illustrative only. It is not intended to represent the full project scope of any specific project, nor to imply that this is the only way to organize a WBS on this type of project.

Figure 5–4. Sample Work Breakdown Structure for Wastewater Treatment Plant

in the WBS is outside the scope of the project. As with the scope statement, the WBS is often used to develop or confirm a common understanding of project scope. Each descending level represents an increasingly detailed description of the project deliverables. Section 5.3.2.2 describes the most common approach for developing a WBS. A WBS is normally presented in chart form, as illustrated in **Figures 5-2, 5-3**, and **5-4**; however, the WBS should not be confused with the method of presentation—drawing an unstructured activity list in chart form does not make it a WBS.

Each item in the WBS is generally assigned a unique identifier; these identifiers can provide a structure for a hierarchical summation of costs and resources. The items at the lowest level of the WBS may be referred to as *work packages*, especially in organizations that follow earned value management practices. These work packages may in turn be further decomposed in a subproject work breakdown structure. Generally, this type of approach is used when the project manager is assigning a scope of work to another organization, and this other organization

A Guide to the Project Management Body of Knowledge (PMBOK® Guide) 2000 Edition
©2000 Project Management Institute, Four Campus Boulevard, Newtown Square, PA 19073-3299 USA

must plan and manage the scope of work at a more detailed level than the project manager in the main project. These work packages may be further decomposed in the project plan and schedule, as described in Sections 5.3.2.2 and 6.1.2.1.

Work component descriptions are often collected in a *WBS dictionary*. A WBS dictionary will typically include work package descriptions, as well as other planning information such as schedule dates, cost budgets, and staff assignments.

The WBS should not be confused with other kinds of "breakdown" structures used to present project information. Other structures commonly used in some application areas include:

■ Contractual WBS (CWBS), which is used to define the level of reporting that the seller will provide the buyer. The CWBS generally includes less detail than the WBS used by the seller to manage the seller's work.

■ Organizational breakdown structure (OBS), which is used to show which work components have been assigned to which organizational units.

■ Resource breakdown structure (RBS), which is a variation of the OBS and is typically used when work components are assigned to individuals.

■ Bill of materials (BOM), which presents a hierarchical view of the physical assemblies, subassemblies, and components needed to fabricate a manufactured product.

■ Project breakdown structure (PBS), which is fundamentally the same as a properly done WBS. The term *PBS* is widely used in application areas where the term *WBS* is incorrectly used to refer to a BOM.

.2 *Scope statement updates.* Include any modification of the contents of the scope statement (described in Section 5.2.3.1). Appropriate stakeholders must be notified as needed.

5.4 SCOPE VERIFICATION

Scope verification is the process of obtaining formal acceptance of the project scope by the stakeholders (sponsor, client, customer, etc.). It requires reviewing deliverables and work results to ensure that all were completed correctly and satisfactorily. If the project is terminated early, the scope verification process should establish and document the level and extent of completion. Scope verification differs from quality control (described in Section 8.3) in that it is primarily concerned with *acceptance* of the work results while quality control is primarily concerned with the *correctness* of the work results. These processes are generally performed in parallel to ensure both correctness and acceptance.

Inputs	Tools & Techniques	Outputs
.1 Work results .2 Product documentation .3 Work breakdown structure .4 Scope statement .5 Project plan	.1 Inspection	.1 Formal acceptance

5.4.1 Inputs to Scope Verification

.1 Work results. Work results—which deliverables have been fully or partially completed—are an output of project plan execution (discussed in Section 4.2).

.2 Product documentation. Documents produced to describe the project's products must be available for review. The terms used to describe this documentation (plans, specifications, technical documentation, drawings, etc.) vary by application area.

.3 Work breakdown structure. The WBS aids in definition of the scope, and should be used to verify the work of the project (see Section 5.3.3.1).

.4 Scope statement. The scope statement defines the scope in some detail and should be verified (see Section 5.2.3.1).

.5 Project plan. The project plan is described in Section 4.1.3.1.

5.4.2 Tools and Techniques for Scope Verification

.1 Inspection. Inspection includes activities such as measuring, examining, and testing undertaken to determine whether results conform to requirements. Inspections are variously called reviews, product reviews, audits, and walk-throughs; in some application areas, these different terms have narrow and specific meanings.

5.4.3 Outputs from Scope Verification

.1 Formal acceptance. Documentation that the client or sponsor has accepted the product of the project phase or major deliverable(s) must be prepared and distributed. Such acceptance may be conditional, especially at the end of a phase.

5.5 SCOPE CHANGE CONTROL

Scope change control is concerned with a) influencing the factors that create scope changes to ensure that changes are agreed upon, b) determining that a scope change has occurred, and c) managing the actual changes when and if they occur. Scope change control must be thoroughly integrated with the other control processes (schedule control, cost control, quality control, and others, as discussed in Section 4.3).

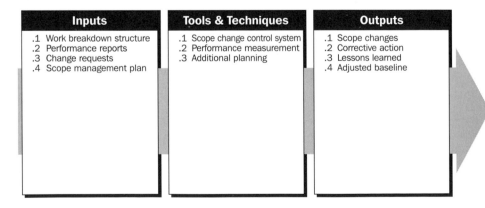

Inputs	Tools & Techniques	Outputs
.1 Work breakdown structure .2 Performance reports .3 Change requests .4 Scope management plan	.1 Scope change control system .2 Performance measurement .3 Additional planning	.1 Scope changes .2 Corrective action .3 Lessons learned .4 Adjusted baseline

A Guide to the Project Management Body of Knowledge (PMBOK® Guide) 2000 Edition
©2000 Project Management Institute, Four Campus Boulevard, Newtown Square, PA 19073-3299 USA

5.5.1 Inputs to Scope Change Control

.1 Work breakdown structure. The WBS is described in Section 5.3.3.1. It defines the project's scope baseline.

.2 Performance reports. Performance reports, discussed in Section 10.3.3.1, provide information on scope performance, such as which interim deliverables have been completed and which have not. Performance reports may also alert the project team to issues that may cause problems in the future.

.3 Change requests. Change requests may occur in many forms—oral or written, direct or indirect, externally or internally initiated, and legally mandated or optional. Changes may require expanding the scope or may allow shrinking it. Most change requests are the result of:

- An external event (e.g., a change in a government regulation).
- An error or omission in defining the scope of the product (e.g., failure to include a required feature in the design of a telecommunications system).
- An error or omission in defining the scope of the project (e.g., using a BOM instead of a WBS).
- A value-adding change (e.g., an environmental remediation project is able to reduce costs by taking advantage of technology that was not available when the scope was originally defined).
- Implementing a contingency plan or workaround plan to respond to a risk, as described in Section 11.6.3.3.

.4 Scope management plan. The scope management plan is described in Section 5.2.3.3.

5.5.2 Tools and Techniques for Scope Change Control

.1 Scope change control system. A scope change control system defines the procedures by which the project scope may be changed. It includes the paperwork, tracking systems, and approval levels necessary for authorizing changes. The scope change control system should be integrated with the integrated change control described in Section 4.3 and, in particular, with any system or systems in place to control product scope. When the project is done under contract, the scope change control system must also comply with all relevant contractual provisions.

.2 Performance measurement. Performance measurement techniques, described in Section 10.3.2, help to assess the magnitude of any variations that do occur. Determining what is causing the variance relative to the baseline and deciding if the variance requires corrective action are important parts of scope change control.

.3 Additional planning. Few projects run exactly according to plan. Prospective scope changes may require modifications to the WBS or analysis of alternative approaches (see Sections 5.3.3.1 and 5.2.2.3, respectively).

5.5.3 Outputs from Scope Change Control

.1 Scope changes. A scope change is any modification to the agreed-upon project scope as defined by the approved WBS. Scope changes often require adjustments to cost, time, quality, or other project objectives.

Project scope changes are fed back through the planning process, technical and planning documents are updated as needed, and stakeholders are notified as appropriate.

.2 *Corrective action.* Corrective action is anything done to bring expected future project performance in line with the project plan.

.3 *Lessons learned.* The causes of variances, the reasoning behind the corrective action chosen, and other types of lessons learned from scope change control should be documented, so that this information becomes part of the historical database for both this project and other projects of the performing organization.

.4 *Adjusted baseline.* Depending upon the nature of the change, the corresponding baseline document may be revised and reissued to reflect the approved change and form the new baseline for future changes.

A Guide to the Project Management Body of Knowledge (PMBOK® Guide) 2000 Edition
©2000 Project Management Institute, Four Campus Boulevard, Newtown Square, PA 19073-3299 USA

Chapter 6

Project Time Management

Project Time Management includes the processes required to ensure timely completion of the project. **Figure 6-1** provides an overview of the following major processes in developing the project time schedule:

6.1 Activity Definition—identifying the specific activities that must be performed to produce the various project deliverables.

6.2 Activity Sequencing—identifying and documenting interactivity dependencies.

6.3 Activity Duration Estimating—estimating the number of work periods that will be needed to complete individual activities.

6.4 Schedule Development—analyzing activity sequences, activity durations, and resource requirements to create the project schedule.

6.5 Schedule Control—controlling changes to the project schedule.

These processes interact with each other and with the processes in the other knowledge areas as well. Each process may involve effort from one or more individuals or groups of individuals, based on the needs of the project. Each process generally occurs at least once in every project phase.

Although the processes are presented here as discrete elements with well-defined interfaces, in practice they may overlap and interact in ways not detailed here. Process interactions are discussed in detail in Chapter 3.

On some projects, especially smaller ones, activity sequencing, activity duration estimating, and schedule development are so tightly linked that they are viewed as a single process (e.g., they may be performed by a single individual over a relatively short period of time). They are presented here as distinct processes because the tools and techniques for each are different.

6.1 ACTIVITY DEFINITION

Activity definition involves identifying and documenting the specific activities that must be performed to produce the deliverables and subdeliverables identified in the Work Breakdown Structure (WBS). Implicit in this process is the need to define the activities such that the project objectives will be met.

Figure 6–1 | 6.1.3.1

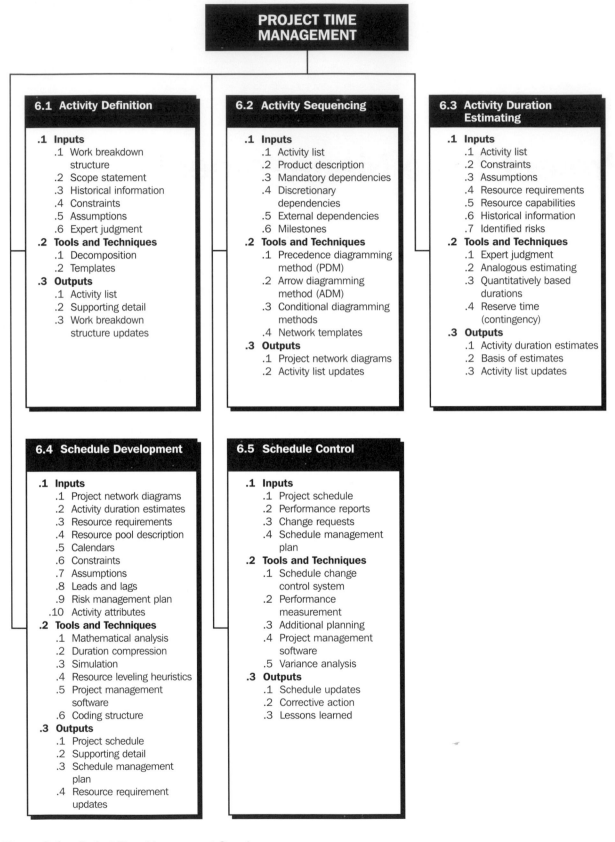

PROJECT TIME MANAGEMENT

6.1 Activity Definition

.1 Inputs
.1 Work breakdown structure
.2 Scope statement
.3 Historical information
.4 Constraints
.5 Assumptions
.6 Expert judgment

.2 Tools and Techniques
.1 Decomposition
.2 Templates

.3 Outputs
.1 Activity list
.2 Supporting detail
.3 Work breakdown structure updates

6.2 Activity Sequencing

.1 Inputs
.1 Activity list
.2 Product description
.3 Mandatory dependencies
.4 Discretionary dependencies
.5 External dependencies
.6 Milestones

.2 Tools and Techniques
.1 Precedence diagramming method (PDM)
.2 Arrow diagramming method (ADM)
.3 Conditional diagramming methods
.4 Network templates

.3 Outputs
.1 Project network diagrams
.2 Activity list updates

6.3 Activity Duration Estimating

.1 Inputs
.1 Activity list
.2 Constraints
.3 Assumptions
.4 Resource requirements
.5 Resource capabilities
.6 Historical information
.7 Identified risks

.2 Tools and Techniques
.1 Expert judgment
.2 Analogous estimating
.3 Quantitatively based durations
.4 Reserve time (contingency)

.3 Outputs
.1 Activity duration estimates
.2 Basis of estimates
.3 Activity list updates

6.4 Schedule Development

.1 Inputs
.1 Project network diagrams
.2 Activity duration estimates
.3 Resource requirements
.4 Resource pool description
.5 Calendars
.6 Constraints
.7 Assumptions
.8 Leads and lags
.9 Risk management plan
.10 Activity attributes

.2 Tools and Techniques
.1 Mathematical analysis
.2 Duration compression
.3 Simulation
.4 Resource leveling heuristics
.5 Project management software
.6 Coding structure

.3 Outputs
.1 Project schedule
.2 Supporting detail
.3 Schedule management plan
.4 Resource requirement updates

6.5 Schedule Control

.1 Inputs
.1 Project schedule
.2 Performance reports
.3 Change requests
.4 Schedule management plan

.2 Tools and Techniques
.1 Schedule change control system
.2 Performance measurement
.3 Additional planning
.4 Project management software
.5 Variance analysis

.3 Outputs
.1 Schedule updates
.2 Corrective action
.3 Lessons learned

Figure 6–1. Project Time Management Overview

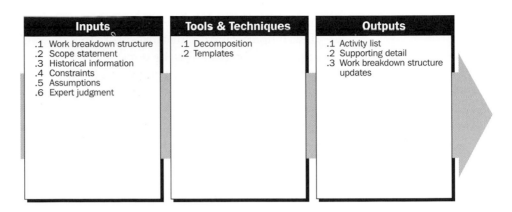

6.1.1 Inputs to Activity Definition

.1 *Work breakdown structure.* The WBS is the primary input to activity definition (see Section 5.3.3.1 for a more detailed discussion of the WBS).

.2 *Scope statement.* The project justification and the project objectives contained in the scope statement must be considered explicitly during activity definition (see Section 5.2.3.1 for a more detailed discussion of the scope statement).

.3 *Historical information.* Historical information (what activities were actually required on previous, similar projects) should be considered in defining project activities.

.4 *Constraints.* Constraints are factors that will limit the project management team's options; an example would be the use of desired maximum activity durations.

.5 *Assumptions.* See Section 4.1.1.5.

.6 *Expert judgment.* Expert judgment is discussed in Sections 5.1.2.2 and 6.3.2.1.

6.1.2 Tools and Techniques for Activity Definition

.1 *Decomposition.* Within the context of the process of Activity Definition, decomposition involves subdividing project work packages into smaller, more manageable components to provide better management control. The technique of decomposition is described in more detail in Section 5.3.2.2. The major difference between decomposition here and in Scope Definition is that the final outputs here are described as activities rather than as deliverables. The WBS and the activity list are usually developed sequentially, with the WBS being the basis for development of the final activity list. In some application areas, the WBS and the activity list are developed concurrently.

.2 *Templates.* An activity list (described in Section 6.1.3.1), or a portion of an activity list from a previous project, is often usable as a template for a new project. The activities in templates can also contain a list of resource skills and their required hours of effort, identification of risks, expected deliverables, and other descriptive information.

6.1.3 Outputs from Activity Definition

.1 *Activity list.* The activity list must include all activities that will be performed on the project. It should be organized as an extension to the WBS to help ensure that it is complete, and that it does not include any activities that are not required as part of the project scope. As with the WBS, the activity list should include descriptions of each activity to ensure that the project team members will understand how the work is to be done.

.2 *Supporting detail.* Supporting detail for the activity list should be documented and organized as needed to facilitate its use by other project management processes. Supporting detail should always include documentation of all identified assumptions and constraints. The amount of additional detail varies by application area.

.3 *Work breakdown structure updates.* In using the WBS to identify which activities are needed, the project team may identify missing deliverables, or may determine that the deliverable descriptions need to be clarified or corrected. Any such updates must be reflected in the WBS and related documentation, such as cost estimates. These updates are often called *refinements* and are most likely when the project involves new or unproven technology.

6.2 ACTIVITY SEQUENCING

Activity sequencing involves identifying and documenting interactivity logical relationships. Activities must be sequenced accurately to support later development of a realistic and achievable schedule. Sequencing can be performed with the aid of a computer (e.g., by using project management software) or with manual techniques. Manual techniques are often more effective on smaller projects and in the early phases of larger ones when little detail is available. Manual and automated techniques may also be used in combination.

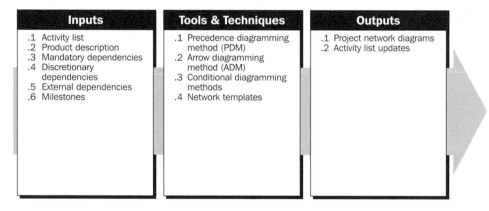

Inputs	Tools & Techniques	Outputs
.1 Activity list .2 Product description .3 Mandatory dependencies .4 Discretionary dependencies .5 External dependencies .6 Milestones	.1 Precedence diagramming method (PDM) .2 Arrow diagramming method (ADM) .3 Conditional diagramming methods .4 Network templates	.1 Project network diagrams .2 Activity list updates

6.2.1 Inputs to Activity Sequencing

.1 *Activity list.* The activity list is described in Section 6.1.3.1.

.2 *Product description.* The product description is discussed in Section 5.1.1.1. Product characteristics often affect activity sequencing (e.g., the physical layout of a plant to be constructed, subsystem interfaces on a software project). While these effects are often apparent in the activity list, the product description should generally be reviewed to ensure accuracy.

.3 *Mandatory dependencies.* Mandatory dependencies are those that are inherent in the nature of the work being done. They often involve physical limitations. (On a construction project, it is impossible to erect the superstructure until after the foundation has been built; on an electronics project, a prototype must be built before it can be tested.) Mandatory dependencies are also called *hard logic*.

A Guide to the Project Management Body of Knowledge (PMBOK® Guide) 2000 Edition
©2000 Project Management Institute, Four Campus Boulevard, Newtown Square, PA 19073-3299 USA

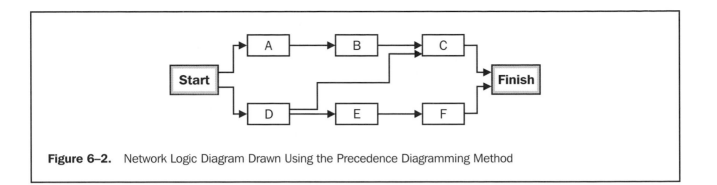

Figure 6–2. Network Logic Diagram Drawn Using the Precedence Diagramming Method

.4 *Discretionary dependencies.* Discretionary dependencies are those that are defined by the project management team. They should be used with care (and fully documented), since they may limit later scheduling options. Discretionary dependencies are usually defined based on knowledge of:
  - "Best practices" within a particular application area.
  - Some unusual aspect of the project where a specific sequence is desired, even though there are other acceptable sequences.

  Discretionary dependencies may also be called *preferred logic, preferential logic,* or *soft logic.*

.5 *External dependencies.* External dependencies are those that involve a relationship between project activities and nonproject activities. For example, the testing activity in a software project may be dependent on delivery of hardware from an external source, or environmental hearings may need to be held before site preparation can begin on a construction project.

.6 *Milestones.* Milestone events need to be part of the activity sequencing to assure that the requirements for meeting the milestone(s) are met.

6.2.2 Tools and Techniques for Activity Sequencing

.1 *Precedence diagramming method (PDM).* This is a method of constructing a project network diagram that uses boxes or rectangles (nodes) to represent the activities and connects them with arrows that show the dependencies (see also Section 6.2.3.1). **Figure 6-2** shows a simple network logic diagram drawn using PDM. This technique is also called *activity-on-node* (AON) and is the method used by most project management software packages. PDM can be done manually or on a computer.

  It includes four types of dependencies or precedence relationships:
  - Finish-to-start—the initiation of the work of the successor depends upon the completion of the work of the predecessor.
  - Finish-to-finish—the completion of the work of the successor depends upon the completion of the work of the predecessor.
  - Start-to-start—the initiation of the work of the successor depends upon the initiation of the work of the predecessor.
  - Start-to-finish—the completion of the successor is dependent upon the initiation of the predecessor.

  In PDM, finish-to-start is the most commonly used type of logical relationship. Start-to-finish relationships are rarely used, and then typically only by professional scheduling engineers. Using start-to-start, finish-to-finish, or start-to-finish relationships with project management software can produce unexpected results, since these types of relationships have not been consistently implemented.

Figure 6–3 | 6.3.1.4

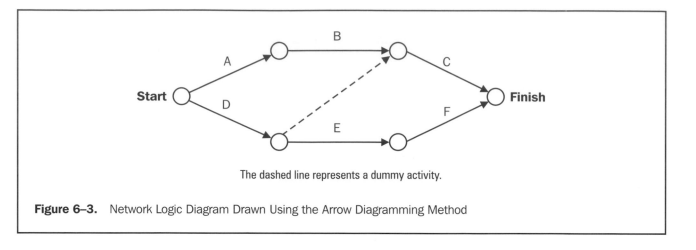

The dashed line represents a dummy activity.

Figure 6–3. Network Logic Diagram Drawn Using the Arrow Diagramming Method

.2 *Arrow diagramming method (ADM).* This method of constructing a project network diagram uses arrows to represent the activities and connects them at nodes to show their dependencies (see also Section 6.2.3.1). **Figure 6-3** shows a simple network logic diagram drawn using ADM. This technique is also called *activity-on-arrow* (AOA) and, although less prevalent than PDM, is still the technique of choice in some application areas. ADM uses only finish-to-start dependencies and may require the use of dummy activities to define all logical relationships correctly. ADM can be done manually or on a computer.

.3 *Conditional diagramming methods.* Diagramming techniques such as Graphical Evaluation and Review Technique (GERT) and System Dynamics models allow for nonsequential activities such as loops (e.g., a test that must be repeated more than once) or conditional branches (e.g., a design update that is only needed if the inspection detects errors). Neither PDM nor ADM allows loops or conditional branches.

.4 *Network templates.* Standardized networks can be used to expedite the preparation of project network diagrams. They can include an entire project or only a portion of it. Portions of a network are often referred to as *subnets* or *fragnets*. Subnets are especially useful when a project includes several identical or nearly identical features, such as floors on a high-rise office building, clinical trials on a pharmaceutical research project, program modules on a software project, or the start-up phase of a development project.

6.2.3 Outputs from Activity Sequencing

.1 *Project network diagrams.* Project network diagrams are schematic displays of the project's activities and the logical relationships (dependencies) among them. **Figures 6-2** and **6-3** illustrate two different approaches to drawing a project network diagram. A project network diagram may be produced manually or on a computer. It may include full project details, or have one or more summary activities (hammocks). The diagram should be accompanied by a summary narrative that describes the basic sequencing approach. Any unusual sequences should be fully described.

A project network diagram is often referred to as a PERT chart. Historically PERT (Program Evaluation and Review Technique) was a specific type of network diagram (see also Section 6.4.2.1).

A Guide to the Project Management Body of Knowledge (PMBOK® Guide) 2000 Edition
©2000 Project Management Institute, Four Campus Boulevard, Newtown Square, PA 19073-3299 USA

.2 *Activity list updates.* In much the same manner that the activity definition process may generate updates to the WBS, preparation of project network diagrams may reveal instances where an activity must be divided or otherwise redefined to diagram the correct logical relationships.

6.3 ACTIVITY DURATION ESTIMATING

Activity duration estimating is the process of taking information on project scope and resources and then developing durations for input to schedules. The inputs for the estimates of duration typically originate from the person or group on the project team who is most familiar with the nature of a specific activity. The estimate is often progressively elaborated, and the process considers the quality and availability of the input data. Thus, the estimate can be assumed to be progressively more accurate and of known quality. The person or group on the project team who is most familiar with the nature of a specific activity should make, or at least approve, the estimate.

Estimating the number of work periods required to complete an activity will often require consideration of elapsed time as well. For example, if "concrete curing" will require four days of elapsed time, it may require from two to four work periods, based on a) which day of the week it begins, and b) whether or not weekend days are treated as work periods. Most computerized scheduling software will handle this problem by using alternative work-period calendars.

Overall project duration may also be estimated using the tools and techniques presented here, but it is more properly calculated as the output of schedule development (described in Section 6.4). The project team can consider the project duration a probability distribution (using probabilistic techniques) or as a single-point estimate (using deterministic techniques).

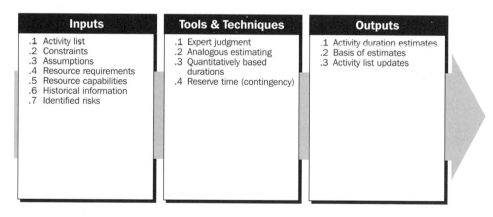

Inputs	Tools & Techniques	Outputs
.1 Activity list	.1 Expert judgment	.1 Activity duration estimates
.2 Constraints	.2 Analogous estimating	.2 Basis of estimates
.3 Assumptions	.3 Quantitatively based	.3 Activity list updates
.4 Resource requirements	durations	
.5 Resource capabilities	.4 Reserve time (contingency)	
.6 Historical information		
.7 Identified risks		

6.3.1 Inputs to Activity Duration Estimating

.1 *Activity list.* The activity list is described in Section 6.1.3.1.

.2 *Constraints.* Constraints are described in Section 6.1.1.4.

.3 *Assumptions.* Assumptions are described in Section 4.1.1.5. An example would be reporting periods for the duration of the project that could dictate maximum durations, i.e., two reporting periods.

.4 *Resource requirements.* Resource requirements are described in Section 7.1.3.1. The duration of most activities will be significantly influenced by the resources assigned to them. For example, two people working together may be able to complete a design activity in half the time it takes either of them individually, while a person working half time on an activity will generally take at least twice as much time as the same person working full time. However, as additional resources are added, projects can experience communication overload, which reduces productivity and causes production to improve proportionally less than the increase in resource.

.5 *Resource capabilities.* The duration of most activities will be significantly influenced by the capabilities of the human and material resources assigned to them. For example, if both are assigned full time, a senior staff member can generally be expected to complete a given activity in less time than a junior staff member.

.6 *Historical information.* Historical information on the likely durations of many categories of activities is often available from one or more of the following sources:

- Project files—one or more of the organizations involved in the project may maintain records of previous project results that are detailed enough to aid in developing duration estimates. In some application areas, individual team members may maintain such records.

- Commercial duration estimating databases—historical information is often available commercially. These databases tend to be especially useful when activity durations are not driven by the actual work content (e.g., how long it takes concrete to cure; how long a government agency usually takes to respond to certain types of requests).

- Project team knowledge—the individual members of the project team may remember previous actuals or estimates. While such recollections may be useful, they are generally far less reliable than documented results.

.7 *Identified risks.* The project team considers information on identified risks (see Section 11.2) when producing estimates of activity durations, since risks (either threats or opportunities) can have a significant influence on duration. The project team considers the extent to which the effect of risks is included in the baseline duration estimate for each activity, including risks with high probabilities or impact.

6.3.2 Tools and Techniques for Activity Duration Estimating

.1 *Expert judgment.* Expert judgment is described in Section 5.1.2.2. Durations are often difficult to estimate because of the number of factors that can influence them (e.g., resource levels, resource productivity). Expert judgment guided by historical information should be used whenever possible. If such expertise is not available, the estimates are inherently uncertain and risky (see Chapter 11, Project Risk Management).

.2 *Analogous estimating.* Analogous estimating, also called *top-down estimating*, means using the actual duration of a previous, similar activity as the basis for estimating the duration of a future activity. It is frequently used to estimate project duration when there is a limited amount of detailed information about the project (e.g., in the early phases). Analogous estimating is a form of expert judgment (described in Section 6.3.2.1).

Analogous estimating is most reliable when a) the previous activities are similar in fact and not just in appearance, and b) the individuals preparing the estimates have the needed expertise.

A Guide to the Project Management Body of Knowledge (PMBOK® Guide) 2000 Edition
©2000 Project Management Institute, Four Campus Boulevard, Newtown Square, PA 19073-3299 USA

.3 *Quantitatively based durations.* The quantities to be performed for each specific work category (i.e., number of drawing, meters of cable, tons of steel, etc.) defined by the engineering/design effort, when multiplied by the productivity unit rate (i.e., hours per drawing, meters of cable per hour, etc.), can be used to estimate activity durations.

.4 *Reserve time (contingency).* Project teams may choose to incorporate an additional time frame, called time *reserve, contingency,* or *buffer,* that can be added to the activity duration or elsewhere in the schedule as recognition of schedule risk. This reserve time can be a percentage of the estimated duration, or a fixed number of work periods. The reserve time can later be reduced or eliminated, as more precise information about the project becomes available. Such reserve time should be documented along with other data and assumptions.

6.3.3 Outputs from Activity Duration Estimating

.1 *Activity duration estimates.* Activity duration estimates are quantitative assessments of the likely number of work periods that will be required to complete an activity.

Activity duration estimates should always include some indication of the range of possible results. For example:

- 2 weeks ± 2 days to indicate that the activity will take at least eight days and no more than twelve (assuming a five-day workweek).
- 15 percent probability of exceeding three weeks to indicate a high probability—85 percent—that the activity will take three weeks or less.

Chapter 11 on Project Risk Management includes a more detailed discussion of estimating uncertainty.

.2 *Basis of estimates.* Assumptions made in developing the estimates must be documented.

.3 *Activity list updates.* Activity list updates are described in Section 6.2.3.2.

6.4 SCHEDULE DEVELOPMENT

Schedule development means determining start and finish dates for project activities. If the start and finish dates are not realistic, then the project is unlikely to be finished as scheduled. The schedule development process must often be iterated (along with the processes that provide inputs, especially duration estimating and cost estimating) prior to determination of the project schedule.

Inputs	Tools & Techniques	Outputs
.1 Project network diagrams	.1 Mathematical analysis	.1 Project schedule
.2 Activity duration estimates	.2 Duration compression	.2 Supporting detail
.3 Resource requirements	.3 Simulation	.3 Schedule management plan
.4 Resource pool description	.4 Resource leveling heuristics	.4 Resource requirement updates
.5 Calendars	.5 Project management software	
.6 Constraints	.6 Coding structure	
.7 Assumptions		
.8 Leads and lags		
.9 Risk management plan		
.10 Activity attributes		

6.4.1 Inputs to Schedule Development

.1 *Project network diagrams.* Project network diagrams are described in Section 6.2.3.1.

.2 *Activity duration estimates.* Activity duration estimates are described in Section 6.3.3.1.

.3 *Resource requirements.* Resource requirements are described in Section 6.3.1.4.

.4 *Resource pool description.* Knowledge of what resources will be available at what times and in what patterns is necessary for schedule development. For example, shared or critical resources can be especially difficult to schedule since their availability may be highly variable. The amount of detail and the level of specificity in the resource pool description will vary. For example, one need only know that two consultants will be available in a particular time frame for preliminary schedule development of a consulting project. The final schedule for the same project, however, identifies which specific consultants will be available.

.5 *Calendars.* Project and resource calendars identify periods when work is allowed. *Project calendars* affect all resources (e.g., some projects will work only during normal business hours, while others will work a full three shifts). A five-day workweek is an example of calendar usage. *Resource calendars* affect a specific resource or category of resources (e.g., a project team member may be on vacation or in a training program; a labor contract may limit certain workers to certain days of the week).

.6 *Constraints.* Constraints are factors that will limit the project management team's options. There are two major categories of time constraints considered during schedule development:

■ Imposed dates—imposed dates on activity starts or finishes can be used to restrict the start or finish to occur either no earlier than a specified date or no later than a specified date. While all four date constraints are typically available in project management software, the "Start No Earlier Than" and the "Finish No Later Than" constraints are the most commonly used. Typical uses of date constraints include such situations as a market window on a technology project, weather restrictions on outdoor activities, government-mandated compliance with environmental remediation, delivery of material from parties not represented in the project schedule, etc.

■ Key events or major milestones—completion of certain deliverables by a specified date may be *requested* by the project sponsor, the project customer, or other stakeholders. Once scheduled, these dates become expected and often may be moved only with great difficulty. Milestones may also be used to indicate interfaces with work outside of the project. Such work is typically not in the project database, and milestones with constraint dates can provide the appropriate schedule interface.

.7 *Assumptions.* See Section 4.1.1.5.

.8 *Leads and lags.* Any of the dependencies may require specification of a lead or a lag to accurately define the relationship. An example of a lag: there might be a desire to schedule a two-week delay (lag) between ordering a piece of equipment and installing or using it. An example of a lead, in a finish-to-start dependency with a ten-day lead: the successor activity starts ten days before the predecessor has completed.

.9 *Risk management plan.* The risk management plan is discussed in 11.1.3.

.10 *Activity attributes.* Attributes of the activities—including responsibility (i.e., who will perform the work), geographic area or building (where the work has to be performed), and activity type (i.e., summary or detailed)—are very important for

A Guide to the Project Management Body of Knowledge (PMBOK® Guide) 2000 Edition
©2000 Project Management Institute, Four Campus Boulevard, Newtown Square, PA 19073-3299 USA

further selection and sorting of the planned activities in a convenient way for the users. WBS classification is also an important attribute that allows useful activity ordering and sorting.

6.4.2 Tools and Techniques for Schedule Development

.1 *Mathematical analysis.* Mathematical analysis involves calculating theoretical early and late start and finish dates for all project activities without regard for any resource pool limitations. The resulting dates are not the schedule, but rather indicate the time periods within which the activity *could* be scheduled given resource limits and other known constraints. The most widely known mathematical analysis techniques are:

- Critical Path Method (CPM)—calculates a single, deterministic early and late start and finish date for each activity based on specified, sequential network logic and a single duration estimate. The focus of CPM is calculating *float* to determine which activities have the least scheduling flexibility. The underlying CPM algorithms are often used in other types of mathematical analysis.
- Graphical Evaluation and Review Technique (GERT)—allows for probabilistic treatment of both network logic and activity duration estimates (i.e., some activities may not be performed at all, some may be performed only in part, and others may be performed more than once).
- Program Evaluation and Review Technique (PERT)—uses a weighted average duration estimate to calculate activity durations. Although there are surface differences, PERT differs from CPM primarily in that it uses the distribution's mean (expected value) instead of the most likely estimate originally used in CPM (see **Figure 6-4**). PERT itself is seldom used today.

.2 *Duration compression.* Duration compression is a special case of mathematical analysis that looks for ways to shorten the project schedule without changing the project scope (e.g., to meet imposed dates or other schedule objectives). Duration compression includes techniques such as:

- Crashing—in which cost and schedule tradeoffs are analyzed to determine how, if at all, to obtain the greatest amount of compression for the least incremental cost. Crashing does not always produce a viable alternative and often results in increased cost.
- Fast tracking—doing activities in parallel that would normally be done in sequence (e.g., starting to write code on a software project before the design is complete, or starting to build the foundation for a petroleum processing plant before the 25 percent engineering point is reached). Fast tracking often results in rework and usually increases risk.

.3 *Simulation.* Simulation involves calculating multiple project durations with different sets of activity assumptions. The most common technique is Monte Carlo Analysis, in which a distribution of probable results is defined for each activity and used to calculate a distribution of probable results for the total project (see also Section 11.4.2.4). In addition, *what-if* analyses can be made using the logic network to simulate different scenarios, such as delaying a major component delivery, extending specific engineering durations, or introducing external factors (such as a strike, or a change in the permitting process). The outcome of the what-if simulations can be used to assess the feasibility of the schedule under adverse conditions, and in preparing contingency/response plans to overcome or mitigate the impact of unexpected situations.

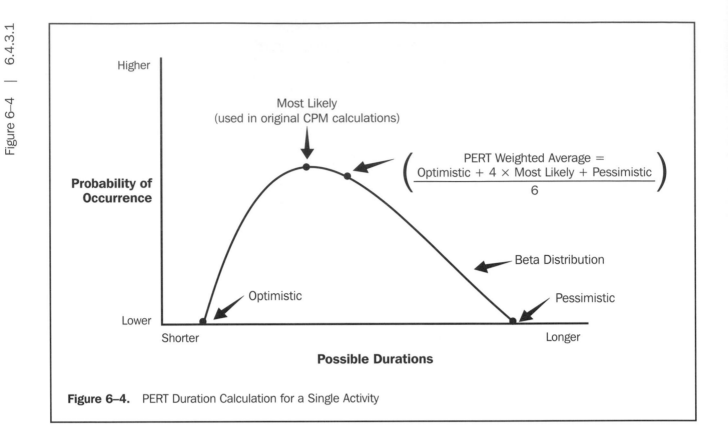

Figure 6–4. PERT Duration Calculation for a Single Activity

.4 *Resource leveling heuristics.* Mathematical analysis often produces a preliminary *early-start* schedule that requires more resources during certain time periods than are available, or requires changes in resource levels that are not manageable. Heuristics, such as, "Allocate scarce resources to critical path activities first," can be applied to develop a schedule that reflects such constraints. Resource leveling often results in a project duration that is longer than the preliminary schedule. This technique is sometimes called the *resource-based method*, especially when implemented with computerized optimization. Resource reallocation from non-critical to critical activities is a common way to bring the schedule back, or as close as possible, to its originally intended overall duration. Utilization of extended hours, weekends, or multiple shifts should also be considered to reduce the durations of critical activities. Productivity increases based on the use of different technologies and/or machinery (i.e., automatic welding, electrical pipe cutters, etc.) are another way to shorten durations that have extended the preliminary schedule. Fast tracking, if feasible (as described in Section 6.4.2.2), is another way to reduce the overall project duration. Some projects may have a finite and critical project resource, requiring that this resource be scheduled in reverse from the project ending date; this is known as *reverse resource allocation scheduling*. Critical chain is a technique that modifies the project schedule to account for limited resources.

.5 *Project management software.* Project management software is widely used to assist with schedule development. Other software may be capable of interacting directly or indirectly within themselves, or with other software, to carry out the requirements of other knowledge areas. These products automate the calculation

A Guide to the Project Management Body of Knowledge (PMBOK® Guide) 2000 Edition
©2000 Project Management Institute, Four Campus Boulevard, Newtown Square, PA 19073-3299 USA

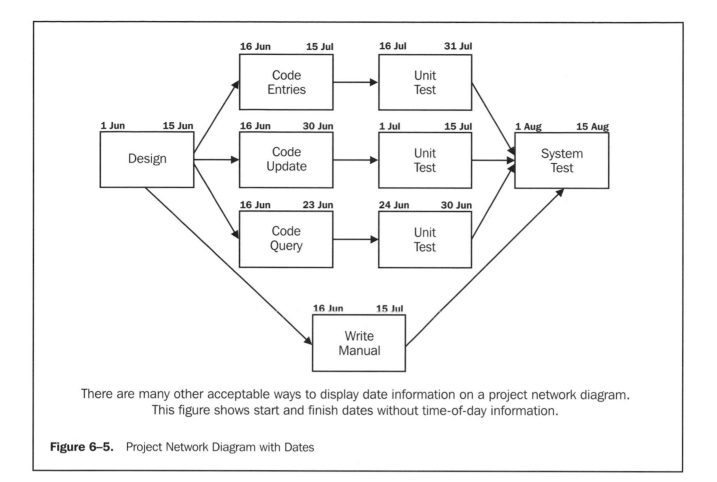

There are many other acceptable ways to display date information on a project network diagram. This figure shows start and finish dates without time-of-day information.

Figure 6–5. Project Network Diagram with Dates

of the mathematical analysis and resource leveling, and thus allow for rapid consideration of many schedule alternatives. They are also widely used to print or display the outputs of schedule development.

.6 *Coding structure.* The activities should have a coding structure that will allow sorting and/or extractions based on different attributes assigned to the activities, such as responsibility, geographic area or building, project phase, schedule level, activity type, and WBS classification.

6.4.3 Outputs from Schedule Development

.1 *Project schedule.* The project schedule includes at least planned start and expected finish dates for each activity. (Note: The project schedule remains preliminary until resource assignments have been confirmed. This would usually happen no later than the completion of Project Plan Development, Section 4.1.)

The project schedule may be presented in summary form (the *master schedule*), or in detail. Although it can be presented in tabular form, it is more often presented graphically, using one or more of the following formats:

■ Project network diagrams with date information added (see **Figure 6-5**). These charts usually show both the project logic and the project's critical path activities (see Section 6.2.3.1 for more information on project network diagrams).

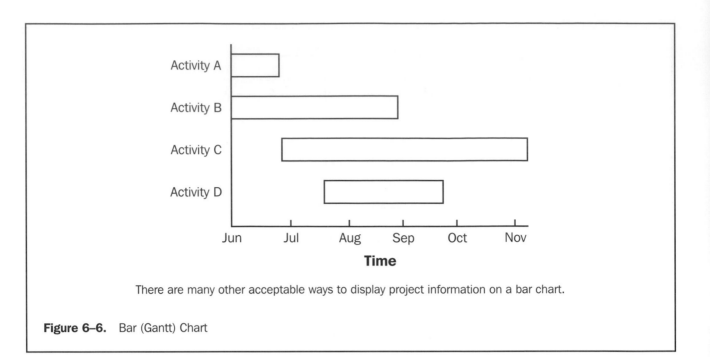

There are many other acceptable ways to display project information on a bar chart.

Figure 6–6. Bar (Gantt) Chart

■ Bar charts, also called *Gantt charts* (see **Figure 6-6**), show activity start and end dates, as well as expected durations, and sometimes show dependencies. They are relatively easy to read, and are frequently used in management presentations.

■ Milestone charts (see **Figure 6-7**) are similar to bar charts, but only identify the scheduled start or completion of major deliverables and key external interfaces.

.2 *Supporting detail.* Supporting detail for the project schedule includes at least documentation of all identified assumptions and constraints. The amount of additional detail varies by application area. For example:

■ On a construction project, it will most likely include such items as resource histograms, cash-flow projections, and order and delivery schedules.

■ On an electronics project, it will most likely include resource histograms only. Information frequently supplied as supporting detail includes, but is not limited to:

■ Resource requirements by time period, often in the form of a resource histogram.

■ Alternative schedules (e.g., best case or worst case, resource leveled or not, with or without imposed dates).

■ Schedule contingency reserves (see Section 11.4).

.3 *Schedule management plan.* A schedule management plan defines how changes to the schedule will be managed. It may be formal or informal, highly detailed or broadly framed, based on the needs of the project. It is a subsidiary element of the overall project plan (see Section 4.1).

.4 *Resource requirement updates.* Resource leveling updates may have a significant effect on preliminary estimates of resource requirements.

A Guide to the Project Management Body of Knowledge (PMBOK® Guide) 2000 Edition
©2000 Project Management Institute, Four Campus Boulevard, Newtown Square, PA 19073-3299 USA

Figure 6-6 | 6.5.1.1

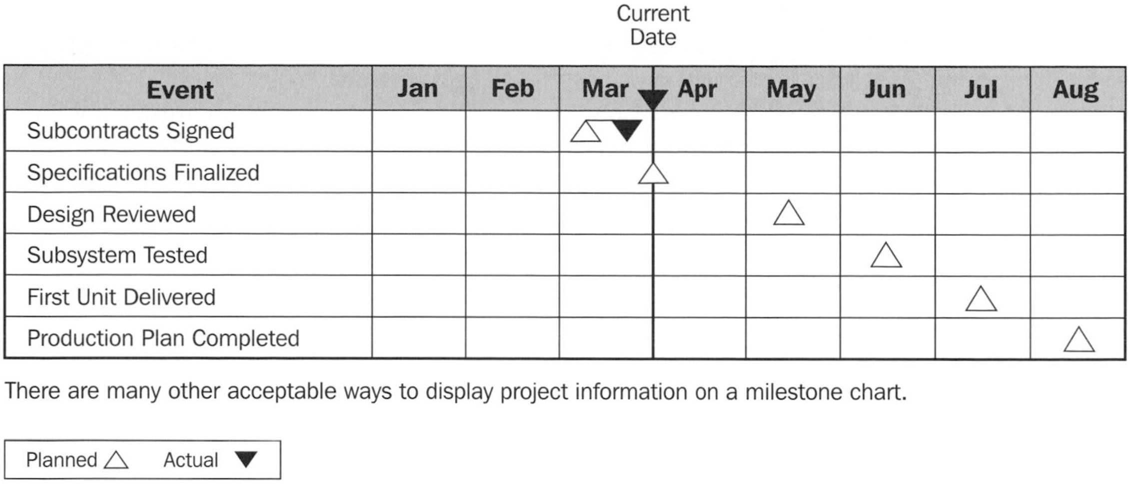

Event	Jan	Feb	Mar	Apr	May	Jun	Jul	Aug
Subcontracts Signed			△ ▼					
Specifications Finalized				△				
Design Reviewed					△			
Subsystem Tested						△		
First Unit Delivered							△	
Production Plan Completed								△

Current Date

There are many other acceptable ways to display project information on a milestone chart.

Planned △   Actual ▼

Figure 6–7. Milestone Chart

6.5 SCHEDULE CONTROL

Schedule control is concerned with a) influencing the factors that create schedule changes to ensure that changes are agreed upon, b) determining that the schedule has changed, and c) managing the actual changes when and as they occur. Schedule control must be thoroughly integrated with the other control processes, as described in Section 4.3, Integrated Change Control.

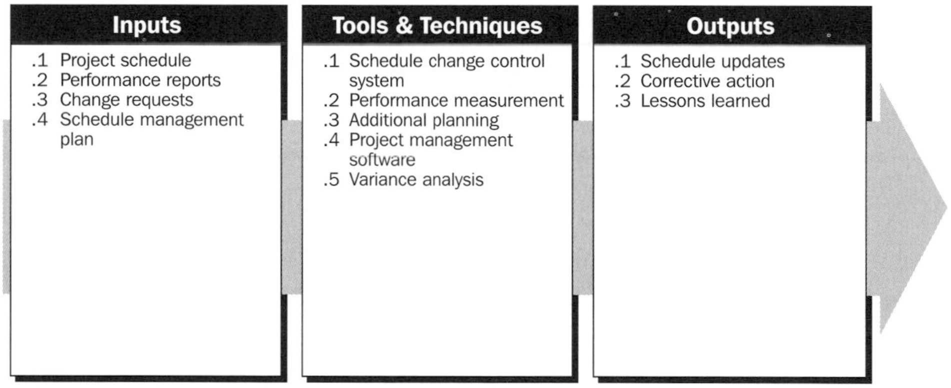

Inputs	Tools & Techniques	Outputs
.1 Project schedule .2 Performance reports .3 Change requests .4 Schedule management plan	.1 Schedule change control system .2 Performance measurement .3 Additional planning .4 Project management software .5 Variance analysis	.1 Schedule updates .2 Corrective action .3 Lessons learned

6.5.1 Inputs to Schedule Control

.1 Project schedule. The project schedule is described in Section 6.4.3.1. The approved project schedule, called the *schedule baseline* (which must be feasible technically and in terms of resources), is a component of the project plan described in Section 4.1.3.1. It provides the basis for measuring and reporting schedule performance.

.2 *Performance reports.* Performance reports, discussed in Section 10.3.3.1, provide information on schedule performance, such as which planned dates have been met and which have not. Performance reports may also alert the project team to issues that may cause problems in the future.

.3 *Change requests.* Change requests may occur in many forms—oral or written, direct or indirect, externally or internally initiated, and legally mandated or optional. Changes may require extending the schedule or may allow accelerating it (see Section 4.3.1.3).

.4 *Schedule management plan.* The schedule management plan is described in Section 6.4.3.3.

6.5.2 Tools and Techniques for Schedule Control

.1 *Schedule change control system.* A schedule change control system defines the procedures by which the project schedule may be changed. It includes the paperwork, tracking systems, and approval levels necessary for authorizing changes. Schedule change control should be integrated with the integrated change control system described in Section 4.3.

.2 *Performance measurement.* Performance measurement techniques such as those described in Section 10.3.2 help to assess the magnitude of any variations that do occur. An important part of schedule control is to decide if the schedule variation requires corrective action. For example, a major delay on a noncritical activity may have little effect on the overall project, while a much shorter delay on a critical or near-critical activity may require immediate action.

.3 *Additional planning.* Few projects run exactly according to plan. Prospective changes may require new or revised activity duration estimates, modified activity sequences, or analysis of alternative schedules.

.4 *Project management software.* Project management software is described in Section 6.4.2.5. The ability of project management software to track planned dates versus actual dates and to forecast the effects of schedule changes, real or potential, makes it a useful tool for schedule control.

.5 *Variance analysis.* Performance of the variance analysis during the schedule-monitoring process is a key element for time control. Comparing target dates with the actual/forecast start and finish dates provides useful information for the detection of deviations and for the implementation of corrective solutions in case of delays. The float variance is also an essential planning component to evaluate project time-performance. Particular attention has to be given to critical and subcritical activities (i.e., analyzing the ten subcritical paths, in order of ascending float).

6.5.3 Outputs from Schedule Control

.1 *Schedule updates.* A schedule update is any modification to the schedule information that is used to manage the project. Appropriate stakeholders must be notified as needed. Schedule updates may or may not require adjustments to other aspects of the project plan.

   Revisions are a special category of schedule updates. Revisions are changes to the schedule start and finish dates in the approved project schedule. These changes are generally incorporated in response to scope changes or changes to estimates. In some cases, schedule delays may be so severe that *rebaselining* is needed to provide realistic data to measure performance. However, care must be taken before rebaselining, as historical data will be lost for the project schedule. Rebaselining should only be used as a last resort in controlling the schedule; new target schedules should be the normal mode of schedule revision.

.2 *Corrective action.* Corrective action is anything done to bring expected future schedule performance in line with the project plan. Corrective action in the area of time management often involves expediting: special actions taken to ensure completion of an activity on time or with the least possible delay. Corrective action frequently requires root-cause analysis to identify the cause of the variation, and schedule recovery can be planned and executed for activities delineated later in the schedule and need not only address the activity causing the deviation.

.3 *Lessons learned.* The causes of variances, the reasoning behind the corrective action chosen, and other types of lessons learned from schedule control should be documented, so that they become part of the historical database for both this project and other projects of the performing organization.

Chapter 7

Project Cost Management

Project Cost Management includes the processes required to ensure that the project is completed within the approved budget. **Figure 7-1** provides an overview of the following major processes:

7.1 Resource Planning—determining what resources (people, equipment, materials) and what quantities of each should be used to perform project activities.

7.2 Cost Estimating—developing an approximation (estimate) of the costs of the resources needed to complete project activities.

7.3 Cost Budgeting—allocating the overall cost estimate to individual work activities.

7.4 Cost Control—controlling changes to the project budget.

These processes interact with each other and with the processes in the other knowledge areas as well. Each process may involve effort from one or more individuals or groups of individuals, based on the needs of the project. Each process generally occurs at least once in every project phase.

Although the processes are presented here as discrete elements with well-defined interfaces, in practice they may overlap and interact in ways not detailed here. Process interactions are discussed in detail in Chapter 3.

Project cost management is primarily concerned with the cost of the resources needed to complete project activities. However, project cost management should also consider the effect of project decisions on the cost of using the project's product. For example, limiting the number of design reviews may reduce the cost of the project at the expense of an increase in the customer's operating costs. This broader view of project cost management is often called *life-cycle costing*. Life-cycle costing together with Value Engineering techniques are used to reduce cost and time, improve quality and performance, and optimize the decision-making.

In many application areas, predicting and analyzing the prospective financial performance of the project's product is done outside the project. In others (e.g., capital facilities projects), project cost management also includes this work. When such predictions and analyses are included, project cost management will include additional processes and numerous general management techniques such as return on investment, discounted cash flow, payback analysis, and others.

Project cost management should consider the information needs of the project stakeholders—different stakeholders may measure project costs in different ways and at different times. For example, the cost of a procurement item may be measured when committed, ordered, delivered, incurred, or recorded for accounting purposes.

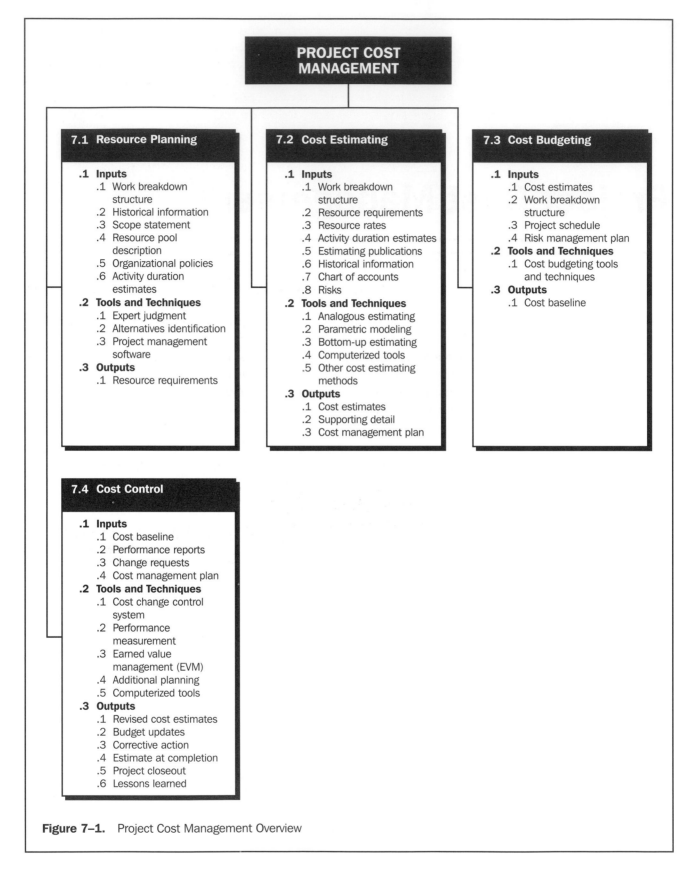

Figure 7–1. Project Cost Management Overview

A Guide to the Project Management Body of Knowledge (PMBOK® Guide) 2000 Edition
©2000 Project Management Institute, Four Campus Boulevard, Newtown Square, PA 19073-3299 USA

When project costs are used as a component of a reward and recognition system (discussed in Section 9.3.2.3), controllable and uncontrollable costs should be estimated and budgeted separately to ensure that rewards reflect actual performance.

On some projects, especially smaller ones, resource planning, cost estimating, and cost budgeting are so tightly linked that they are viewed as a single process (e.g., they may be performed by a single individual over a relatively short period of time). They are presented here as distinct processes because the tools and techniques for each are different. The ability to influence cost is greatest at the early stages of the project, and this is why early scope definition is critical, as well as thorough requirements identification and execution of a sound plan.

7.1 RESOURCE PLANNING

Resource planning involves determining what physical resources (people, equipment, materials) and what quantities of each should be used and when they would be needed to perform project activities. It must be closely coordinated with cost estimating (described in Section 7.2). For example:

- A construction project team will need to be familiar with local building codes. Such knowledge is often readily available from local sellers. However, if the local labor pool lacks experience with unusual or specialized construction techniques, the additional cost for a consultant might be the most effective way to secure knowledge of the local building codes.
- An automotive design team should be familiar with the latest in automated assembly techniques. The requisite knowledge might be obtained by hiring a consultant, by sending a designer to a seminar on robotics, or by including someone from manufacturing as a member of the team.

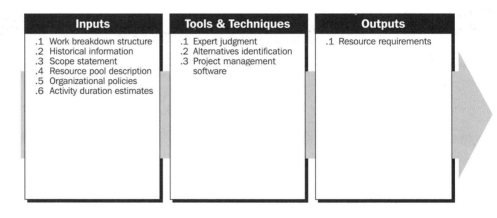

Inputs	Tools & Techniques	Outputs
.1 Work breakdown structure .2 Historical information .3 Scope statement .4 Resource pool description .5 Organizational policies .6 Activity duration estimates	.1 Expert judgment .2 Alternatives identification .3 Project management software	.1 Resource requirements

7.1.1 Inputs to Resource Planning

.1 *Work breakdown structure.* The work breakdown structure (WBS, described in Section 5.3.3.1) identifies the project deliverables and processes that will need resources, and thus is the primary input to resource planning. Any relevant outputs from other planning processes should be provided through the WBS to ensure proper control.

.2 *Historical information.* Historical information regarding what types of resources were required for similar work on previous projects should be used if available.

.3 *Scope statement.* The scope statement (described in Section 5.2.3.1) contains the project justification and the project objectives, both of which should be considered explicitly during resource planning.

.4 *Resource pool description.* Knowledge of what resources (people, equipment, material) are potentially available is necessary for resource planning. The amount of detail and the level of specificity of the resource pool description will vary. For example, during the early phases of an engineering design project, the pool may include "junior and senior engineers" in large numbers. During later phases of the same project, however, the pool may be limited to those individuals who are knowledgeable about the project as a result of having worked on the earlier phases.

.5 *Organizational policies.* The policies of the performing organization regarding staffing and the rental or purchase of supplies and equipment must be considered during resource planning.

.6 *Activity duration estimates.* Time durations (described in Section 6.3.3.1).

7.1.2 Tools and Techniques for Resource Planning

.1 *Expert judgment.* Expert judgment will often be required to assess the inputs to this process. Such expertise may be provided by any group or individual with specialized knowledge or training, and is available from many sources including:
- Other units within the performing organization.
- Consultants.
- Professional and technical associations.
- Industry groups.

.2 *Alternatives identification.* Alternatives identification is discussed in Section 5.2.2.3.

.3 *Project management software.* Project management software has the capability to help organize resource pools. Depending upon the sophistication of the software, resource availabilities and rates can be defined, as well as resource calendars.

7.1.3 Outputs from Resource Planning

.1 *Resource requirements.* The output of the resource planning process is a description of what types of resources are required and in what quantities for each element at the lowest level of the WBS. Resource requirements for higher levels within the WBS can be calculated based on the lower-level values. These resources will be obtained either through staff acquisition (described in Section 9.2) or procurement (described in Chapter 12).

7.2 COST ESTIMATING

Cost estimating involves developing an approximation (estimate) of the costs of the resources needed to complete project activities. In approximating cost, the estimator considers the causes of variation of the final estimate for purposes of better managing the project.

When a project is performed under contract, care should be taken to distinguish cost estimating from pricing. Cost estimating involves developing an assessment of the likely quantitative result—how much will it cost the performing organization to provide the product or service involved? Pricing is a business decision—how much will the performing organization charge for the product or service—that uses the cost estimate as but one consideration of many.

A Guide to the Project Management Body of Knowledge (PMBOK® Guide) 2000 Edition
©2000 Project Management Institute, Four Campus Boulevard, Newtown Square, PA 19073-3299 USA

Cost estimating includes identifying and considering various costing alternatives. For example, in most application areas, additional work during a design phase is widely held to have the potential for reducing the cost of the production phase. The cost-estimating process must consider whether the cost of the additional design work will be offset by the expected savings.

Inputs	Tools & Techniques	Outputs
.1 Work breakdown structure .2 Resource requirements .3 Resource rates .4 Activity duration estimates .5 Estimating publications .6 Historical information .7 Chart of accounts .8 Risks	.1 Analogous estimating .2 Parametric modeling .3 Bottom-up estimating .4 Computerized tools .5 Other cost estimating methods	.1 Cost estimates .2 Supporting detail .3 Cost management plan

7.2.1 Inputs to Cost Estimating

.1 *Work breakdown structure.* The WBS is described in Section 5.3.3.1. It is used to organize the cost estimates and to ensure that all identified work has been estimated.

.2 *Resource requirements.* Resource requirements are described in Section 7.1.3.1.

.3 *Resource rates.* The individual or group preparing the estimates must know the unit rates (e.g., staff cost per hour, bulk material cost per cubic yard) for each resource to calculate project costs. If actual rates are not known, the rates themselves may have to be estimated.

.4 *Activity duration estimates.* Activity duration estimates (described in Section 6.3.3.1) will affect cost estimates on any project where the project budget includes an allowance for the cost of financing (i.e., interest charges).

.5 *Estimating publications.* Commercially available data on cost estimating.

.6 *Historical information.* Information on the cost of many categories of resources is often available from one or more of the following sources:

- Project files—one or more of the organizations involved in the project may maintain records of previous project results that are detailed enough to aid in developing cost estimates. In some application areas, individual team members may maintain such records.

- Commercial cost-estimating databases—historical information is often available commercially.

- Project team knowledge—the individual members of the project team may remember previous actuals or estimates. While such recollections may be useful, they are generally far less reliable than documented results.

.7 *Chart of accounts.* A chart of accounts describes the coding structure used by the performing organization to report financial information in its general ledger. Project cost estimates must be assigned to the correct accounting category.

.8 *Risks.* The project team considers information on risks (see Section 11.2.3.1) when producing cost estimates, since risks (either threats or opportunities) can have a significant impact on cost. The project team considers the extent to which the effect of risk is included in the cost estimates for each activity.

7.2.2 Tools and Techniques for Cost Estimating

  .1 *Analogous estimating.* Analogous estimating, also called *top-down estimating,* means using the actual cost of a previous, similar project as the basis for estimating the cost of the current project. It is frequently used to estimate total project costs when there is a limited amount of detailed information about the project (e.g., in the early phases). Analogous estimating is a form of expert judgment (described in Section 7.1.2.1).

       Analogous estimating is generally less costly than other techniques, but it is also generally less accurate. It is most reliable when a) the previous projects are similar in fact and not just in appearance, and b) the individuals or groups preparing the estimates have the needed expertise.

  .2 *Parametric modeling.* Parametric modeling involves using project characteristics (parameters) in a mathematical model to predict project costs. Models may be simple (residential home construction will cost a certain amount per square foot of living space) or complex (one model of software development costs uses thirteen separate adjustment factors, each of which has five to seven points on it).

       Both the cost and accuracy of parametric models vary widely. They are most likely to be reliable when a) the historical information used to develop the model was accurate, b) the parameters used in the model are readily quantifiable, and c) the model is scalable (i.e., it works as well for a very large project as for a very small one).

  .3 *Bottom-up estimating.* This technique involves estimating the cost of individual activities or work packages, then summarizing or rolling up the individual estimates to get a project total.

       The cost and accuracy of bottom-up estimating is driven by the size and complexity of the individual activity or work package: smaller activities increase both cost and accuracy of the estimating process. The project management team must weigh the additional accuracy against the additional cost.

  .4 *Computerized tools.* Computerized tools, such as project management software, spreadsheets and simulation/statistical tools, are widely used to assist with cost estimating. Such products can simplify the use of the tools described earlier and thereby facilitate rapid consideration of many costing alternatives.

  .5 *Other cost estimating methods.* For example, vendor bid analysis.

7.2.3 Outputs from Cost Estimating

  .1 *Cost estimates.* Cost estimates are quantitative assessments of the likely costs of the resources required to complete project activities. They may be presented in summary or in detail.

       Costs must be estimated for all resources that will be charged to the project. This includes, but is not limited to, labor, materials, supplies, and special categories such as an inflation allowance or cost reserve.

       Cost estimates are generally expressed in units of currency (dollars, euros, yen, etc.) to facilitate comparisons both within and across projects. In some cases, the estimator may use units of measure to estimate cost, such as staff hours or staff days, along with their cost estimates to facilitate appropriate management control. Cost estimating generally includes considering appropriate risk response planning, such as contingency plans.

A Guide to the Project Management Body of Knowledge (PMBOK® Guide) 2000 Edition
©2000 Project Management Institute, Four Campus Boulevard, Newtown Square, PA 19073-3299 USA

Cost estimates may benefit from being refined during the course of the project to reflect the additional detail available. In some application areas, there are guidelines for when such refinements should be made and what degree of accuracy is expected. For example, The Association for the Advancement of Cost Engineering (AACE) International has identified a progression of five types of estimates of construction costs during engineering: order of magnitude, conceptual, preliminary, definitive, and control.

.2 *Supporting detail.* Supporting detail for the cost estimates should include:

- A description of the scope of work estimated. This is often provided by a reference to the WBS.
- Documentation of the basis for the estimate; i.e., how it was developed.
- Documentation of any assumptions made.
- An indication of the range of possible results; for example, $10,000 ± $1,000 to indicate that the item is expected to cost between $9,000 and $11,000.

The amount and type of additional details vary by application area. Retaining even rough notes may prove valuable by providing a better understanding of how the estimate was developed.

.3 *Cost management plan.* The cost management plan describes how cost variances will be managed (e.g., different responses to major problems than to minor ones). A cost management plan may be formal or informal, highly detailed or broadly framed, based on the needs of the project stakeholders. It is a subsidiary element of the project plan (discussed in Section 4.1.3.1).

7.3 COST BUDGETING

Cost budgeting involves allocating the overall cost estimates to individual activities or work packages to establish a cost baseline for measuring project performance. Reality may dictate that estimates are done after budgetary approval is provided, but estimates should be done prior to budget request wherever possible.

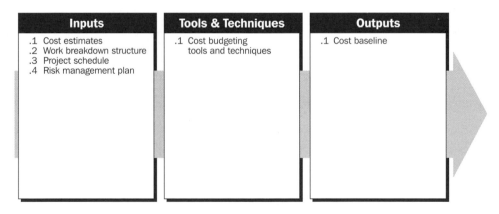

Inputs	Tools & Techniques	Outputs
.1 Cost estimates .2 Work breakdown structure .3 Project schedule .4 Risk management plan	.1 Cost budgeting tools and techniques	.1 Cost baseline

7.3.1 Inputs to Cost Budgeting

.1 *Cost estimates.* Cost estimates are described in Section 7.2.3.1.

.2 *Work breakdown structure.* The WBS (described in Section 5.3.3.1) identifies the project elements to which costs will be allocated.

Figure 7–2 | 7.4.2.2

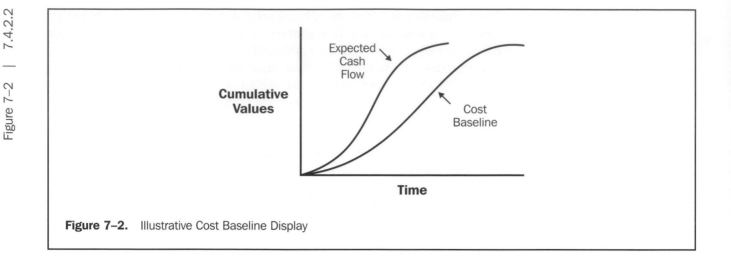

Figure 7–2. Illustrative Cost Baseline Display

.3 *Project schedule.* The project schedule (described in Section 6.4.3.1) includes planned start and expected finish dates for the project components to which costs will be allocated. This information is needed to assign costs to the time period when the cost will be incurred.

.4 *Risk management plan.* The risk management plan is discussed in Section 11.1.3. In addition to this, the risk management plan often includes cost contingency, which can be determined on the basis of the expected accuracy of the estimate.

7.3.2 Tools and Techniques for Cost Budgeting

.1 *Cost budgeting tools and techniques.* The tools and techniques described in Section 7.2.2 for developing project cost estimates are used to develop budgets for activities or work packages as well.

7.3.3 Outputs from Cost Budgeting

.1 *Cost baseline.* The cost baseline is a time-phased budget that will be used to measure and monitor cost performance on the project. It is developed by summing estimated costs by period and is usually displayed in the form of an S-curve, as illustrated in **Figure 7-2**.

   Many projects, especially larger ones, may have multiple cost baselines to measure different aspects of cost performance. For example, a spending plan or cash-flow forecast is a cost baseline for measuring disbursements.

7.4 COST CONTROL

Cost control is concerned with a) influencing the factors that create changes to the cost baseline to ensure that changes are agreed upon, b) determining that the cost baseline has changed, and c) managing the actual changes when and as they occur. Cost control includes:

A Guide to the Project Management Body of Knowledge (PMBOK® Guide) 2000 Edition
©2000 Project Management Institute, Four Campus Boulevard, Newtown Square, PA 19073-3299 USA

- Monitoring cost performance to detect and understand variances from plan.
- Ensuring that all appropriate changes are recorded accurately in the cost baseline.
- Preventing incorrect, inappropriate, or unauthorized changes from being included in the cost baseline.
- Informing appropriate stakeholders of authorized changes.
- Acting to bring expected costs within acceptable limits.

Cost control includes searching out the "whys" of both positive and negative variances. It must be thoroughly integrated with the other control processes (scope change control, schedule control, quality control, and others, as discussed in Section 4.3). For example, inappropriate responses to cost variances can cause quality or schedule problems, or produce an unacceptable level of risk later in the project.

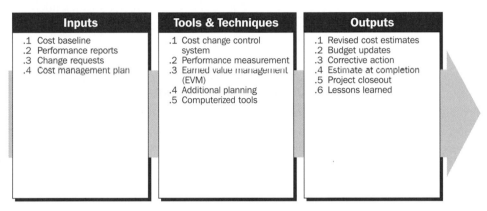

Inputs	Tools & Techniques	Outputs
.1 Cost baseline .2 Performance reports .3 Change requests .4 Cost management plan	.1 Cost change control system .2 Performance measurement .3 Earned value management (EVM) .4 Additional planning .5 Computerized tools	.1 Revised cost estimates .2 Budget updates .3 Corrective action .4 Estimate at completion .5 Project closeout .6 Lessons learned

7.4.1 Inputs to Cost Control

.1 Cost baseline. The cost baseline is described in Section 7.3.3.1.

.2 Performance reports. Performance reports (discussed in Section 10.3.3.1) provide information on project scope and cost performance, such as which budgets have been met and which have not. Performance reports may also alert the project team to issues that may cause problems in the future.

.3 Change requests. Change requests may occur in many forms—oral or written, direct or indirect, externally or internally initiated, and legally mandated or optional. Changes may require increasing the budget or may allow decreasing it.

.4 Cost management plan. The cost management plan is described in Section 7.2.3.3.

7.4.2 Tools and Techniques for Cost Control

.1 Cost change control system. A cost change control system defines the procedures by which the cost baseline may be changed. It includes the paperwork, tracking systems, and approval levels necessary for authorizing changes. The cost change control system should be integrated with the integrated change control system, discussed in Section 4.3.

.2 Performance measurement. Performance measurement techniques, described in Section 10.3.2, help to assess the magnitude of any variations that do occur. Earned Value Management (EVM), described in Sections 7.4.2.3 and 10.3.2.4, is especially useful for cost control. An important part of cost control is to determine what is causing the variance and to decide if the variance requires corrective action.

.3 *Earned value management (EVM).* All EVM Control Account Plans (CAPs) must continuously measure project performance by relating three independent variables: 1) The Planned Value, the physical work scheduled to be performed, including the estimated value of this work (previously called the Budgeted Costs for Work Scheduled [BCWS]), as compared against the 2) The Earned Value, physical work actually accomplished, including the estimated value of this work (previously called the Budgeted Costs for Work Performed [BCWP]), and to the 3) Actual Costs incurred to accomplish the Earned Value. The relationship of 2) Earned Value less 1) Planned Value constitutes the Schedule Variance (SV). The relationship of 2) Earned Value less 3) Actual Costs constitutes the Cost Variance (CV) for the project. See also Section 10.3.2.4.

.4 *Additional planning.* Few projects run exactly according to plan. Prospective changes may require new or revised cost estimates or analysis of alternative approaches.

.5 *Computerized tools.* Computerized tools, such as project management software and spreadsheets, are often used to track planned costs versus actual costs, and to forecast the effects of cost changes.

7.4.3 Outputs from Cost Control

.1 *Revised cost estimates.* Revised cost estimates are modifications to the cost information used to manage the project. Appropriate stakeholders must be notified as needed. Revised cost estimates may or may not require adjustments to other aspects of the project plan.

.2 *Budget updates.* Budget updates are a special category of revised cost estimates. Budget updates are changes to an approved cost baseline. These numbers are generally revised only in response to scope changes. In some cases, cost variances may be so severe that *rebaselining* is needed to provide a realistic measure of performance.

.3 *Corrective action.* Corrective action is anything done to bring expected future project performance in line with the project plan.

.4 *Estimate at completion.* An Estimate at Completion (EAC) is a forecast of most likely total project costs based on project performance and risk quantification, described in Section 11.4.3. The most common forecasting techniques are some variation of:

- EAC = Actuals to date plus a new estimate for all remaining work. This approach is most often used when past performance shows that the original estimating assumptions were fundamentally flawed, or that they are no longer relevant to a change in conditions. Formula: EAC = AC + ETC.

- EAC = Actuals to date plus remaining budget (BAC – EV). This approach is most often used when current variances are seen as atypical and the project management team expectations are that similar variances will not occur in the future. Formula: EAC = AC + BAC – EV.

- EAC = Actuals to date plus the remaining project budget (BAC – EV) modified by a performance factor, often the cumulative cost performance index (CPI). This approach is most often used when current variances are seen as typical of future variances. Formula: EAC = AC + ((BAC – EV)/CPI)—this CPI is the cumulative CPI.

Each of these approaches may be the correct approach for any given project and will provide the project management team with a signal if the EAC forecasts go beyond acceptable tolerances.

.5 *Project closeout.* Processes and procedures should be developed for the closing or canceling of projects. For example, the Statement of Position (SOP 98-1 issued by the American Institute of Certified Public Accountants—AICPA) requires that all the costs for a failed information technology project be written off in the quarter that the project is canceled.

.6 *Lessons learned.* The causes of variances, the reasoning behind the corrective action chosen, and other types of lessons learned from cost control should be documented so that they become part of the historical database for both this project and other projects of the performing organization (see Section 4.3.3.3).

Chapter 8

Project Quality Management

Project Quality Management includes the processes required to ensure that the project will satisfy the needs for which it was undertaken. It includes "all activities of the overall management function that determine the quality policy, objectives, and responsibilities and implements them by means such as quality planning, quality assurance, quality control, and quality improvement, within the quality system" (1). **Figure 8-1** provides an overview of the following major project quality management processes:

8.1 Quality Planning—identifying which quality standards are relevant to the project and determining how to satisfy them.

8.2 Quality Assurance—evaluating overall project performance on a regular basis to provide confidence that the project will satisfy the relevant quality standards.

8.3 Quality Control—monitoring specific project results to determine if they comply with relevant quality standards and identifying ways to eliminate causes of unsatisfactory performance.

These processes interact with each other and with the processes in the other knowledge areas as well. Each process may involve effort from one or more individuals or groups of individuals, based on the needs of the project. Each process generally occurs at least once in every project phase.

Although the processes are presented here as discrete elements with well-defined interfaces, in practice they may overlap and interact in ways not detailed here. Process interactions are discussed in detail in Chapter 3.

The basic approach to quality management described in this section is intended to be compatible with that of the International Organization for Standardization (ISO), as detailed in the ISO 9000 and 10000 series of standards and guidelines. This generalized approach should also be compatible with a) proprietary approaches to quality management such as those recommended by Deming, Juran, Crosby, and others, and b) nonproprietary approaches such as Total Quality Management (TQM), Continuous Improvement, and others.

Project quality management must address both the management of the project and the product of the project. The generic term *product* is occasionally used, in literature regarding quality, to refer to both goods and services. Failure to meet quality requirements in either dimension can have serious negative consequences for any or all of the project stakeholders. For example:

Figure 8–1 | 8.1

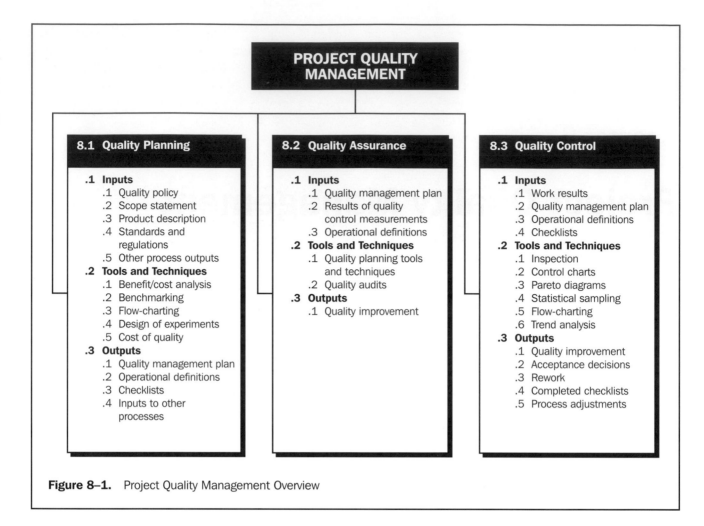

Figure 8–1. Project Quality Management Overview

- Meeting customer requirements by overworking the project team may produce negative consequences in the form of increased employee attrition.
- Meeting project schedule objectives by rushing planned quality inspections may produce negative consequences when errors go undetected.

Quality is "the totality of characteristics of an entity that bear on its ability to satisfy stated or implied needs" (2). Stated and implied needs are the inputs to developing project requirements. A critical aspect of quality management in the project context is the necessity to turn implied needs into requirements through project scope management, which is described in Chapter 5.

The project management team must be careful not to confuse *quality* with *grade*. Grade is "a category or rank given to entities having the same functional use but different technical characteristics" (3). Low quality is always a problem; low grade may not be. For example, a software product may be of high quality (no obvious bugs, readable manual) and low grade (a limited number of features), or of low quality (many bugs, poorly organized user documentation) and high grade (numerous features). Determining and delivering the required levels of both quality and grade are the responsibilities of the project manager and the project management team.

The project management team should also be aware that modern quality management complements project management. For example, both disciplines recognize the importance of:

A Guide to the Project Management Body of Knowledge (PMBOK® Guide) 2000 Edition
©2000 Project Management Institute, Four Campus Boulevard, Newtown Square, PA 19073-3299 USA

■ Customer satisfaction—understanding, managing, and influencing needs so that customer expectations are met. This requires a combination of *conformance to requirements* (the project must produce what it said it would produce) and *fitness for use* (the product or service produced must satisfy real needs).

■ Prevention over inspection—the cost of preventing mistakes is always much less than the cost of correcting them, as revealed by inspection.

■ Management responsibility—success requires the *participation* of all members of the team, but it remains the *responsibility* of management to provide the resources needed to succeed.

■ Processes within phases—the repeated plan-do-check-act cycle described by Deming and others is highly similar to the combination of phases and processes discussed in Chapter 3, Project Management Processes.

In addition, quality improvement initiatives undertaken by the performing organization (e.g., TQM, Continuous Improvement, and others) can improve the quality of the project's management as well as the quality of the project's product.

However, there is an important difference of which the project management team must be acutely aware—the temporary nature of the project means that investments in product quality improvement, especially defect prevention and appraisal, must often be borne by the performing organization since the project may not last long enough to reap the rewards.

8.1 QUALITY PLANNING

Quality planning involves identifying which quality standards are relevant to the project and determining how to satisfy them. It is one of the key facilitating processes during project planning (see Section 3.3.2, Planning Processes) and should be performed regularly and in parallel with the other project planning processes. For example, the changes in the product of the project required to meet identified quality standards may require cost or schedule adjustments, or the desired product quality may require a detailed risk analysis of an identified problem. Prior to development of the ISO 9000 Series, the activities described here as *quality planning* were widely discussed as part of *quality assurance*.

The quality planning techniques discussed here are those most frequently used on projects. There are many others that may be useful on certain projects or in some application areas.

The project team should also be aware of one of the fundamental tenets of modern quality management—quality is planned in, not inspected in.

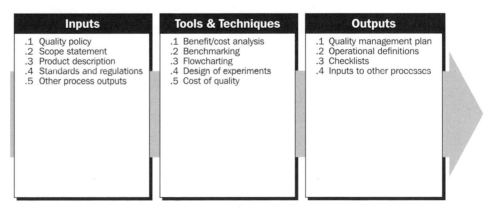

Inputs	Tools & Techniques	Outputs
.1 Quality policy	.1 Benefit/cost analysis	.1 Quality management plan
.2 Scope statement	.2 Benchmarking	.2 Operational definitions
.3 Product description	.3 Flowcharting	.3 Checklists
.4 Standards and regulations	.4 Design of experiments	.4 Inputs to other processes
.5 Other process outputs	.5 Cost of quality	

8.1.1 Inputs to Quality Planning

.1 *Quality policy.* Quality policy is "the overall intentions and direction of an organization with regard to quality, as formally expressed by top management" (4). The quality policy of the performing organization can often be adopted "as is" for use by the project. However, if the performing organization lacks a formal quality policy, or if the project involves multiple performing organizations (as with a joint venture), then the project management team will need to develop a quality policy for the project.

Regardless of the origin of the quality policy, the project management team is responsible for ensuring that the project stakeholders are fully aware of it (e.g., through appropriate information distribution, as described in Section 10.2).

.2 *Scope statement.* The scope statement (described in Section 5.2.3.1) is a key input to quality planning since it documents major project deliverables, as well as the project objectives that serve to define important stakeholder requirements.

.3 *Product description.* Although elements of the product description (described in Section 5.1.1.1) may be embodied in the scope statement, the product description will often contain details of technical issues and other concerns that may affect quality planning.

.4 *Standards and regulations.* The project management team must consider any application area-specific standards or regulations that may affect the project. Section 2.5.1 discusses standards and regulations.

.5 *Other process outputs.* In addition to the scope statement and product description, processes in other knowledge areas may produce outputs that should be considered as part of quality planning. For example, procurement planning (described in Section 12.1) may identify contractor quality requirements that should be reflected in the overall quality management plan.

8.1.2 Tools and Techniques for Quality Planning

.1 *Benefit/cost analysis.* The quality planning process must consider benefit/cost tradeoffs, as described in Section 5.2.2.2. The primary benefit of meeting quality requirements is less rework, which means higher productivity, lower costs, and increased stakeholder satisfaction. The primary cost of meeting quality requirements is the expense associated with project quality management activities. It is axiomatic of the quality management discipline that the benefits outweigh the costs.

.2 *Benchmarking.* Benchmarking involves comparing actual or planned project practices to those of other projects to generate ideas for improvement and to provide a standard by which to measure performance. The other projects may be within the performing organization or outside of it, and may be within the same application area or in another.

.3 *Flowcharting.* A flow chart is any diagram that shows how various elements of a system relate. Flowcharting techniques commonly used in quality management include:

- *Cause-and-effect diagrams*, also called *Ishikawa diagrams* or *fishbone diagrams*, which illustrate how various factors might be linked to potential problems or effects. **Figure 8-2** is an example of a generic cause-and-effect diagram.
- *System* or *process flow charts*, which show how various elements of a system interrelate. **Figure 8-3** is an example of a process flow chart for design reviews.

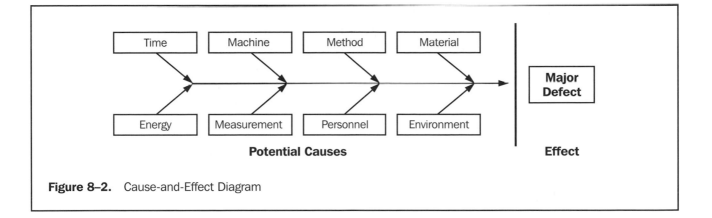

Figure 8–2. Cause-and-Effect Diagram

Flowcharting can help the project team anticipate what and where quality problems might occur, and thus can help develop approaches for dealing with them.

.4 *Design of experiments.* Design of experiments is a statistical method that helps identify which factors might influence specific variables. The technique is applied most frequently to the product of the project (e.g., automotive designers might wish to determine which combination of suspension and tires will produce the most desirable ride characteristics at a reasonable cost).

However, it can also be applied to project management issues, such as cost and schedule tradeoffs. For example, senior engineers will cost more than junior engineers, but can also be expected to complete the assigned work in less time. An appropriately designed "experiment" (in this case, computing project costs and durations for various combinations of senior and junior engineers) will often allow determination of an optimal solution from a relatively limited number of cases.

.5 *Cost of quality.* Cost of quality refers to the total cost of all efforts to achieve product/service quality, and includes all work to ensure conformance to requirements, as well as all work resulting from nonconformance to requirements. There are three types of costs that are incurred: prevention costs, appraisal costs, and failure costs, where the latter is broken down into internal and external costs.

8.1.3 Outputs from Quality Planning

.1 *Quality management plan.* The quality management plan should describe how the project management team will implement its quality policy. In ISO 9000 terminology, it should describe the *project quality system*: "the organizational structure, responsibilities, procedures, processes, and resources needed to implement quality management" (5).

The quality management plan provides input to the overall project plan (described in Section 4.1, Project Plan Development), and must address quality control, quality assurance, and quality improvement for the project.

The quality management plan may be formal or informal, highly detailed, or broadly framed, based on the requirements of the project.

Figure 8–3 | 8.2.2.2

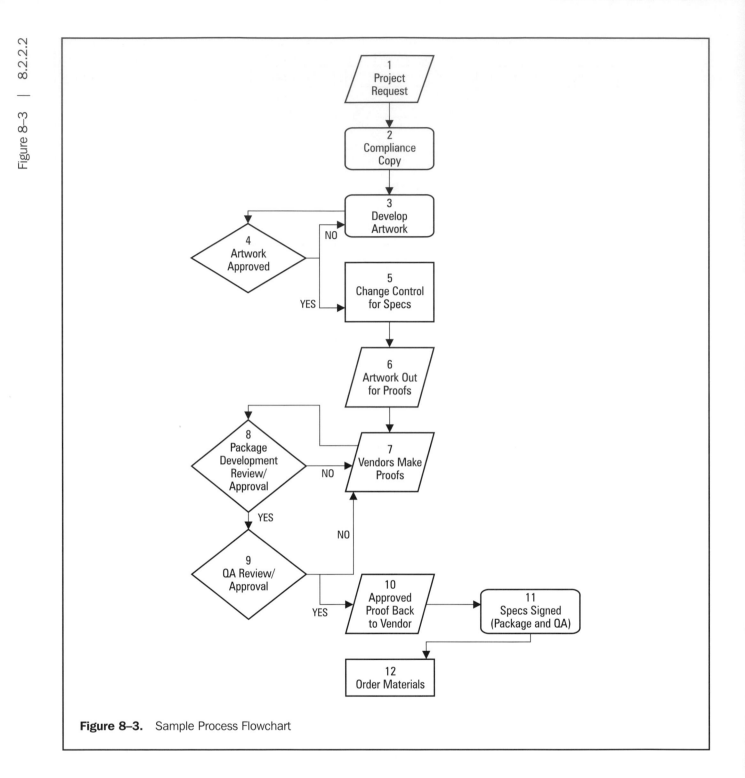

Figure 8–3. Sample Process Flowchart

.2 *Operational definitions.* An operational definition describes, in very specific terms, what something is and how it is measured by the quality control process. For example, it is not enough to say that meeting the planned schedule dates is a measure of management quality; the project management team must also indicate whether every activity must start on time or only finish on time; whether individual activities will be measured, or only certain deliverables, and if so, which ones. Operational definitions are also called *metrics* in some application areas.

A Guide to the Project Management Body of Knowledge (PMBOK® Guide) 2000 Edition
©2000 Project Management Institute, Four Campus Boulevard, Newtown Square, PA 19073-3299 USA

.3 *Checklists.* A checklist is a structured tool, usually item specific, used to verify that a set of required steps has been performed. Checklists may be simple or complex. They are usually phrased as imperatives ("Do this!") or interrogatories ("Have you done this?"). Many organizations have standardized checklists available to ensure consistency in frequently performed tasks. In some application areas, checklists are also available from professional associations or commercial service providers.

.4 *Inputs to other processes.* The quality planning process may identify a need for further activity in another area.

8.2 QUALITY ASSURANCE

Quality assurance is all the planned and systematic activities implemented within the quality system to provide confidence that the project will satisfy the relevant quality standards (6). It should be performed throughout the project. Prior to development of the ISO 9000 Series, the activities described under quality planning were widely included as part of quality assurance.

Quality assurance is often provided by a Quality Assurance Department or similarly titled organizational unit, but it does not have to be.

Assurance may be provided to the project management team and to the management of the performing organization (internal quality assurance), or it may be provided to the customer and others not actively involved in the work of the project (external quality assurance).

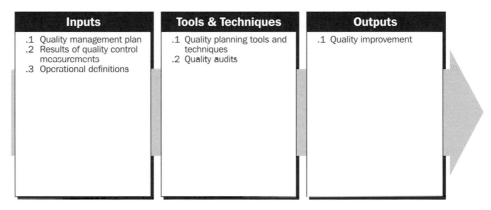

Inputs	Tools & Techniques	Outputs
.1 Quality management plan .2 Results of quality control measurements .3 Operational definitions	.1 Quality planning tools and techniques .2 Quality audits	.1 Quality improvement

8.2.1 Inputs to Quality Assurance

.1 *Quality management plan.* The quality management plan is described in Section 8.1.3.1.

.2 *Results of quality control measurements.* Quality control measurements are records of quality control testing and measurement in a format for comparison and analysis.

.3 *Operational definitions.* Operational definitions are described in Section 8.1.3.2.

8.2.2 Tools and Techniques for Quality Assurance

.1 *Quality planning tools and techniques.* The quality planning tools and techniques described in Section 8.1.2 can be used for quality assurance as well.

.2 *Quality audits.* A quality audit is a structured review of other quality management activities. The objective of a quality audit is to identify lessons learned that can improve performance of this project or of other projects within the performing organization. Quality audits may be scheduled or random, and they may be carried out by properly trained in-house auditors or by third parties, such as quality system registration agencies.

8.2.3 Outputs from Quality Assurance

.1 Quality improvement. Quality improvement includes taking action to increase the effectiveness and efficiency of the project to provide added benefits to the project stakeholders. In most cases, implementing quality improvements will require preparation of change requests or taking of corrective action, and will be handled according to procedures for integrated change control, as described in Section 4.3.

8.3 QUALITY CONTROL

Quality control involves monitoring specific project results to determine if they comply with relevant quality standards, and identifying ways to eliminate causes of unsatisfactory results. It should be performed throughout the project. Project results include both *product* results, such as deliverables, and *project management* results, such as cost and schedule performance. Quality control is often performed by a Quality Control Department or similarly titled organizational unit, but it does not have to be.

The project management team should have a working knowledge of statistical quality control, especially sampling and probability, to help it evaluate quality control outputs. Among other subjects, the team may find it useful to know the differences between:

- Prevention (keeping errors out of the process) and inspection (keeping errors out of the hands of the customer).
- Attribute sampling (the result conforms, or it does not) and variables sampling (the result is rated on a continuous scale that measures the degree of conformity).
- Special causes (unusual events) and random causes (normal process variation).
- Tolerances (the result is acceptable if it falls within the range specified by the tolerance) and control limits (the process is in control if the result falls within the control limits).

Inputs	Tools & Techniques	Outputs
.1 Work results	.1 Inspection	.1 Quality improvement
.2 Quality management plan	.2 Control charts	.2 Acceptance decisions
.3 Operational definitions	.3 Pareto diagrams	.3 Rework
.4 Checklists	.4 Statistical sampling	.4 Completed checklists
	.5 Flowcharting	.5 Process adjustments
	.6 Trend analysis	

A Guide to the Project Management Body of Knowledge (PMBOK® Guide) 2000 Edition
©2000 Project Management Institute, Four Campus Boulevard, Newtown Square, PA 19073-3299 USA

8.3.1 Inputs to Quality Control

.1 *Work results.* Work results (described in Section 4.2.3.1) include both *process* results and *product* results. Information about the planned or expected results (from the project plan) should be available along with information about the actual results.

.2 *Quality management plan.* The quality management plan is described in Section 8.1.3.1.

.3 *Operational definitions.* Operational definitions are described in Section 8.1.3.2.

.4 *Checklists.* Checklists are described in Section 8.1.3.3.

8.3.2 Tools and Techniques for Quality Control

.1 *Inspection.* Inspection includes activities such as measuring, examining, and testing undertaken to determine whether results conform to requirements. Inspections may be conducted at any level (e.g., the results of a single activity may be inspected, or the final product of the project may be inspected). Inspections are variously called *reviews, product reviews, audits,* and *walkthroughs*; in some application areas, these terms have narrow and specific meanings.

.2 *Control charts.* Control charts are a graphic display of the results, over time, of a process. They are used to determine if the process is "in control" (e.g., are differences in the results created by random variations, or are unusual events occurring whose causes must be identified and corrected?). When a process is in control, the process should not be adjusted. The process may be *changed* to provide improvements, but it should not be adjusted when it is in control.

Control charts may be used to monitor any type of output variable. Although used most frequently to track repetitive activities, such as manufactured lots, control charts can also be used to monitor cost and schedule variances, volume and frequency of scope changes, errors in project documents, or other management results to help determine if the *project management process* is in control. **Figure 8-4** is a control chart of project schedule performance.

.3 *Pareto diagrams.* A Pareto diagram is a histogram, ordered by frequency of occurrence, that shows how many results were generated by type or category of identified cause (see **Figure 8-5**). Rank ordering is used to guide corrective action—the project team should take action to fix the problems that are causing the greatest number of defects first. Pareto diagrams are conceptually related to Pareto's Law, which holds that a relatively small number of causes will typically produce a large majority of the problems or defects. This is commonly referred to as the *80/20 principle*, where 80 percent of the problems are due to 20 percent of the causes.

.4 *Statistical sampling.* Statistical sampling involves choosing part of a population of interest for inspection (e.g., selecting ten engineering drawings at random from a list of seventy-five). Appropriate sampling can often reduce the cost of quality control. There is a substantial body of knowledge on statistical sampling; in some application areas, it is necessary for the project management team to be familiar with a variety of sampling techniques.

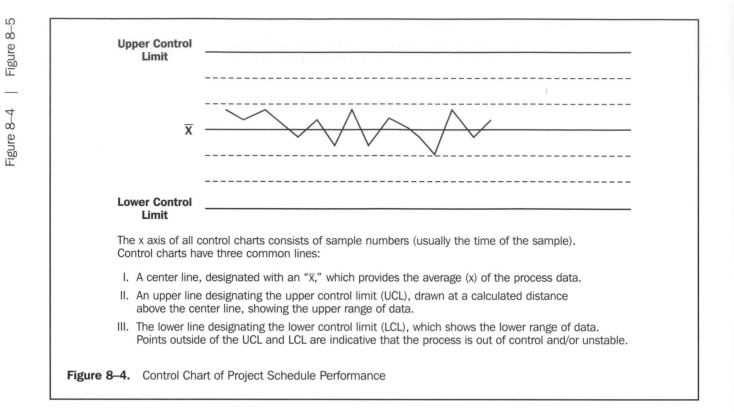

The x axis of all control charts consists of sample numbers (usually the time of the sample). Control charts have three common lines:

I. A center line, designated with an "x̄," which provides the average (x) of the process data.

II. An upper line designating the upper control limit (UCL), drawn at a calculated distance above the center line, showing the upper range of data.

III. The lower line designating the lower control limit (LCL), which shows the lower range of data. Points outside of the UCL and LCL are indicative that the process is out of control and/or unstable.

Figure 8–4. Control Chart of Project Schedule Performance

.5 *Flowcharting.* Flowcharting is described in Section 8.1.2.3. Flowcharting is used in quality control to help analyze how problems occur.

.6 *Trend analysis.* Trend analysis involves using mathematical techniques to forecast future outcomes based on historical results. Trend analysis is often used to monitor:

■ Technical performance—how many errors or defects have been identified, how many remain uncorrected.

■ Cost and schedule performance—how many activities per period were completed with significant variances.

8.3.3 Outputs from Quality Control

.1 *Quality improvement.* Quality improvement is described in Section 8.2.3.1.

.2 *Acceptance decisions.* The items inspected will be either accepted or rejected. Rejected items may require rework (described in Section 8.3.3.3).

.3 *Rework.* Rework is action taken to bring a defective or nonconforming item into compliance with requirements or specifications. Rework, especially unanticipated rework, is a frequent cause of project overruns in most application areas. The project team should make every reasonable effort to minimize rework.

.4 *Completed checklists.* See Section 8.1.3.3. When checklists are used, the completed checklists should become part of the project's records.

.5 *Process adjustments.* Process adjustments involve immediate corrective or preventive action as a result of quality control measurements. In some cases, the process adjustment may need to be handled according to procedures for integrated change control, as described in Section 4.3.

A Guide to the Project Management Body of Knowledge (PMBOK® Guide) 2000 Edition
©2000 Project Management Institute, Four Campus Boulevard, Newtown Square, PA 19073-3299 USA

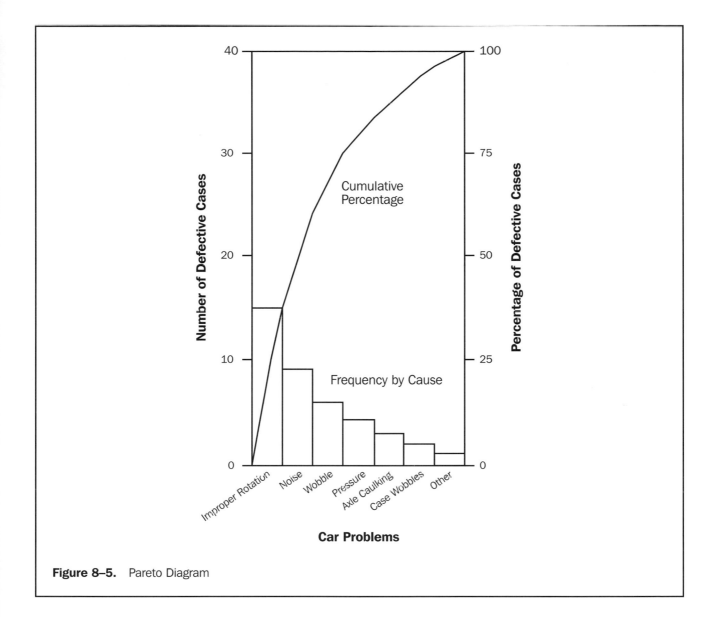

Figure 8–5. Pareto Diagram

Chapter 9

Project Human Resource Management

Project Human Resource Management includes the processes required to make the most effective use of the people involved with the project. It includes all the project stakeholders—sponsors, customers, partners, individual contributors, and others described in Section 2.2. **Figure 9-1** provides an overview of the following major processes:

9.1 **Organizational Planning**—identifying, documenting, and assigning project roles, responsibilities, and reporting relationships.

9.2 **Staff Acquisition**—getting the human resources needed assigned to and working on the project.

9.3 **Team Development**—developing individual and group competencies to enhance project performance.

These processes interact with each other and with the processes in the other knowledge areas as well. Each process may involve effort from one or more individuals or groups of individuals, based on the needs of the project.

Although the processes are presented here as discrete elements with well-defined interfaces, in practice they may overlap and interact in ways not detailed here. Process interactions are discussed in detail in Chapter 3.

There is a substantial body of literature about dealing with people in an operational, ongoing context. Some of the many topics include:

■ Leading, communicating, negotiating, and others discussed in Section 2.4, Key General Management Skills.

■ Delegating, motivating, coaching, mentoring, and other subjects related to dealing with individuals.

■ Team building, dealing with conflict, and other subjects related to dealing with groups.

■ Performance appraisal, recruitment, retention, labor relations, health and safety regulations, and other subjects related to administering the human resource function.

Most of this material is directly applicable to leading and managing people on projects, and the project manager and project management team should be familiar with it. However, they must also be sensitive as to how this knowledge is applied on the project. For example:

Figure 9–1 | 9.1.1.2

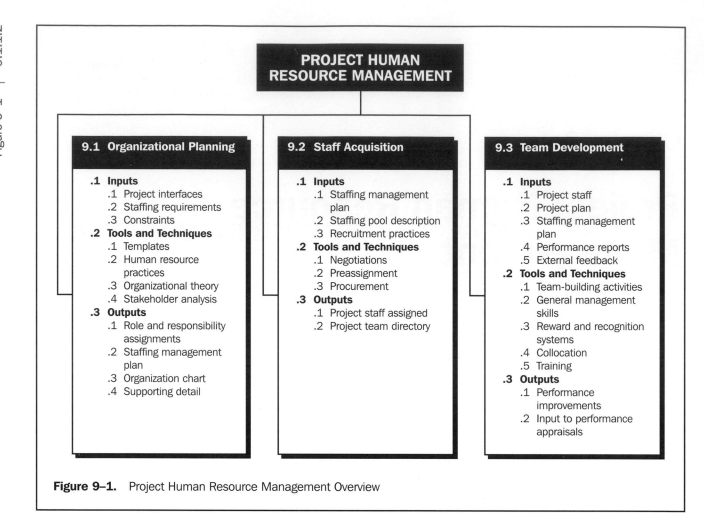

Figure 9–1. Project Human Resource Management Overview

■ The temporary nature of projects means that the personal and organizational relationships will generally be both temporary and new. The project management team must take care to select techniques that are appropriate for such transient relationships.

■ The nature and number of project stakeholders will often change as the project moves from phase to phase of its life cycle. As a result, techniques that are effective in one phase may not be effective in another. The project management team must take care to use techniques that are appropriate to the current needs of the project.

■ Human resource administrative activities are seldom a direct responsibility of the project management team. However, the team must be sufficiently aware of administrative requirements to ensure compliance.

Note: Project managers may also have responsibilities for human resource redeployment and release, depending upon the industry or organization to which they belong.

9.1 ORGANIZATIONAL PLANNING

Organizational planning involves identifying, documenting, and assigning project roles, responsibilities, and reporting relationships. Roles, responsibilities, and

A Guide to the Project Management Body of Knowledge (PMBOK® Guide) 2000 Edition
©2000 Project Management Institute, Four Campus Boulevard, Newtown Square, PA 19073-3299 USA

reporting relationships may be assigned to individuals or to groups. The individuals and groups may be part of the organization performing the project, or they may be external to it. Internal groups are often associated with a specific functional department such as engineering, marketing, or accounting.

On most projects, the majority of organizational planning is done as part of the earliest project phases. However, the results of this process should be reviewed regularly throughout the project to ensure continued applicability. If the initial organization is no longer effective, then it should be revised promptly.

Organizational planning is often tightly linked with communications planning (described in Section 10.1), since the project's organizational structure will have a major effect on the project's communications requirements.

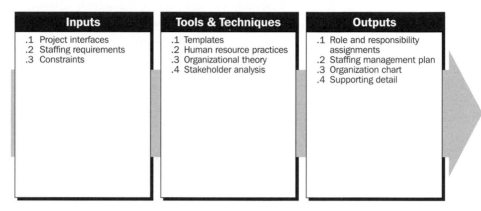

Inputs	Tools & Techniques	Outputs
.1 Project interfaces .2 Staffing requirements .3 Constraints	.1 Templates .2 Human resource practices .3 Organizational theory .4 Stakeholder analysis	.1 Role and responsibility assignments .2 Staffing management plan .3 Organization chart .4 Supporting detail

9.1.1 Inputs to Organizational Planning

.1 *Project interfaces.* Project interfaces generally fall into one of three categories:

- Organizational interfaces—formal and informal reporting relationships among different organizational units. Organizational interfaces may be highly complex or very simple. For example, developing a complex telecommunications system may require coordinating numerous subcontractors over several years, while fixing a programming error in a system installed at a single site may require little more than notifying the user and the operations staff upon completion.

- Technical interfaces—formal and informal reporting relationships among different technical disciplines. Technical interfaces occur both within project phases (e.g., the site design developed by the civil engineers must be compatible with the superstructure developed by the structural engineers) and between project phases (e.g., when an automotive design team passes the results of its work along to the retooling team that must create the manufacturing capability for the vehicle).

- Interpersonal interfaces—formal and informal reporting relationships among different individuals working on the project.

  These interfaces often occur simultaneously, as when an architect employed by a design firm explains key design considerations to an unrelated construction contractor's project management team.

.2 *Staffing requirements.* Staffing requirements define what kinds of competencies are required from what kinds of individuals or groups and in what time frames. Staffing requirements are a subset of the overall resource requirements identified during resource planning (described in Section 7.1).

.3 *Constraints.* Constraints are factors that limit the project team's options. A project's organizational options may be constrained in many ways. Common factors that may constrain how the team is organized include, but are not limited to, the following:

- Organizational structure of the performing organization—an organization whose basic structure is a *strong matrix* means a relatively stronger role for the project manager than one whose basic structure is a *weak matrix* (see Section 2.3.3 for a more detailed discussion of organizational structures).
- Collective bargaining agreements—contractual agreements with unions or other employee groups may require certain roles or reporting relationships (in essence, the employee group is a stakeholder).
- Preferences of the project management team—if members of the project management team have had success with certain structures in the past, then they are likely to advocate similar structures in the future.
- Expected staff assignments—how the project is organized is often influenced by the competencies of specific individuals.

9.1.2 Tools and Techniques for Organizational Planning

.1 *Templates.* Although each project is unique, most projects will resemble another project to some extent. Using the role and responsibility definitions or reporting relationships of a similar project can help expedite the process of organizational planning.

.2 *Human resource practices.* Many organizations have a variety of policies, guidelines, and procedures that can help the project management team with various aspects of organizational planning. For example, an organization that views managers as "coaches" is likely to have documentation on how the role of "coach" is to be performed.

.3 *Organizational theory.* There is a substantial body of literature describing how organizations can and should be structured. Although only a small subset of this body of literature is specifically targeted toward project organizations, the project management team should be generally familiar with the subject of organizational theory so as to be better able to respond to project requirements.

.4 *Stakeholder analysis.* The identification of stakeholders and the needs of the various stakeholders should be analyzed to ensure that their needs will be met. Section 10.1.2.1 discusses stakeholder analysis in more detail.

9.1.3 Outputs from Organizational Planning

.1 *Role and responsibility assignments.* Project roles (who does what) and responsibilities (who decides what) must be assigned to the appropriate project stakeholders. Roles and responsibilities may vary over time. Most roles and responsibilities will be assigned to stakeholders who are actively involved in the work of the project, such as the project manager, other members of the project management team, and the individual contributors.

The roles and responsibilities of the project manager are generally critical on most projects, but vary significantly by application area.

Project roles and responsibilities should be closely linked to the project scope definition. A Responsibility Assignment Matrix (or RAM, see **Figure 9-2**) is often used for this purpose. On larger projects, RAMs may be developed at various

A Guide to the Project Management Body of Knowledge (PMBOK® Guide) 2000 Edition
©2000 Project Management Institute, Four Campus Boulevard, Newtown Square, PA 19073-3299 USA

PHASE \ PERSON	A	B	C	D	E	F	...
Requirements	S	R	A	P	P		
Functional	S		A	P		P	
Design	S		R	A	I		P
Development		R	S	A		P	P
Testing			S	P	I	A	P

P = Participant   A = Accountable   R = Review Required
I = Input Required   S = Sign-off Required

Figure 9–2. Responsibility Assignment Matrix

levels. For example, a high-level RAM may define which group or unit is responsible for each component of the work breakdown structure, while lower-level RAMs are used within the group to assign roles and responsibilities for specific activities to particular individuals.

.2 *Staffing management plan.* The staffing management plan describes when and how human resources will be brought onto and taken off of the project team. The staffing plan may be formal or informal, highly detailed or broadly framed, based on the needs of the project. It is a subsidiary element of the overall project plan (see Section 4.1, Project Plan Development).

The staffing management plan often includes resource histograms, as illustrated in **Figure 9-3**.

Particular attention should be paid to how project team members (individuals or groups) will be released when they are no longer needed on the project. Appropriate reassignment procedures may:

■ Reduce costs by reducing or eliminating the tendency to "make work" to fill the time between this assignment and the next.

■ Improve morale by reducing or eliminating uncertainty about future employment opportunities.

.3 *Organization chart.* An organization chart is any graphic display of project reporting relationships. It may be formal or informal, highly detailed or broadly framed, based on the needs of the project. For example, the organization chart for a three- to four-person internal service project is unlikely to have the rigor and detail of the organization chart for a 3,000-person disaster response team.

An Organizational Breakdown Structure (OBS) is a specific type of organization chart that shows which organizational units are responsible for which work packages.

.4 *Supporting detail.* Supporting detail for organizational planning varies by application area and project size. Information frequently supplied as supporting detail includes, but is not limited to:

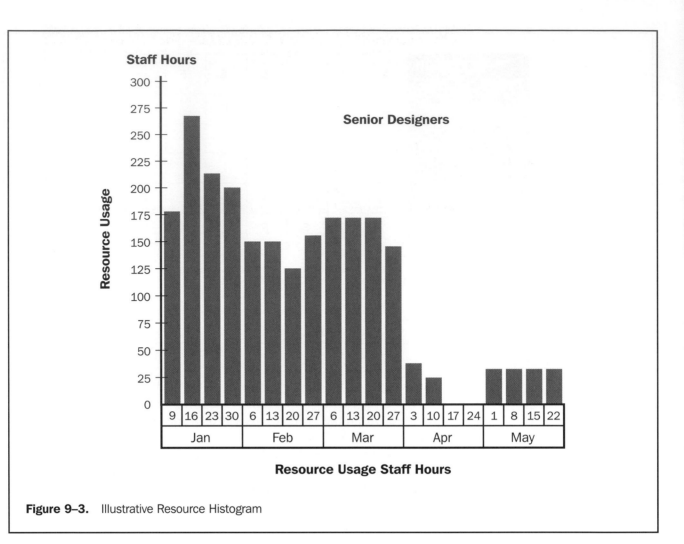

Figure 9–3. Illustrative Resource Histogram

■ Organizational impact—what alternatives are precluded by organizing in this manner.

■ Job descriptions—written outlines by job title of the competencies, responsibilities, authority, physical environment, and other characteristics involved in performing a given job. Also called *position descriptions*.

■ Training needs—if the staff to be assigned is not expected to have the competencies needed by the project, those competencies will need to be developed as part of the project.

9.2 STAFF ACQUISITION

Staff acquisition involves getting the needed human resources (individuals or groups) assigned to and working on the project. In most environments, the "best" resources may not be available, and the project management team must take care to ensure that the resources that are available will meet project requirements.

A Guide to the Project Management Body of Knowledge (PMBOK® Guide) 2000 Edition
©2000 Project Management Institute, Four Campus Boulevard, Newtown Square, PA 19073-3299 USA

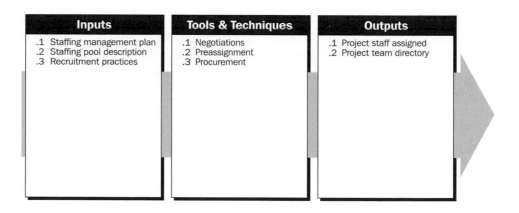

Inputs	Tools & Techniques	Outputs
.1 Staffing management plan .2 Staffing pool description .3 Recruitment practices	.1 Negotiations .2 Preassignment .3 Procurement	.1 Project staff assigned .2 Project team directory

9.2.1 Inputs to Staff Acquisition

.1 *Staffing management plan.* The staffing management plan is described in Section 9.1.3.2. It includes the project's staffing requirements, as described in Section 9.1.1.2.

.2 *Staffing pool description.* When the project management team is able to influence or direct staff assignments, it must consider the characteristics of the potentially available staff. Considerations include, but are not limited to:

- Previous experience—have the individuals or groups done similar or related work before? Have they done it well?
- Personal interests—are the individuals or groups interested in working on this project?
- Personal characteristics—are the individuals or groups likely to work well together as a team?
- Availability—will the most desirable individuals or groups be available in the necessary time frames?
- Competencies and proficiency—what competencies are required and at what level?

.3 *Recruitment practices.* One or more of the organizations involved in the project may have policies, guidelines, or procedures governing staff assignments. When they exist, such practices act as a constraint on the staff-acquisition process.

9.2.2 Tools and Techniques for Staff Acquisition

.1 *Negotiations.* Staff assignments must be negotiated on most projects. For example, the project management team may need to negotiate with:

- Responsible functional managers to ensure that the project receives appropriately competent staff in the necessary time frame.
- Other project management teams within the performing organization to assign scarce or specialized resources appropriately.

The team's influencing competencies (see Section 2.4.5, Influencing the Organization) play an important role in negotiating staff assignments, as do the politics of the organizations involved. For example, a functional manager may be rewarded based on staff utilization. This creates an incentive for the manager to assign available staff who may not meet all of the project's requirements.

9.2.2.2 — 9.3.2.4

.2 *Preassignment.* In some cases, staff may be preassigned to the project. This is often the case when a) the project is the result of a competitive proposal, and specific staff were promised as part of the proposal, or b) the project is an internal service project, and staff assignments were defined within the project charter.

.3 *Procurement.* Project procurement management (described in Chapter 12) can be used to obtain the services of specific individuals or groups of individuals to perform project activities. Procurement is required when the performing organization lacks the in-house staff needed to complete the project (e.g., as a result of a conscious decision not to hire such individuals as full-time employees, as a result of having all appropriately competent staff previously committed to other projects, or as a result of other circumstances).

9.2.3 Outputs from Staff Acquisition

.1 *Project staff assigned.* The project is staffed when appropriate people have been reliably assigned to work on it. Staff may be assigned full time, part time, or variably, based on the needs of the project.

.2 *Project team directory.* A project team directory lists all the project team members and other stakeholders. The directory may be formal or informal, highly detailed or broadly framed, based on the needs of the project.

9.3 TEAM DEVELOPMENT

Team development includes both enhancing the ability of stakeholders to contribute as individuals as well as enhancing the ability of the team to function as a team. Individual development (managerial and technical) is the foundation necessary to develop the team. Development as a team is critical to the project's ability to meet its objectives.

Team development on a project is often complicated when individual team members are accountable to both a functional manager and the project manager (see Section 2.3.3 for a discussion of matrix organizational structures). Effective management of this dual reporting relationship is often a critical success factor for the project, and is generally the responsibility of the project manager.

Although team development is positioned in Chapter 3 as one of the executing processes, team development occurs throughout the project.

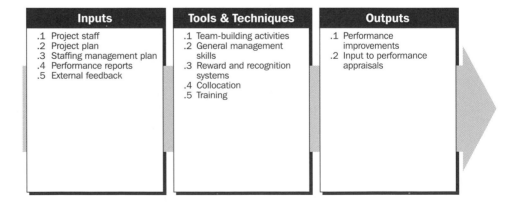

A Guide to the Project Management Body of Knowledge (PMBOK® Guide) 2000 Edition
©2000 Project Management Institute, Four Campus Boulevard, Newtown Square, PA 19073-3299 USA

9.3.1 Inputs to Team Development

.1 *Project staff.* Project staffing is described in Section 9.2.3.1. The staff assignments implicitly define the individual competencies and team competencies available upon which to build.

.2 *Project plan.* The project plan is described in Section 4.1.3.1. The project plan describes the technical context within which the team operates.

.3 *Staffing management plan.* The staffing management plan is described in Section 9.1.3.2.

.4 *Performance reports.* Performance reports (described in Section 10.3.3.1) provide feedback to the project team about performance against the project plan.

.5 *External feedback.* The project team must periodically measure itself against the expectations of those outside the project.

9.3.2 Tools and Techniques for Team Development

.1 *Team-building activities.* Team-building activities include management and individual actions taken specifically and primarily to improve team performance. Many actions—such as involving nonmanagement-level team members in the planning process, or establishing ground rules for surfacing and dealing with conflict—may enhance team performance as a secondary effect. Team-building activities can vary from a five-minute agenda item in a regular status review meeting to an extended, off-site, professionally facilitated experience designed to improve interpersonal relationships among key stakeholders.

There is a substantial body of literature on team building. The project management team should be generally familiar with a variety of team-building activities.

.2 *General management skills.* General management skills (discussed in Section 2.4) are of particular importance to team development.

.3 *Reward and recognition systems.* Reward and recognition systems are formal management actions that promote or reinforce desired behavior. To be effective, such systems must make the link between project performance and reward clear, explicit, and achievable. For example, a project manager who is to be rewarded for meeting the project's cost objective should have an appropriate level of control over staffing and procurement decisions.

Projects must often have their own reward and recognition systems since the systems of the performing organization may not be appropriate. For example, the willingness to work overtime to meet an aggressive schedule objective *should* be rewarded or recognized; needing to work overtime as the result of poor planning *should not* be.

Reward and recognition systems must also consider cultural differences. For example, developing an appropriate team reward mechanism in a culture that prizes individualism may be very difficult.

.4 *Collocation.* Collocation involves placing all, or almost all, of the most active project team members in the same physical location to enhance their ability to perform as a team. Collocation is widely used on larger projects and can also be effective for smaller projects (e.g., with a *war room*, where the team congregates and posts schedules, updates, etc.). On some projects, collocation may not be an option; where it is not viable, an alternative may be scheduling frequent face-to-face meetings to encourage interaction.

.5 *Training.* Training includes all activities designed to enhance the competencies of the project team. Some authors distinguish among training, education, and development, but the distinctions are neither consistent nor widely accepted. Training may be formal (e.g., classroom training, computer-based training) or informal (e.g., feedback from other team members). There is a substantial body of literature on how to provide training to adults.

If the project team members lack necessary management or technical skills, such skills must be developed as part of the project, or steps must be taken to restaff the project appropriately. Direct and indirect costs for training are generally paid by the performing organization.

9.3.3 Outputs from Team Development

.1 *Performance improvements.* Team performance improvements can come from many sources and can affect many areas of project performance; for example:

■ Improvements in individual skills may allow a specific person to perform assigned activities more effectively.

■ Improvements in team behaviors (e.g., surfacing and dealing with conflict) may allow project team members to devote a greater percentage of their efforts to technical activities.

■ Improvements in either individual or team competencies may facilitate identifying and developing better ways of doing project work.

.2 *Input to performance appraisals.* Project staff should generally provide input to the appraisals of any project staff members with whom they interact in a significant way.

A Guide to the Project Management Body of Knowledge (PMBOK® Guide) 2000 Edition
©2000 Project Management Institute, Four Campus Boulevard, Newtown Square, PA 19073-3299 USA

Chapter 10

Project Communications Management

Project Communications Management includes the processes required to ensure timely and appropriate generation, collection, dissemination, storage, and ultimate disposition of project information. It provides the critical links among people, ideas, and information that are necessary for success. Everyone involved in the project must be prepared to send and receive communications, and must understand how the communications in which they are involved as individuals affect the project as a whole. **Figure 10-1** provides an overview of the following major processes:

10.1 Communications Planning—determining the information and communications needs of the stakeholders: who needs what information, when they will need it, and how it will be given to them.

10.2 Information Distribution—making needed information available to project stakeholders in a timely manner.

10.3 Performance Reporting—collecting and disseminating performance information. This includes status reporting, progress measurement, and forecasting.

10.4 Administrative Closure—generating, gathering, and disseminating information to formalize a phase or project completion.

These processes interact with each other and with the processes in the other knowledge areas as well. Each process may involve effort from one or more individuals or groups of individuals, based on the needs of the project. Each process generally occurs at least once in every project phase.

Although the processes are presented here as discrete elements with well-defined interfaces, in practice they may overlap and interact in ways not detailed here. Process interactions are discussed in detail in Chapter 3.

The general management skill of communicating (discussed in Section 2.4.2) is related to, but not the same as, project communications management. Communicating is a broader subject and involves a substantial body of knowledge that is not unique to the project context. For example:

■ Sender-receiver models—feedback loops, barriers to communications, etc.
■ Choice of media—when to communicate in writing versus when to communicate orally, when to write an informal memo versus when to write a formal report, etc.

Figure 10–1 | 10.1.1.1

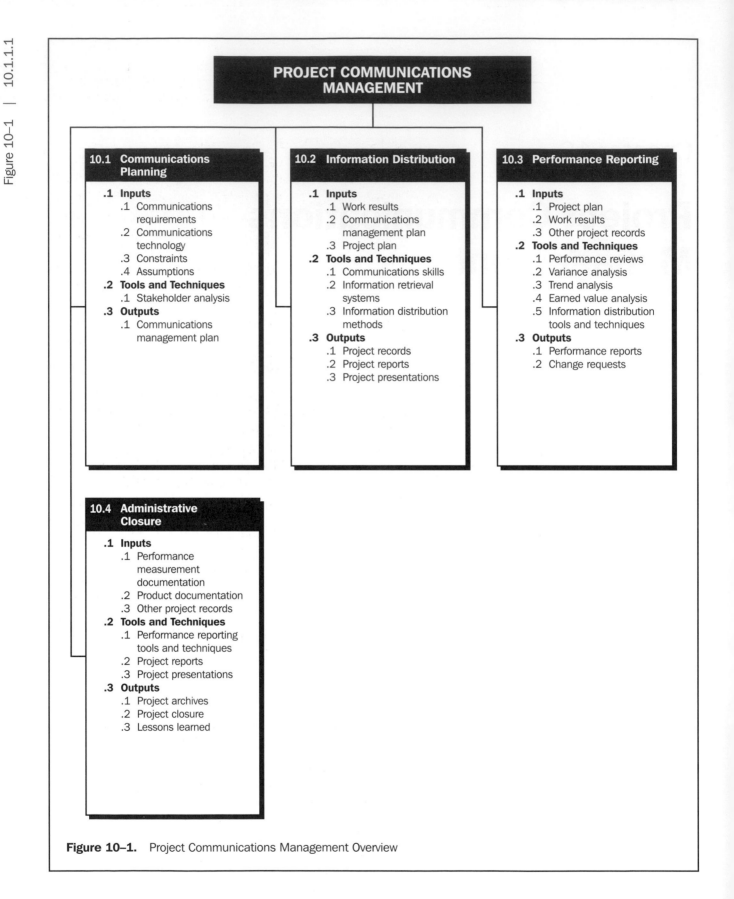

Figure 10–1. Project Communications Management Overview

A Guide to the Project Management Body of Knowledge (PMBOK® Guide) 2000 Edition
©2000 Project Management Institute, Four Campus Boulevard, Newtown Square, PA 19073-3299 USA

- Writing style—active versus passive voice, sentence structure, word choice, etc.
- Presentation techniques—body language, design of visual aids, etc.
- Meeting management techniques—preparing an agenda, dealing with conflict, etc.

10.1 COMMUNICATIONS PLANNING

Communications planning involves determining the information and communications needs of the stakeholders: who needs what information, when they will need it, how it will be given to them, and by whom. While all projects share the need to communicate project information, the informational needs and the methods of distribution vary widely. Identifying the informational needs of the stakeholders and determining a suitable means of meeting those needs is an important factor for project success.

On most projects, the majority of communications planning is done as part of the earliest project phases. However, the results of this process should be reviewed regularly throughout the project and revised as needed to ensure continued applicability.

Communications planning is often tightly linked with organizational planning (described in Section 9.1) since the project's organizational structure will have a major effect on the project's communications requirements.

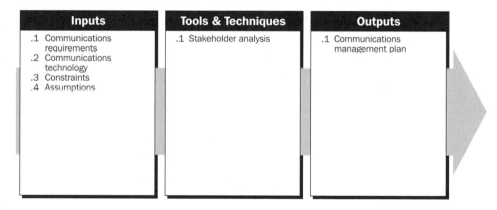

Inputs	Tools & Techniques	Outputs
.1 Communications requirements .2 Communications technology .3 Constraints .4 Assumptions	.1 Stakeholder analysis	.1 Communications management plan

10.1.1 Inputs to Communications Planning

.1 *Communications requirements.* Communications requirements are the sum of the information requirements of the project stakeholders. Requirements are defined by combining the type and format of information required with an analysis of the value of that information. Project resources should be expended only on communicating information that contributes to success or where a lack of communication can lead to failure. Information typically required to determine project communications requirements includes:

- Project organization and stakeholder responsibility relationships.
- Disciplines, departments, and specialties involved in the project.
- Logistics of how many individuals will be involved with the project and at which locations.
- External information needs (e.g., communicating with the media).

.2 *Communications technology.* The technologies or methods used to transfer information back and forth among project stakeholders can vary significantly: from brief conversations to extended meetings, from simple written documents to immediately accessible online schedules and databases.

Communications technology factors that may affect the project include:

■ The immediacy of the need for information—is project success dependent upon having frequently updated information available on a moment's notice, or would regularly issued written reports suffice?

■ The availability of technology—are the systems that are already in place appropriate, or do project needs warrant change?

■ The expected project staffing—are the proposed communications systems compatible with the experience and expertise of the project participants, or will extensive training and learning be required?

■ The length of the project—is the available technology likely to change before the project is over?

.3 *Constraints.* Constraints are factors that will limit the project management team's options. For example, if substantial project resources will be procured, more consideration will need to be given to handling contract information.

When a project is performed under contract, there are often specific contractual provisions that affect communications planning.

.4 *Assumptions.* See Section 4.1.1.5.

10.1.2 Tools and Techniques for Communications Planning

.1 *Stakeholder analysis.* The information needs of the various stakeholders should be analyzed to develop a methodical and logical view of their information needs and sources to meet those needs (project stakeholders are discussed in more detail in Section 2.2). The analysis should consider methods and technologies suited to the project that will provide the information needed. Care should be taken to avoid wasting resources on unnecessary information or inappropriate technology.

10.1.3 Outputs from Communications Planning

.1 *Communications management plan.* A communications management plan is a document that provides:

■ A collection and filing structure that details what methods will be used to gather and store various types of information. Procedures should also cover collecting and disseminating updates and corrections to previously distributed material.

■ A distribution structure that details to whom information (status reports, data, schedule, technical documentation, etc.) will flow, and what methods (written reports, meetings, etc.) will be used to distribute various types of information. This structure must be compatible with the responsibilities and reporting relationships described by the project organization chart.

■ A description of the information to be distributed, including format, content, level of detail, and conventions/definitions to be used.

■ Production schedules showing when each type of communication will be produced.

■ Methods for accessing information between scheduled communications.

■ A method for updating and refining the communications management plan as the project progresses and develops.

A Guide to the Project Management Body of Knowledge (PMBOK® Guide) 2000 Edition
©2000 Project Management Institute, Four Campus Boulevard, Newtown Square, PA 19073-3299 USA

The communications management plan may be formal or informal, highly detailed or broadly framed, based on the needs of the project. It is a subsidiary component of the overall project plan (described in Section 4.1).

10.2 INFORMATION DISTRIBUTION

Information distribution involves making needed information available to project stakeholders in a timely manner. It includes implementing the communications management plan, as well as responding to unexpected requests for information.

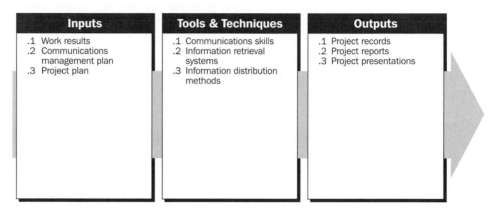

Inputs	Tools & Techniques	Outputs
.1 Work results .2 Communications management plan .3 Project plan	.1 Communications skills .2 Information retrieval systems .3 Information distribution methods	.1 Project records .2 Project reports .3 Project presentations

10.2.1 Inputs to Information Distribution

.1 *Work results.* Work results are described in Section 4.2.3.1.

.2 *Communications management plan.* The communications management plan is described in Section 10.1.3.1.

.3 *Project plan.* The project plan is described in Section 4.1.3.1.

10.2.2 Tools and Techniques for Information Distribution

.1 *Communications skills.* Communications skills are used to exchange information. The sender is responsible for making the information clear, unambiguous, and complete, so that the receiver can receive it correctly, and for confirming that it is properly understood. The receiver is responsible for making sure that the information is received in its entirety and understood correctly. Communicating has many dimensions:

■ Written and oral, listening and speaking.
■ Internal (within the project) and external (to the customer, the media, the public, etc.).
■ Formal (reports, briefings, etc.) and informal (memos, ad hoc conversations, etc.).
■ Vertical (up and down the organization) and horizontal (with peers).

.2 *Information retrieval systems.* Information can be shared by team members and stakeholders through a variety of methods including manual filing systems, electronic databases, project management software, and systems that allow access to technical documentation such as engineering drawings, design specifications, test plans, etc.

.3 *Information distribution methods.* Project information may be distributed using a variety of methods including project meetings, hard-copy document distribution, shared access to networked electronic databases, fax, electronic mail, voice mail, videoconferencing, and project intranet.

10.2.3 Outputs from Information Distribution

.1 *Project records.* Project records may include correspondence, memos, and documents describing the project. This information should, to the extent possible and appropriate, be maintained in an organized fashion. Project team members may often maintain personal records in a project notebook.

.2 *Project reports.* Formal project reports on project status and/or issues.

.3 *Project presentations.* The project team provides information formally, or informally, to any or all of the project stakeholders. The information is relevant to the needs of the audience, and the method of presentation is appropriate.

10.3 PERFORMANCE REPORTING

Performance reporting involves collecting and disseminating performance information to provide stakeholders with information about how resources are being used to achieve project objectives. This process includes:

- Status reporting—describing where the project now stands—for example, status related to schedule and budget metrics.
- Progress reporting—describing what the project team has accomplished—for example, percent complete to schedule, or what is completed versus what is in process.
- Forecasting—predicting future project status and progress.

Performance reporting should generally provide information on scope, schedule, cost, and quality. Many projects also require information on risk and procurement. Reports may be prepared comprehensively or on an exception basis.

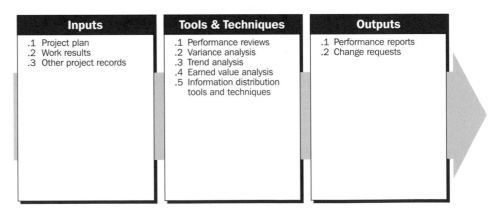

Inputs	Tools & Techniques	Outputs
.1 Project plan .2 Work results .3 Other project records	.1 Performance reviews .2 Variance analysis .3 Trend analysis .4 Earned value analysis .5 Information distribution tools and techniques	.1 Performance reports .2 Change requests

10.3.1 Inputs to Performance Reporting

.1 *Project plan.* The project plan is discussed in Section 4.1.3.1. The project plan contains the various baselines that will be used to assess project performance.

A Guide to the Project Management Body of Knowledge (PMBOK® Guide) 2000 Edition
©2000 Project Management Institute, Four Campus Boulevard, Newtown Square, PA 19073-3299 USA

.2 *Work results.* Work results—which deliverables have been fully or partially completed, what costs (and/or resources) have been incurred or committed, etc.—are an output of project plan execution (discussed in Section 4.2.3.1). Work results should be reported within the framework provided by the communications management plan. Accurate, uniform information on work results is essential to useful performance reporting.

.3 *Other project records.* Project records are discussed in Section 10.2.3.1. In addition to the project plan and the project's work results, other project documents often contain information pertaining to the project context that should be considered when assessing project performance.

10.3.2 Tools and Techniques for Performance Reporting

.1 *Performance reviews.* Performance reviews are meetings held to assess project status and/or progress. Performance reviews are typically used in conjunction with one or more of the performance-reporting techniques described below.

.2 *Variance analysis.* Variance analysis involves comparing actual project results to planned or expected results. Cost and schedule variances are the most frequently analyzed, but variances from plan in the areas of scope, resource, quality, and risk are often of equal or greater importance.

.3 *Trend analysis.* Trend analysis involves examining project results over time to determine if performance is improving or deteriorating.

.4 *Earned value analysis.* Earned value analysis in its various forms is the most commonly used method of performance measurement. It integrates scope, cost (or resource), and schedule measures to help the project management team assess project performance. Earned value analysis involves calculating three key values for each activity:

■ The Planned Value (PV), previously called the budgeted cost of work scheduled (BCWS), is that portion of the approved cost estimate planned to be spent on the activity during a given period.

■ The Actual Cost (AC), previously called the actual cost of work performed (ACWP), is the total of costs incurred in accomplishing work on the activity during a given period. This Actual Cost must correspond to whatever was budgeted for the PV and the EV (example: direct hours only, direct costs only, or all costs including indirect costs).

■ The EV, previously called the budgeted cost of work performed (BCWP), is the value of the work actually completed.

These three values are used in combination to provide measures of whether or not work is being accomplished as planned. The most commonly used measures are the cost variance (CV) ($CV = EV - AC$), and the schedule variance (SV) ($SV = EV - PV$). These two values, the CV and SV, can be converted to efficiency indicators to reflect the cost and schedule performance of any project. The cost performance index ($CPI = EV/AC$) is the most commonly used cost-efficiency indicator. The cumulative CPI (the sum of all individual EV budgets divided by the sum of all individual ACs) is widely used to forecast project costs at completion. Also, the schedule performance index ($SPI = EV/PV$) is sometimes used in conjunction with the CPI to forecast the project completion estimates.

.5 *Information distribution tools and techniques.* Performance reports are distributed using the tools and techniques described in Section 10.2.2.

Figure 10–2 | 10.4.3.1

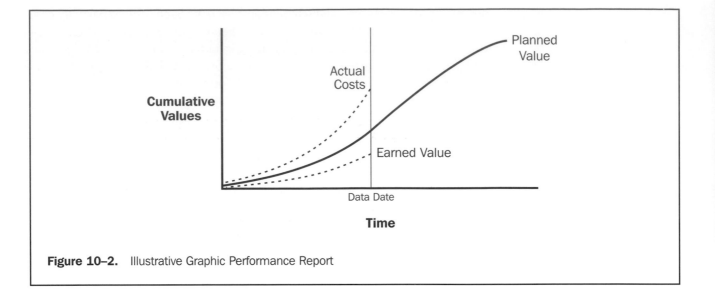

Figure 10–2. Illustrative Graphic Performance Report

WBS Element	Planned Budget ($) (PV)	Earned Earned Value ($) (EV)	Cost Actual Cost ($) (AC)	Cost Variance ($) (EV − AC)	Cost Variance (%) (CV ÷ EV)	Schedule Variance ($) (EV − PV)	Schedule Variance (%) (SV ÷ PV)	Performance Index Cost CPI (EV ÷ AC)	Performance Index Schedule SPI (EV ÷ PV)
1.0 Pre-Pilot Plan	63,000	58,000	62,500	−4,500	−7.8	−5,000	−7.9	0.93	0.92
2.0 Checklists	64,000	48,000	46,800	1,200	2.5	−16,000	−25.0	1.03	0.75
3.0 Curriculum	23,000	20,000	23,500	−3,500	−17.5	−3,000	−13.0	0.85	0.87
4.0 Mid-Term Evaluation	68,000	68,000	72,500	−4,500	−6.6	0	0.0	0.94	1.00
5.0 Implementation Support	12,000	10,000	10,000	0	0.0	−2,000	−16.7	1.00	0.83
6.0 Manual of Practice	7,000	6,200	6,000	200	3.2	−800	−11.4	1.03	0.89
7.0 Roll-Out Plan	20,000	13,500	18,100	−4,600	−34.1	−6,500	−32.5	.075	0.68
Totals	**257,000**	**223,700**	**239,400**	**−15,700**	**−7.0**	**−33,300**	**−13.0**	**0.93**	**0.87**

Note: All figures are project-to-date.

*Other units of measure that may be used in these calculations may include: labor hours, cubic yards of concrete, etc.

Figure 10–3. Illustrative Tabular Performance Report

10.3.3 Outputs from Performance Reporting

.1 *Performance reports.* Performance reports organize and summarize the information gathered and present the results of any analysis. Reports should provide the kinds of information and the level of detail required by various stakeholders, as documented in the communications management plan.

Common formats for performance reports include bar charts (also called Gantt charts), S-curves, histograms, and tables. **Figure 10-2** uses S-curves to display cumulative EV analysis data, while **Figure 10-3** displays a different set of EV data in tabular form.

.2 *Change requests.* Analysis of project performance often generates a request for a change to some aspect of the project. These change requests are handled as described in the various change control processes (e.g., scope change management, schedule control, etc.).

A Guide to the Project Management Body of Knowledge (PMBOK® Guide) 2000 Edition
©2000 Project Management Institute, Four Campus Boulevard, Newtown Square, PA 19073-3299 USA

10.4 ADMINISTRATIVE CLOSURE

The project or phase, after either achieving its objectives or being terminated for other reasons, requires closure. Administrative closure consists of documenting project results to formalize acceptance of the product of the project by the sponsor, or customer. It includes collecting project records; ensuring that they reflect final specifications; analyzing project success, effectiveness, and lessons learned; and archiving such information for future use.

Administrative closure activities should not be delayed until project completion. Each phase of the project should be properly closed to ensure that important and useful information is not lost. In addition, employee skills in the staff pool database should be updated to reflect new skills and proficiency increases.

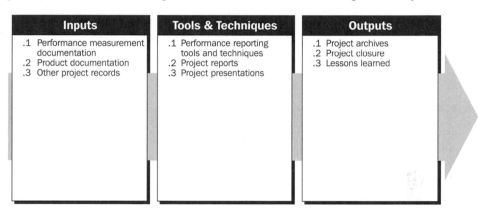

Inputs	Tools & Techniques	Outputs
.1 Performance measurement documentation .2 Product documentation .3 Other project records	.1 Performance reporting tools and techniques .2 Project reports .3 Project presentations	.1 Project archives .2 Project closure .3 Lessons learned

10.4.1 Inputs to Administrative Closure

.1 Performance measurement documentation. All documentation produced to record and analyze project performance, including the planning documents that established the framework for performance measurement, must be available for review during administrative closure.

.2 Product documentation. Documents produced to describe the product of the project (plans, specifications, technical documentation, drawings, electronic files, etc.—the terminology varies by application area) must also be available for review during administrative closure.

.3 Other project records. Project records are discussed in Section 10.2.3.1.

10.4.2 Tools and Techniques for Administrative Closure

.1 Performance reporting tools and techniques. Performance reporting tools and techniques are discussed in Section 10.3.2.

.2 Project reports. See Section 10.2.3.2.

.3 Project presentations. See Section 10.2.3.3.

10.4.3 Outputs from Administrative Closure

.1 Project archives. A complete set of indexed project records should be prepared for archiving by the appropriate parties. Any project-specific or programwide historical databases pertinent to the project should be updated. When projects are done under contract, or when they involve significant procurement, particular attention must be paid to archiving of financial records.

.2 *Project closure.* Confirmation that the project has met all customer requirements for the product of the project (the customer has formally accepted the project results and deliverables and the requirements of the delivering organization—for example, staff evaluations, budget reports, lessons learned, etc.).

.3 *Lessons learned.* Lessons learned are discussed in Section 4.3.3.3.

A Guide to the Project Management Body of Knowledge (PMBOK® Guide) 2000 Edition
©2000 Project Management Institute, Four Campus Boulevard, Newtown Square, PA 19073-3299 USA

Chapter 11

Project Risk Management

Risk management is the systematic process of identifying, analyzing, and responding to project risk. It includes maximizing the probability and consequences of positive events and minimizing the probability and consequences of adverse events to project objectives. **Figure 11-1** provides an overview of the following major processes:

11.1 Risk Management Planning—deciding how to approach and plan the risk management activities for a project.

11.2 Risk Identification—determining which risks might affect the project and documenting their characteristics.

11.3 Qualitative Risk Analysis—performing a qualitative analysis of risks and conditions to prioritize their effects on project objectives.

11.4 Quantitative Risk Analysis—measuring the probability and consequences of risks and estimating their implications for project objectives.

11.5 Risk Response Planning—developing procedures and techniques to enhance opportunities and reduce threats to the project's objectives.

11.6 Risk Monitoring and Control—monitoring residual risks, identifying new risks, executing risk reduction plans, and evaluating their effectiveness throughout the project life cycle.

These processes interact with each other and with the processes in the other knowledge areas. Each process generally occurs at least once in every project. Although processes are presented here as discrete elements with well-defined interfaces, in practice they may overlap and interact in ways not detailed here. Process interactions are discussed in detail in Chapter 3.

Project risk is an uncertain event or condition that, if it occurs, has a positive or a negative effect on a project objective. A risk has a cause and, if it occurs, a consequence. For example, a cause may be requiring a permit or having limited personnel assigned to the project. The risk event is that the permit may take longer than planned, or the personnel may not be adequate for the task. If either of these uncertain events occur, there will be a consequence on the project cost, schedule, or quality. Risk conditions could include aspects of the project environment that may contribute to project risk such as poor project management practices, or dependency on external participants that cannot be controlled.

Project risk includes both threats to the project's objectives and opportunities to improve on those objectives. It has its origins in the uncertainty that is present in all projects. Known risks are those that have been identified and analyzed, and

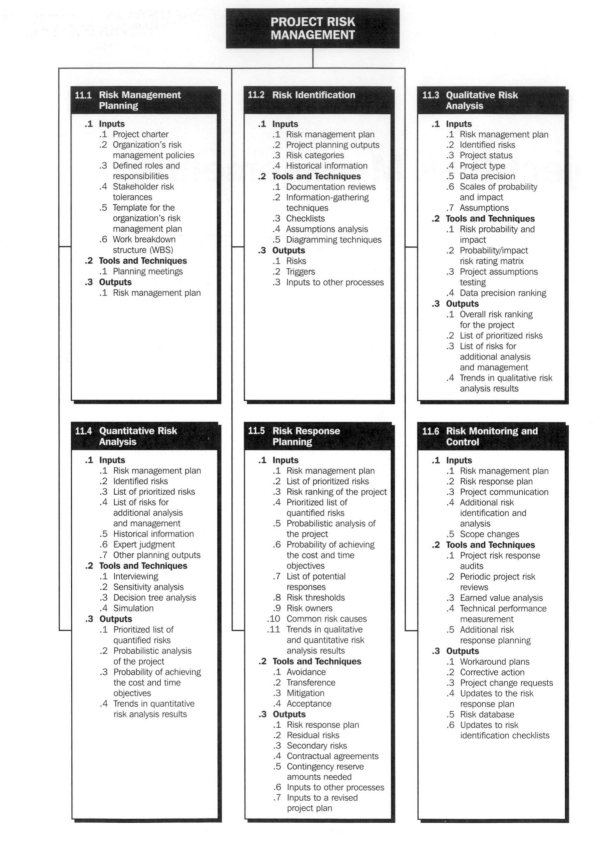

PROJECT RISK MANAGEMENT

11.1 Risk Management Planning

.1 Inputs
- .1 Project charter
- .2 Organization's risk management policies
- .3 Defined roles and responsibilities
- .4 Stakeholder risk tolerances
- .5 Template for the organization's risk management plan
- .6 Work breakdown structure (WBS)

.2 Tools and Techniques
- .1 Planning meetings

.3 Outputs
- .1 Risk management plan

11.2 Risk Identification

.1 Inputs
- .1 Risk management plan
- .2 Project planning outputs
- .3 Risk categories
- .4 Historical information

.2 Tools and Techniques
- .1 Documentation reviews
- .2 Information-gathering techniques
- .3 Checklists
- .4 Assumptions analysis
- .5 Diagramming techniques

.3 Outputs
- .1 Risks
- .2 Triggers
- .3 Inputs to other processes

11.3 Qualitative Risk Analysis

.1 Inputs
- .1 Risk management plan
- .2 Identified risks
- .3 Project status
- .4 Project type
- .5 Data precision
- .6 Scales of probability and impact
- .7 Assumptions

.2 Tools and Techniques
- .1 Risk probability and impact
- .2 Probability/impact risk rating matrix
- .3 Project assumptions testing
- .4 Data precision ranking

.3 Outputs
- .1 Overall risk ranking for the project
- .2 List of prioritized risks
- .3 List of risks for additional analysis and management
- .4 Trends in qualitative risk analysis results

11.4 Quantitative Risk Analysis

.1 Inputs
- .1 Risk management plan
- .2 Identified risks
- .3 List of prioritized risks
- .4 List of risks for additional analysis and management
- .5 Historical information
- .6 Expert judgment
- .7 Other planning outputs

.2 Tools and Techniques
- .1 Interviewing
- .2 Sensitivity analysis
- .3 Decision tree analysis
- .4 Simulation

.3 Outputs
- .1 Prioritized list of quantified risks
- .2 Probabilistic analysis of the project
- .3 Probability of achieving the cost and time objectives
- .4 Trends in quantitative risk analysis results

11.5 Risk Response Planning

.1 Inputs
- .1 Risk management plan
- .2 List of prioritized risks
- .3 Risk ranking of the project
- .4 Prioritized list of quantified risks
- .5 Probabilistic analysis of the project
- .6 Probability of achieving the cost and time objectives
- .7 List of potential responses
- .8 Risk thresholds
- .9 Risk owners
- .10 Common risk causes
- .11 Trends in qualitative and quantitative risk analysis results

.2 Tools and Techniques
- .1 Avoidance
- .2 Transference
- .3 Mitigation
- .4 Acceptance

.3 Outputs
- .1 Risk response plan
- .2 Residual risks
- .3 Secondary risks
- .4 Contractual agreements
- .5 Contingency reserve amounts needed
- .6 Inputs to other processes
- .7 Inputs to a revised project plan

11.6 Risk Monitoring and Control

.1 Inputs
- .1 Risk management plan
- .2 Risk response plan
- .3 Project communication
- .4 Additional risk identification and analysis
- .5 Scope changes

.2 Tools and Techniques
- .1 Project risk response audits
- .2 Periodic project risk reviews
- .3 Earned value analysis
- .4 Technical performance measurement
- .5 Additional risk response planning

.3 Outputs
- .1 Workaround plans
- .2 Corrective action
- .3 Project change requests
- .4 Updates to the risk response plan
- .5 Risk database
- .6 Updates to risk identification checklists

Figure 11-1. Project Risk Management Overview

A Guide to the Project Management Body of Knowledge (PMBOK® Guide) 2000 Edition
©2000 Project Management Institute, Four Campus Boulevard, Newtown Square, PA 19073-3299 USA

it may be possible to plan for them. Unknown risks cannot be managed, although project managers may address them by applying a general contingency based on past experience with similar projects.

Organizations perceive risk as it relates to threats to project success. Risks that are threats to the project may be accepted if they are in balance with the reward that may be gained by taking the risk. For example, adopting a fast-track schedule that may be overrun is a risk taken to achieve an earlier completion date. Risks that are opportunities may be pursued to benefit the project's objectives.

To be successful, the organization must be committed to addressing risk management throughout the project. One measure of the organizational commitment is its dedication to gathering high-quality data on project risks and their characteristics.

11.1 RISK MANAGEMENT PLANNING

Risk management planning is the process of deciding how to approach and plan the risk management activities for a project. It is important to plan for the risk management processes that follow to ensure that the level, type, and visibility of risk management are commensurate with both the risk and importance of the project to the organization.

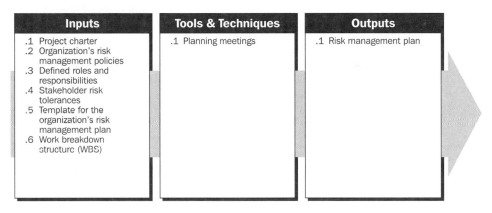

Inputs	Tools & Techniques	Outputs
.1 Project charter .2 Organization's risk management policies .3 Defined roles and responsibilities .4 Stakeholder risk tolerances .5 Template for the organization's risk management plan .6 Work breakdown structure (WBS)	.1 Planning meetings	.1 Risk management plan

11.1.1 Inputs to Risk Management Planning

.1 Project charter. The project charter is discussed in Section 5.1.3.1.

.2 Organization's risk management policies. Some organizations may have predefined approaches to risk analysis and response that have to be tailored to a particular project.

.3 Defined roles and responsibilities. Predefined roles, responsibilities, and authority levels for decision-making will influence planning.

.4 Stakeholder risk tolerances. Different organizations and different individuals have different tolerances for risk. These may be expressed in policy statements or revealed in actions.

.5 Template for the organization's risk management plan. Some organizations have developed templates (or a pro-forma standard) for use by the project team. The organization will continuously improve the template, based on its application and usefulness in the project.

.6 Work breakdown structure (WBS). The WBS is described in Section 5.3.3.1.

11.1.2 Tools and Techniques for Risk Management Planning

.1 Planning meetings. Project teams hold planning meetings to develop the risk management plan. Attendees include the project manager, the project team leaders, anyone in the organization with responsibility to manage the risk planning and execution activities, key stakeholders, and others, as needed. They use the risk management templates and other inputs as appropriate.

11.1.3 Outputs from Risk Management Planning

.1 Risk management plan. The risk management plan describes how risk identification, qualitative and quantitative analysis, response planning, monitoring, and control will be structured and performed during the project life cycle. The risk management plan does not address responses to individual risks—this is accomplished in the risk response plan, which is discussed in Section 11.5.3.1. The risk management plan may include the following.

- *Methodology.* Defines the approaches, tools, and data sources that may be used to perform risk management on this project. Different types of assessments may be appropriate, depending upon the project stage, amount of information available, and flexibility remaining in risk management.
- *Roles and responsibilities.* Defines the lead, support, and risk management team membership for each type of action in the risk management plan. Risk management teams organized outside of the project office may be able to perform more independent, unbiased risk analyses of project than those from the sponsoring project team.
- *Budgeting.* Establishes a budget for risk managment for the project.
- *Timing.* Defines how often the risk management process will be performed throughout the project life cycle. Results should be developed early enough to affect decisions. The decisions should be revisited periodically during project execution.
- *Scoring and interpretation.* The scoring and interpretation methods appropriate for the type and timing of the qualitative and quantitative risk analysis being performed. Methods and scoring must be determined in advance to ensure consistency.
- *Thresholds.* The threshold criteria for risks that will be acted upon, by whom, and in what manner. The project owner, customer, or sponsor may have a different risk threshold. The acceptable threshold forms the target against which the project team will measure the effectiveness of the risk response plan execution.
- *Reporting formats.* Describes the content and format of the risk response plan described in Section 11.5.3.1. Defines how the results of the risk management processes will be documented, analyzed, and communicated to the project team, internal and external stakeholders, sponsors, and others.
- *Tracking.* Documents how all facets of risk activities will be recorded for the benefit of the current project, future needs, and lessons learned. Documents if and how risk processes will be audited.

A Guide to the Project Management Body of Knowledge (PMBOK® Guide) 2000 Edition
©2000 Project Management Institute, Four Campus Boulevard, Newtown Square, PA 19073-3299 USA

11.2 RISK IDENTIFICATION

Risk identification involves determining which risks might affect the project and documenting their characteristics.

Participants in risk identification generally include the following, as possible: project team, risk management team, subject matter experts from other parts of the company, customers, end users, other project managers, stakeholders, and outside experts.

Risk identification is an iterative process. The first iteration may be performed by a part of the project team, or by the risk management team. The entire project team and primary stakeholders may make a second iteration. To achieve an unbiased analysis, persons who are not involved in the project may perform the final iteration.

Often simple and effective risk responses can be developed and even implemented as soon as the risk is identified.

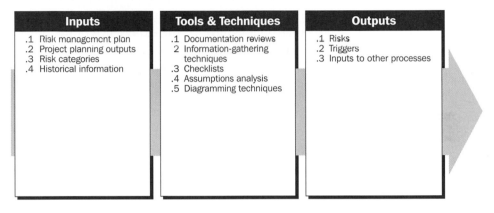

11.2.1 Inputs to Risk Identification

.1 *Risk management plan.* This plan is described in Section 11.1.3.

.2 *Project planning outputs.* Risk identification requires an understanding of the project's mission, scope, and objectives of the owner, sponsor, or stakeholders. Outputs of other processes should be reviewed to identify possible risks across the entire project. These may include, but are not limited to:

■ Project charter.
■ WBS.
■ Product description.
■ Schedule and cost estimates.
■ Resource plan.
■ Procurement plan.
■ Assumption and constraint lists.

.3 *Risk categories.* Risks that may affect the project for better or worse can be identified and organized into risk categories. Risk categories should be well defined and should reflect common sources of risk for the industry or application area. Categories include the following:

■ Technical, quality, or performance risks—such as reliance on unproven or complex technology, unrealistic performance goals, changes to the technology used or to industry standards during the project.

- Project-management risks—such as poor allocation of time and resources, inadequate quality of the project plan, poor use of project management disciplines.
- Organizational risks—such as cost, time, and scope objectives that are internally inconsistent, lack of prioritization of projects, inadequacy or interruption of funding, and resource conflicts with other projects in the organization.
- External risks—such as shifting legal or regulatory environment, labor issues, changing owner priorities, country risk, and weather. *Force majeure* risks such as earthquakes, floods, and civil unrest generally require disaster recovery actions rather than risk management.

.4 *Historical information.* Information on prior projects may be available from the following sources:

- Project files—one or more of the organizations involved in the project may maintain records of previous project results that can be used to identify risks. These may be final project reports or risk response plans. They may include organized lessons learned that describe problems and their resolutions, or be available through the experience of the project stakeholders or others in the organization.
- Published information—commercial databases, academic studies, benchmarking, and other published studies may be available for many application areas.

11.2.2 Tools and Techniques for Risk Identification

.1 *Documentation reviews.* Performing a structured review of project plans and assumptions, both at the total project and detailed scope levels, prior project files, and other information is generally the initial step taken by project teams.

.2 *Information-gathering techniques.* Examples of information-gathering techniques used in risk identification can include brainstorming; Delphi; interviewing; and strengths, weaknesses, opportunities, and threats (SWOT) analysis.

- *Brainstorming*. Brainstorming is probably the most frequently used risk identification technique. The goal is to obtain a comprehensive list of risks that can be addressed later in the qualitative and quantitative risk analysis processes.

  The project team usually performs brainstorming, although a multidisciplinary set of experts can also perform this technique. Under the leadership of a facilitator, these people generate ideas about project risk. Sources of risk are identified in broad scope and posted for all to examine during the meeting. Risks are then categorized by type of risk, and their definitions are sharpened.

- *Delphi technique*. The Delphi technique is a way to reach a consensus of experts on a subject such as project risk. Project risk experts are identified but participate anonymously.

  A facilitator uses a questionnaire to solicit ideas about the important project risks. The responses are submitted and are then circulated to the experts for further comment. Consensus on the main project risks may be reached in a few rounds of this process. The Delphi technique helps reduce bias in the data and keeps any person from having undue influence on the outcome.

- *Interviewing*. Risks can be identified by interviews of experienced project managers or subject-matter experts. The person responsible for risk identification identifies the appropriate individuals, briefs them on the project, and provides

A Guide to the Project Management Body of Knowledge (PMBOK® Guide) 2000 Edition
©2000 Project Management Institute, Four Campus Boulevard, Newtown Square, PA 19073-3299 USA

information such as the WBS and the list of assumptions. The interviewees identify risks on the project based on their experience, project information, and other sources that they find useful.

■ *Strengths, weaknesses, opportunities, and threats (SWOT) analysis*. Ensures examination of the project from each of the SWOT perspectives to increase the breadth of the risks considered.

.3 *Checklists.* Checklists for risk identification can be developed based on historical information and knowledge that has been accumulated from previous similar projects and from other sources of information. One advantage of using a checklist is that risk identification is quick and simple. One disadvantage is that it is impossible to build an exhaustive checklist of risks, and the user may be effectively limited to the categories in the list. Care should be taken to explore items that do not appear on a standard checklist if they seem relevant to the specific project. The checklist should itemize all types of possible risks to the project. It is important to review the checklist as a formal step of every project-closing procedure to improve the list of potential risks, to improve the description of risks.

.4 *Assumptions analysis.* Every project is conceived and developed based on a set of hypotheses, scenarios, or assumptions. Assumptions analysis is a technique that explores the assumptions' validity. It identifies risks to the project from inaccuracy, inconsistency, or incompleteness of assumptions.

.5 *Diagramming techniques.* Diagramming techniques may include:

■ Cause-and-effect diagrams (also known as *Ishikawa* or *fishbone* diagrams)—useful for identifying causes of risks (described in Section 8.1.2.3).

■ System or process flow charts—show how various elements of a system interrelate and the mechanism of causation (described in Section 8.1.2.3).

■ Influence diagrams—a graphical representation of a problem showing causal influences, time ordering of events, and other relationships among variables and outcomes.

11.2.3 Outputs from Risk Identification

.1 *Risks.* A risk is an uncertain event or condition that, if it occurs, has a positive or negative effect on a project objective.

.2 *Triggers.* Triggers, sometimes called risk symptoms or warning signs, are indications that a risk has occurred or is about to occur. For example, failure to meet intermediate milestones may be an early warning signal of an impending schedule delay.

.3 *Inputs to other processes.* Risk identification may identify a need for further action in another area. For example, the WBS may not have sufficient detail to allow adequate identification of risks, or the schedule may not be complete or entirely logical.

11.3 QUALITATIVE RISK ANALYSIS

Qualitative risk analysis is the process of assessing the impact and likelihood of identified risks. This process prioritizes risks according to their potential effect on project objectives. Qualitative risk analysis is one way to determine the importance of addressing specific risks and guiding risk responses. The time-criticality of risk-related actions may magnify the importance of a risk. An evaluation of the quality of the available information also helps modify the assessment of the risk. Qualitative risk analysis requires that the probability and consequences of the risks be evaluated using established qualitative-analysis methods and tools.

Trends in the results when qualitative analysis is repeated can indicate the need for more or less risk-management action. Use of these tools helps correct biases that are often present in a project plan. Qualitative risk analysis should be revisited during the project's life cycle to stay current with changes in the project risks. This process can lead to further analysis in quantitative risk analysis (11.4) or directly to risk response planning (11.5).

Inputs	Tools & Techniques	Outputs
.1 Risk management plan .2 Identified risks .3 Project status .4 Project type .5 Data precision .6 Scales of probability and impact .7 Assumptions	.1 Risk probability and impact .2 Probability/impact risk rating matrix .3 Project assumptions testing .4 Data precision ranking	.1 Overall risk ranking for the project .2 List of prioritized risks .3 List of risks for additional analysis and management .4 Trends in qualitative risk analysis results

11.3.1 Inputs to Qualitative Risk Analysis

.1 Risk management plan. This plan is described in 11.1.3.

.2 Identified risks. Risks discovered during the risk identification process are evaluated along with their potential impacts on the project.

.3 Project status. The uncertainty of a risk often depends on the project's progress through its life cycle. Early in the project, many risks have not surfaced, the design for the project is immature, and changes can occur, making it likely that more risks will be discovered.

.4 Project type. Projects of a common or recurrent type tend to have better understood probability of occurrence of risk events and their consequences. Projects using state-of-the-art or first-of-its-kind technology—or highly complex projects—tend to have more uncertainty.

.5 Data precision. Precision describes the extent to which a risk is known and understood. It measures the extent of data available, as well as the reliability of data. The source of the data that was used to identify the risk must be evaluated.

.6 Scales of probability and impact. These scales, as described in Section 11.3.2.2, are to be used in assessing the two key dimensions of risk, described in Section 11.3.2.1.

.7 Assumptions. Assumptions identified during the risk identification process are evaluated as potential risks (see Sections 4.1.1.5 and 11.2.2.4).

11.3.2 Tools and Techniques for Qualitative Risk Analysis

.1 Risk probability and impact. Risk probability and risk consequences may be described in qualitative terms such as very high, high, moderate, low, and very low.

Risk probability is the likelihood that a risk will occur.

Risk consequences is the effect on project objectives if the risk event occurs.

These two dimensions of risk are applied to specific risk events, not to the overall project. Analysis of risks using probability and consequences helps identify those risks that should be managed aggressively.

A Guide to the Project Management Body of Knowledge (PMBOK® Guide) 2000 Edition
©2000 Project Management Institute, Four Campus Boulevard, Newtown Square, PA 19073-3299 USA

.2 *Probability/impact risk rating matrix.* A matrix may be constructed that assigns risk ratings (very low, low, moderate, high, and very high) to risks or conditions based on combining probability and impact scales. Risks with high probability and high impact are likely to require further analysis, including quantification, and aggressive risk management. The risk rating is accomplished using a matrix and risk scales for each risk.

A risk's *probability scale* naturally falls between 0.0 (no probability) and 1.0 (certainty). Assessing risk probability may be difficult because expert judgment is used, often without benefit of historical data. An ordinal scale, representing relative probability values from very unlikely to almost certain, could be used. Alternatively, specific probabilities could be assigned by using a general scale (e.g., .1 / .3 / .5 / .7 / .9).

The risk's *impact scale* reflects the severity of its effect on the project objective. Impact can be ordinal or cardinal, depending upon the culture of the organization conducting the analysis. Ordinal scales are simply rank-ordered values, such as very low, low, moderate, high, and very high. Cardinal scales assign values to these impacts. These values are usually linear (e.g., .1 / .3 / .5 / .7 / .9), but are often nonlinear (e.g., .05 / .1 / .2 / .4 / .8), reflecting the organization's desire to avoid high-impact risks. The intent of both approaches is to assign a relative value to the impact on project objectives if the risk in question occurs. Well-defined scales, whether ordinal or cardinal, can be developed using definitions agreed upon by the organization. These definitions improve the quality of the data and make the process more repeatable.

Figure 11-2 is an example of evaluating risk impacts by project objective. It illustrates its use for either ordinal or cardinal approach. These scaled descriptors of relative impact should be prepared by the organization before the project begins.

Figure 11-3 is a Probability-Impact (P-I) matrix. It illustrates the simple multiplication of the scale values assigned to estimates of probability and impact, a common way to combine these two dimensions, to determine whether a risk is considered low, moderate, or high. This figure presents a non-linear scale as an example of aversion to high-impact risks, but linear scales are often used. Alternatively, the P-I matrix can be developed using ordinal scales. The organization must determine which combinations of probability and impact result in a risk's being classified as high risk (red condition), moderate risk (yellow condition), and low risk (green condition) for either approach. The risk score helps put the risk into a category that will guide risk response actions.

.3 *Project assumptions testing.* Identified assumptions must be tested against two criteria: assumption stability and the consequences on the project if the assumption is false. Alternative assumptions that may be true should be identified and their consequences on the project objectives tested in the qualitative risk-analysis process.

.4 *Data precision ranking.* Qualitative risk analysis requires accurate and unbiased data if it is to be helpful to project management. Data precision ranking is a technique to evaluate the degree to which the data about risks is useful for risk management. It involves examining:

- Extent of understanding of the risk.
- Data available about the risk.
- Quality of the data.
- Reliability and integrity of the data.

Figure 11-2 | 11.4

Evaluating Impact of a Risk on Major Project Objectives (ordinal scale or cardinal, non-linear scale)					
Project Objective	Very Low .05	Low .1	Moderate .2	High .4	Very High .8
Cost	Insignificant Cost Increase	<5% Cost Increase	5–10% Cost Increase	10–20% Cost Increase	>20% Cost Increase
Schedule	Insignificant Schedule Slippage	Schedule Slippage <5%	Overall Project Slippage 5–10%	Overall Project Slippage 10–20%	Overall Project Schedule Slips >20%
Scope	Scope Decrease Barely Noticeable	Minor Areas of Scope Are Affected	Major Areas of Scope Are Affected	Scope Reduction Unacceptable to the Client	Project End Item Is Effectively Useless
Quality	Quality Degradation Barely Noticeable	Only Very Demanding Applications Are Affected	Quality Reduction Requires Client Approval	Quality Reduction Unacceptable to the Client	Project End Item Is Effectively Unusable

The impacts on project objectives can be assessed on a scale from Very Low to Very High or on a numerical scale. The numerical (cardinal) scale shown here is non-linear, indicating that the organization wishes specifically to avoid risks with high and very-high impact.

Figure 11–2. Rating Impacts for a Risk

The use of data of low precision—for instance, if a risk is not well understood—may lead to a qualitative risk analysis of little use to the project manager. If a ranking of data precision is unacceptable, it may be possible to gather better data.

11.3.3 Outputs from Qualitative Risk Analysis

.1 *Overall risk ranking for the project.* Risk ranking may indicate the overall risk position of a project relative to other projects by comparing the risk scores. It can be used to assign personnel or other resources to projects with different risk rankings, to make a benefit-cost analysis decision about the project, or to support a recommendation for project initiation, continuation, or cancellation.

.2 *List of prioritized risks.* Risks and conditions can be prioritized by a number of criteria. These include rank (high, moderate, and low) or WBS level. Risks may also be grouped by those that require an immediate response and those that can be handled at a later date. Risks that affect cost, schedule, functionality, and quality may be assessed separately with different ratings. Significant risks should have a description of the basis for the assessed probability and impact.

.3 *List of risks for additional analysis and management.* Risks classified as high or moderate would be prime candidates for more analysis, including quantitative risk analysis, and for risk management action.

A Guide to the Project Management Body of Knowledge (PMBOK® Guide) 2000 Edition
©2000 Project Management Institute, Four Campus Boulevard, Newtown Square, PA 19073-3299 USA

Risk Score for a Specific Risk					
Probability	Risk Score = P × I				
0.9	0.05	0.09	0.18	0.36	0.72
0.7	0.04	0.07	0.14	0.28	0.56
0.5	0.03	0.05	0.10	0.20	0.40
0.3	0.02	0.03	0.06	0.12	0.24
0.1	0.01	0.01	0.02	0.04	0.08
	0.05	0.10	0.20	0.40	0.80
	Impact on an Objective (e.g., cost, time, or scope) (Ratio Scale)				

Each risk is rated on its probability of occurring and impact if it does occur. The organization's thresholds for low (dark gray), moderate (light gray) or high (black) risk as shown in the matrix determines the risk's score.

Figure 11–3. Probability-Impact Matrix

.4 Trends in qualitative risk analysis results. As the analysis is repeated, a trend of results may become apparent, and can make risk response or further analysis more or less urgent and important.

11.4 QUANTITATIVE RISK ANALYSIS

The quantitative risk analysis process aims to analyze numerically the probability of each risk and its consequence on project objectives, as well as the extent of overall project risk. This process uses techniques such as Monte Carlo simulation and decision analysis to:

- Determine the probability of achieving a specific project objective.
- Quantify the risk exposure for the project, and determine the size of cost and schedule contingency reserves that may be needed.
- Identify risks requiring the most attention by quantifying their relative contribution to project risk.
- Identify realistic and achievable cost, schedule, or scope targets.

Quantitative risk analysis generally follows qualitative risk analysis. It requires risk identification. The qualitative and quantitative risk analysis processes can be used separately or together. Considerations of time and budget availability and the need for qualitative or quantitative statements about risk and impacts will determine which method(s) to use. Trends in the results when quantitative analysis is repeated can indicate the need for more or less risk management action.

Inputs	Tools & Techniques	Outputs
.1 Risk management plan .2 Identified risks .3 List of prioritized risks .4 List of risks for additional analysis and management .5 Historical information .6 Expert judgment .7 Other planning outputs	.1 Interviewing .2 Sensitivity analysis .3 Decision tree analysis .4 Simulation	.1 Prioritized list of quantified risks .2 Probabilistic analysis of the project .3 Probability of achieving the cost and time objectives .4 Trends in quantitative risk analysis results

11.4.1 Inputs to Quantitative Risk Analysis

.1 Risk management plan. This plan is described in Section 11.1.3.

.2 Identified risks. These are described in Section 11.2.3.1.

.3 List of prioritized risks. This is described in Section 11.3.3.2.

.4 List of risks for additional analysis and management. This is described in Section 11.3.3.3.

.5 Historical information. Information on prior, similar completed projects, studies of similar projects by risk specialists, and risk databases that may be available from industry or proprietary sources (see Section 11.2.1.4).

.6 Expert judgment. Input may come from the project team, other subject matter experts in the organization, and from others outside the organization. Other sources of information include engineering or statistical experts (see Section 5.1.2.2).

.7 Other planning outputs. Most helpful planning outputs are the project logic and duration estimates used in determining schedules, the WBS listing of all cost elements with cost estimates, and models of project technical objectives.

11.4.2 Tools and Techniques for Quantitative Risk Analysis

.1 Interviewing. Interviewing techniques are used to quantify the probability and consequences of risks on project objectives. A risk interview with project stakeholders and subject-matter experts may be the first step in quantifying risks. The information needed depends upon the type of probability distributions that will be used. For instance, information would be gathered on the optimistic (low), pessimistic (high), and the most likely scenarios if triangular distributions are used, or on mean and standard deviation for the normal and log normal distributions. Examples of three-point estimates for a cost estimate are shown in **Figure 11-4**.

Continuous probability distributions are usually used in quantitative risk analysis. Distributions represent both probability and consequences of the project component. Common distribution types include the uniform, normal, triangular, beta, and log normal. Two examples of these distributions are shown in **Figure 11-5** (where the vertical axis refers to probability and the horizontal axis to impact).

Documenting the rationale of the risk ranges is an important component of the risk interview, because it can lead to effective strategies for risk response in the risk response planning process, described in Section 11.5.

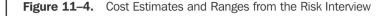

Project Cost Estimates and Ranges			
WBS Element	Low	Most Likely	High
Design	4	6	10
Build	16	20	35
Test	11	15	23
Total Project		41	

The risk interview determines the three-point estimates for each WBS element. The traditional estimate of $41, found by summing the most likely costs, is relatively unlikely, as shown in Figure 11–7.

Figure 11–4. Cost Estimates and Ranges from the Risk Interview

.2 *Sensitivity analysis.* Sensitivity analysis helps to determine which risks have the most potential impact on the project. It examines the extent to which the uncertainty of each project element affects the objective being examined when all other uncertain elements are held at their baseline values.

.3 *Decision tree analysis.* A decision analysis is usually structured as a decision tree. The decision tree is a diagram that describes a decision under consideration and the implications of choosing one or another of the available alternatives. It incorporates probabilities of risks and the costs or rewards of each logical path of events and future decisions. Solving the decision tree indicates which decision yields the greatest expected value to the decision-maker when all the uncertain implications, costs, rewards, and subsequent decisions are quantified. A decision tree is shown in **Figure 11-6**.

.4 *Simulation.* A project simulation uses a model that translates the uncertainties specified at a detailed level into their potential impact on objectives that are expressed at the level of the total project. Project simulations are typically performed using the Monte Carlo technique.

For a cost risk analysis, a simulation may use the traditional project WBS as its model. For a schedule risk analysis, the Precedence Diagramming Method (PDM) schedule is used (see Section 6.2.2.1).

A cost risk simulation result is shown in **Figure 11-7**.

11.4.3 Outputs from Quantitative Risk Analysis

.1 *Prioritized list of quantified risks.* This list of risks includes those that pose the greatest threat or present the greatest opportunity to the project together with a measure of their impact.

.2 *Probabilistic analysis of the project.* Forecasts of potential project schedule and cost results listing the possible completion dates or project duration and costs with their associated confidence levels.

.3 *Probability of achieving the cost and time objectives.* The probability of achieving the project objectives under the current plan and with the current knowledge of the risks facing the project can be estimated using quantitative risk.

.4 *Trends in quantitative risk analysis results.* As the analysis is repeated, a trend of results may become apparent.

Figure 11–5 | 11.5.2

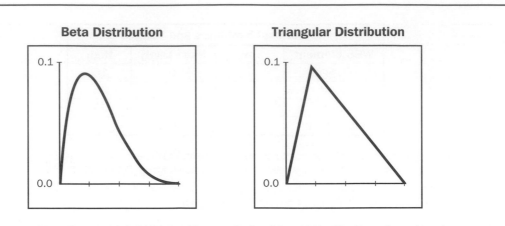

Beta and triangular distributions are frequently used in quantitative risk analysis. The Beta shown here is one example of a family of such distributions. Other distributions that are common include the uniform, normal, and log-normal.

Figure 11–5. Examples of Commonly Used Probability Distributions

11.5 RISK RESPONSE PLANNING

Risk response planning is the process of developing options and determining actions to enhance opportunities and reduce threats to the project's objectives. It includes the identification and assignment of individuals or parties to take responsibility for each agreed risk response. This process ensures that identified risks are properly addressed. The effectiveness of response planning will directly determine whether risk increases or decreases for the project.

Risk response planning must be appropriate to the severity of the risk, cost effective in meeting the challenge, timely to be successful, realistic within the project context, agreed upon by all parties involved, and owned by a responsible person. Selecting the best risk response from several options is often required.

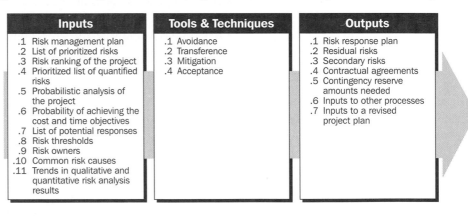

Inputs	Tools & Techniques	Outputs
.1 Risk management plan .2 List of prioritized risks .3 Risk ranking of the project .4 Prioritized list of quantified risks .5 Probabilistic analysis of the project .6 Probability of achieving the cost and time objectives .7 List of potential responses .8 Risk thresholds .9 Risk owners .10 Common risk causes .11 Trends in qualitative and quantitative risk analysis results	.1 Avoidance .2 Transference .3 Mitigation .4 Acceptance	.1 Risk response plan .2 Residual risks .3 Secondary risks .4 Contractual agreements .5 Contingency reserve amounts needed .6 Inputs to other processes .7 Inputs to a revised project plan

11.5.1 Inputs to Risk Response Planning

.1 Risk management plan. This plan is described in Section 11.1.3.

.2 List of prioritized risks. This list from qualitative risk analysis is described in Section 11.3.3.2.

.3 Risk ranking of the project. This is described in Section 11.3.3.1.

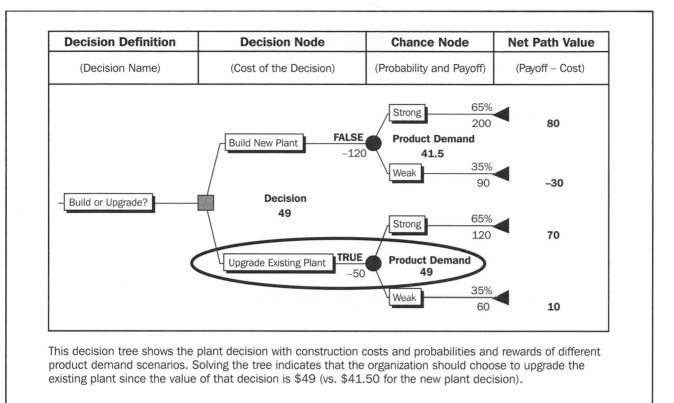

Decision Definition	Decision Node	Chance Node	Net Path Value
(Decision Name)	(Cost of the Decision)	(Probability and Payoff)	(Payoff – Cost)

This decision tree shows the plant decision with construction costs and probabilities and rewards of different product demand scenarios. Solving the tree indicates that the organization should choose to upgrade the existing plant since the value of that decision is $49 (vs. $41.50 for the new plant decision).

Figure 11–6. Decision Tree Analysis

.4 *Prioritized list of quantified risks.* This list from quantitative risk analysis is described in Section 11.4.3.1.

.5 *Probabilistic analysis of the project.* This is described in Section 11.4.3.2.

.6 *Probability of achieving the cost and time objectives.* This is described in Section 11.4.3.3.

.7 *List of potential responses.* In the risk identification process, actions may be identified that respond to individual risks or categories of risks.

.8 *Risk thresholds.* The level of risk that is acceptable to the organization will influence risk response planning (see Section 11.1.3).

.9 *Risk owners.* A list of project stakeholders able to act as owners of risk responses. Risk owners should be involved in developing the risk responses.

.10 *Common risk causes.* Several risks may be driven by a common cause. This situation may reveal opportunities to mitigate two or more project risks with one generic response.

.11 *Trends in qualitative and quantitative risk analysis results.* These are described in Sections 11.3.3.4 and 11.4.3.4. Trends in results can make risk response or further analysis more or less urgent and important.

11.5.2 Tools and Techniques for Risk Response Planning

Several risk response strategies are available. The strategy that is most likely to be effective should be selected for each risk. Then, specific actions should be developed to implement that strategy. Primary and backup strategies may be selected.

Figure 11–7 | 11.5.3.3

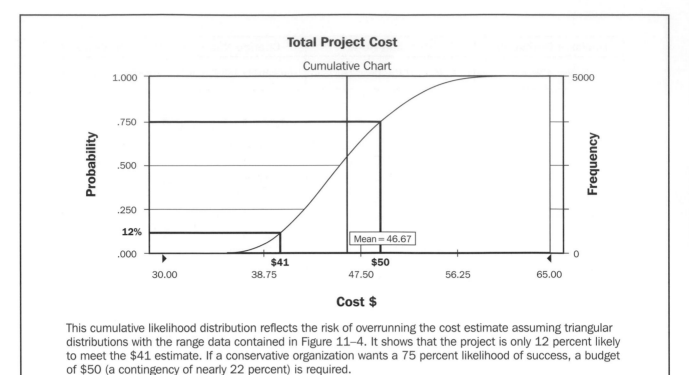

This cumulative likelihood distribution reflects the risk of overrunning the cost estimate assuming triangular distributions with the range data contained in Figure 11–4. It shows that the project is only 12 percent likely to meet the $41 estimate. If a conservative organization wants a 75 percent likelihood of success, a budget of $50 (a contingency of nearly 22 percent) is required.

Figure 11–7. Cost Risk Simulation

.1 *Avoidance.* Risk avoidance is changing the project plan to eliminate the risk or condition or to protect the project objectives from its impact. Although the project team can never eliminate all risk events, some specific risks may be avoided.

Some risk events that arise early in the project can be dealt with by clarifying requirements, obtaining information, improving communication, or acquiring expertise. Reducing scope to avoid high-risk activities, adding resources or time, adopting a familiar approach instead of an innovative one, or avoiding an unfamiliar subcontractor may be examples of avoidance.

.2 *Transference.* Risk transfer is seeking to shift the consequence of a risk to a third party together with ownership of the response. Transferring the risk simply gives another party responsibility for its management; it does not eliminate it.

Transferring liability for risk is most effective in dealing with financial risk exposure. Risk transfer nearly always involves payment of a risk premium to the party taking on the risk. It includes the use of insurance, performance bonds, warranties, and guarantees. Contracts may be used to transfer liability for specified risks to another party. Use of a fixed-price contract may transfer risk to the seller if the project's design is stable. Although a cost-reimbursable contract leaves more of the risk with the customer or sponsor, it may help reduce cost if there are mid-project changes.

.3 *Mitigation.* Mitigation seeks to reduce the probability and/or consequences of an adverse risk event to an acceptable threshold. Taking early action to reduce the probability of a risk's occurring or its impact on the project is more effective than trying to repair the consequences after it has occurred. Mitigation costs should be appropriate, given the likely probability of the risk and its consequences.

A Guide to the Project Management Body of Knowledge (PMBOK® Guide) 2000 Edition
©2000 Project Management Institute, Four Campus Boulevard, Newtown Square, PA 19073-3299 USA

Risk mitigation may take the form of implementing a new course of action that will reduce the problem—e.g., adopting less complex processes, conducting more seismic or engineering tests, or choosing a more stable seller. It may involve changing conditions so that the probability of the risk occurring is reduced—e.g., adding resources or time to the schedule. It may require prototype development to reduce the risk of scaling up from a bench-scale model.

Where it is not possible to reduce probability, a mitigation response might address the risk impact by targeting linkages that determine the severity. For example, designing redundancy into a subsystem may reduce the impact that results from a failure of the original component.

.4 *Acceptance.* This technique indicates that the project team has decided not to change the project plan to deal with a risk or is unable to identify any other suitable response strategy. Active acceptance may include developing a contingency plan to execute, should a risk occur. Passive acceptance requires no action, leaving the project team to deal with the risks as they occur.

A *contingency plan* is applied to identified risks that arise during the project. Developing a contingency plan in advance can greatly reduce the cost of an action should the risk occur. Risk triggers, such as missing intermediate milestones, should be defined and tracked. A *fallback plan* is developed if the risk has a high impact, or if the selected strategy may not be fully effective. This might include allocation of a contingency amount, development of alternative options, or changing project scope.

The most usual risk acceptance response is to establish a *contingency allowance*, or reserve, including amounts of time, money, or resources to account for known risks. The allowance should be determined by the impacts, computed at an acceptable level of risk exposure, for the risks that have been accepted.

11.5.3 Outputs from Risk Response Planning

.1 *Risk response plan.* The risk response plan (sometimes called the *risk register*) should be written to the level of detail at which the actions will be taken. It should include some or all of the following:
- Identified risks, their descriptions, the area(s) of the project (e.g., WBS element) affected, their causes, and how they may affect project objectives.
- Risk owners and assigned responsibilities.
- Results from the qualitative and quantitative risk analysis processes.
- Agreed responses including avoidance, transference, mitigation, or acceptance for each risk in the risk response plan.
- The level of residual risk expected to be remaining after the strategy is implemented.
- Specific actions to implement the chosen response strategy.
- Budget and times for responses.
- Contingency plans and fallback plans.

.2 *Residual risks.* Residual risks are those that remain after avoidance, transfer, or mitigation responses have been taken. They also include minor risks that have been accepted and addressed, e.g., by adding contingency amounts to the cost or time allowable.

.3 *Secondary risks.* Risks that arise as a direct result of implementing a risk response are termed *secondary risks*. These should be identified and responses planned.

.4 *Contractual agreements.* Contractual agreements may be entered into to specify each party's responsibility for specific risks, should they occur, and for insurance, services, and other items as appropriate to avoid or mitigate threats.

.5 *Contingency reserve amounts needed.* The probabilistic analysis of the project (11.4.3.2) and the risk thresholds (11.1.3.1) help the project manager determine the amount of buffer or contingency needed to reduce the risk of overruns of project objectives to a level acceptable to the organization.

.6 *Inputs to other processes.* Most responses to risk involve expenditure of additional time, cost, or resources and require changes to the project plan. Organizations require assurance that spending is justified for the level of risk reduction. Alternative strategies must be fed back into the appropriate processes in other knowledge areas.

.7 *Inputs to a revised project plan.* The results of the response planning process must be incorporated into the project plan, to ensure that agreed actions are implemented and monitored as part of the ongoing project.

11.6 RISK MONITORING AND CONTROL

Risk monitoring and control is the process of keeping track of the identified risks, monitoring residual risks and identifying new risks, ensuring the execution of risk plans, and evaluating their effectiveness in reducing risk. Risk monitoring and control records risk metrics that are associated with implementing contingency plans. Risk monitoring and control is an ongoing process for the life of the project. The risks change as the project matures, new risks develop, or anticipated risks disappear.

Good risk monitoring and control processes provide information that assists with making effective decisions in advance of the risk's occurring. Communication to all project stakeholders is needed to assess periodically the acceptability of the level of risk on the project.

The purpose of risk monitoring is to determine if:

■ Risk responses have been implemented as planned.

■ Risk response actions are as effective as expected, or if new responses should be developed.

■ Project assumptions are still valid.

■ Risk exposure has changed from its prior state, with analysis of trends.

■ A risk trigger has occurred.

■ Proper policies and procedures are followed.

■ Risks have occurred or arisen that were not previously identified.

Risk control may involve choosing alternative strategies, implementing a contingency plan, taking corrective action, or replanning the project. The risk response owner should report periodically to the project manager and the risk team leader on the effectiveness of the plan, any unanticipated effects, and any mid-course correction needed to mitigate the risk.

A Guide to the Project Management Body of Knowledge (PMBOK® Guide) 2000 Edition
©2000 Project Management Institute, Four Campus Boulevard, Newtown Square, PA 19073-3299 USA

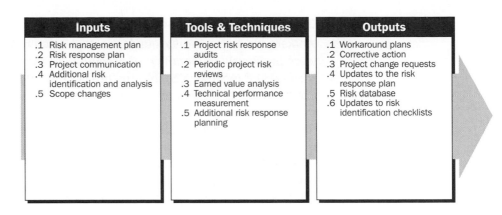

Inputs	Tools & Techniques	Outputs
.1 Risk management plan .2 Risk response plan .3 Project communication .4 Additional risk identification and analysis .5 Scope changes	.1 Project risk response audits .2 Periodic project risk reviews .3 Earned value analysis .4 Technical performance measurement .5 Additional risk response planning	.1 Workaround plans .2 Corrective action .3 Project change requests .4 Updates to the risk response plan .5 Risk database .6 Updates to risk identification checklists

11.6.1 Inputs to Risk Monitoring and Control

.1 Risk management plan. The risk management plan is described in Section 11.1.3.

.2 Risk response plan. The risk response plan is described in Section 11.5.3.1.

.3 Project communication. Work results and other project records described in Section 10.3.1 provide information about project performance and risks. Reports commonly used to monitor and control risks include *Issues Logs, Action-Item Lists, Jeopardy Warnings,* or *Escalation Notices.*

.4 Additional risk identification and analysis. As project performance is measured and reported, potential risks not previously identified may surface. The cycle of the six risk processes should be implemented for these risks.

.5 Scope changes. Scope changes often require new risk analysis and response plans. Scope changes are described in Section 5.5.3.1.

11.6.2 Tools and Techniques for Risk Monitoring and Control

.1 Project risk response audits. Risk auditors examine and document the effectiveness of the risk response in avoiding, transferring, or mitigating risk occurrence as well as the effectiveness of the risk owner. Risk audits are performed during the project life cycle to control risk.

.2 Periodic project risk reviews. Project risk reviews should be regularly scheduled. Project risk should be an agenda item at all team meetings. Risk ratings and prioritization may change during the life of the project. Any changes may require additional qualitative or quantitative analysis.

.3 Earned value analysis. Earned value is used for monitoring overall project performance against a baseline plan. Results from an earned value analysis may indicate potential deviation of the project at completion from cost and schedule targets. When a project deviates significantly from the baseline, updated risk identification and analysis should be performed. Earned value analysis is described in Section 10.3.2.4.

.4 Technical performance measurement. Technical performance measurement compares technical accomplishments during project execution to the project plan's schedule of technical achievement. Deviation, such as not demonstrating functionality as planned at a milestone, can imply a risk to achieving the project's scope.

.5 Additional risk response planning. If a risk emerges that was not anticipated in the risk response plan, or its impact on objectives is greater than expected, the planned response may not be adequate. It will be necessary to perform additional response planning to control the risk.

11.6.3 Outputs from Risk Monitoring and Control

.1 *Workaround plans.* Workarounds are unplanned responses to emerging risks that were previously unidentified or accepted. Workarounds must be properly documented and incorporated into the project plan and risk response plan.

.2 *Corrective action.* Corrective action consists of performing the contingency plan or workaround.

.3 *Project change requests.* Implementing contingency plans or workarounds frequently results in a requirement to change the project plan to respond to risks. The result is issuance of a change request that is managed by integrated change control, as described in Section 4.3.

.4 *Updates to the risk response plan.* Risks may occur or not. Risks that do occur should be documented and evaluated. Implementation of risk controls may reduce the impact or probability of identified risks. Risk rankings must be reassessed so that new, important risks may be properly controlled. Risks that do not occur should be documented and closed in the risk response plan.

.5 *Risk database.* A repository that provides for collection, maintenance, and analysis of data gathered and used in the risk management processes. Use of this database will assist risk management throughout the organization and, over time, form the basis of a risk lessons learned program.

.6 *Updates to risk identification checklists.* Checklists updated from experience will help risk management of future projects.

A Guide to the Project Management Body of Knowledge (PMBOK® Guide) 2000 Edition
©2000 Project Management Institute, Four Campus Boulevard, Newtown Square, PA 19073-3299 USA

Chapter 12

Project Procurement Management

Project Procurement Management includes the processes required to acquire goods and services, to attain project scope, from outside the performing organization. For simplicity, goods and services, whether one or many, will generally be referred to as a *product*. **Figure 12-1** provides an overview of the following major processes:

12.1 Procurement Planning—determining what to procure and when.

12.2 Solicitation Planning—documenting product requirements and identifying potential sources.

12.3 Solicitation—obtaining quotations, bids, offers, or proposals, as appropriate.

12.4 Source Selection—choosing from among potential sellers.

12.5 Contract Administration—managing the relationship with the seller.

12.6 Contract Closeout—completion and settlement of the contract, including resolution of any open items.

These processes interact with each other and with the processes in the other knowledge areas as well. Each process may involve effort from one or more individuals or groups of individuals, based on the needs of the project. Although the processes are presented here as discrete elements with well-defined interfaces, in practice they may overlap and interact in ways not detailed here. Process interactions are discussed in detail in Chapter 3.

Project Procurement Management is discussed from the perspective of the buyer in the buyer-seller relationship. The buyer-seller relationship can exist at many levels on one project. Depending on the application area, the seller may be called a *subcontractor*, a *vendor*, or a *supplier*.

The *seller* will typically manage its work as a project. In such cases:

- The *buyer* becomes the customer, and is thus a key stakeholder for the seller.
- The seller's project management team must be concerned with all the processes of project management, not just with those of this knowledge area.
- The terms and conditions of the contract become a key input to many of the seller's processes. The contract may actually contain the input (e.g., major deliverables, key milestones, cost objectives), or it may limit the project team's options (e.g., buyer approval of staffing decisions is often required on design projects).

A Guide to the Project Management Body of Knowledge (PMBOK® Guide) 2000 Edition
©2000 Project Management Institute, Four Campus Boulevard, Newtown Square, PA 19073-3299 USA

Figure 12–1 | 12.1.1.2

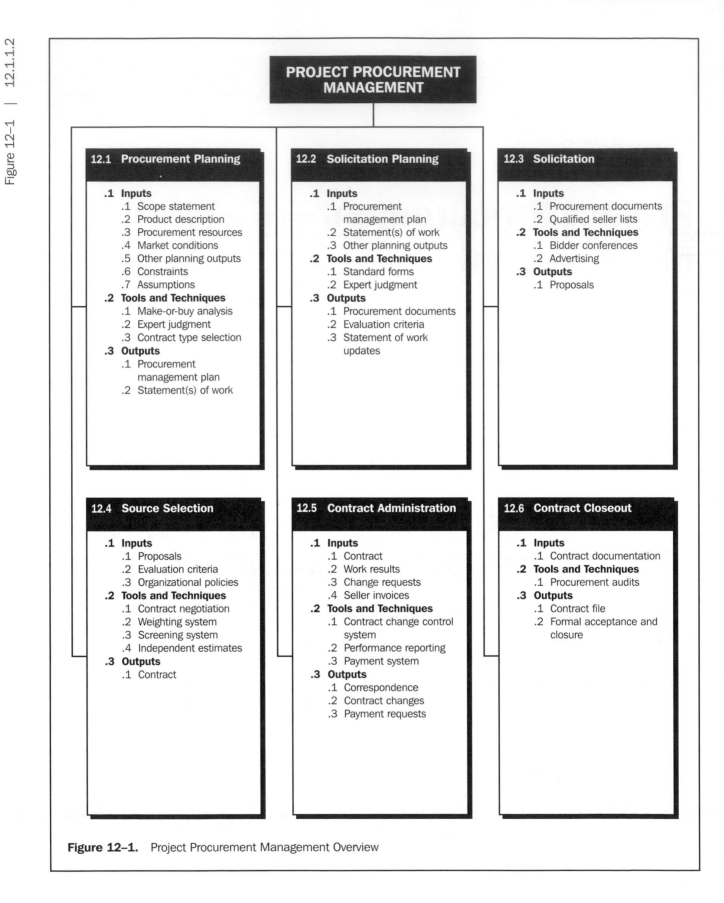

Figure 12–1. Project Procurement Management Overview

A Guide to the Project Management Body of Knowledge (PMBOK® Guide) 2000 Edition
©2000 Project Management Institute, Four Campus Boulevard, Newtown Square, PA 19073-3299 USA

This chapter assumes that the seller is external to the performing organization. Most of the discussion, however, is equally applicable to *formal* agreements entered into with other units of the performing organization. When informal agreements are involved, the processes described in Project Human Resource Management, Chapter 9, and Project Communications Management, Chapter 10, are more likely to apply.

12.1 PROCUREMENT PLANNING

Procurement planning is the process of identifying which project needs can be best met by procuring products or services outside the project organization and should be accomplished during the scope definition effort. It involves consideration of whether to procure, how to procure, what to procure, how much to procure, and when to procure.

When the project obtains products and services (project scope) from outside the performing organization, the processes from solicitation planning (Section 12.2) through contract closeout (Section 12.6) would be performed once for each product or service item. The project management team may want to seek support from specialists in the disciplines of contracting and procurement when needed, and involve them early in the process as a member of the project team.

When the project does not obtain products and services from outside the performing organization, the processes from solicitation planning (Section 12.2) through contract closeout (Section 12.6) would *not* be performed.

Procurement planning should also include consideration of potential sellers, particularly if the buyer wishes to exercise some degree of influence or control over contracting decisions.

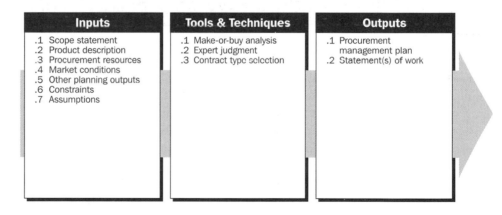

Inputs	Tools & Techniques	Outputs
.1 Scope statement .2 Product description .3 Procurement resources .4 Market conditions .5 Other planning outputs .6 Constraints .7 Assumptions	.1 Make-or-buy analysis .2 Expert judgment .3 Contract type selection	.1 Procurement management plan .2 Statement(s) of work

12.1.1 Inputs to Procurement Planning

   .1 Scope statement. The scope statement (see Section 5.2.3.1) describes the current project boundaries. It provides important information about project needs and strategies that must be considered during procurement planning.

   .2 Product description. The description of the product of the project (described in Section 5.1.1.1) provides important information about any technical issues or concerns that would need to be considered during procurement planning.

The product description is generally broader than a statement of work. A product description describes the ultimate end product of the project; a statement of work (discussed in Section 12.1.3.2) describes the portion of that product to be provided by a seller to the project. However, if the performing organization chooses to procure the entire product, then the distinction between the two terms disappears.

.3 *Procurement resources.* If the performing organization does not have a formal contracting group, then the project team will have to supply both the resources and the expertise to support project procurement activities.

.4 *Market conditions.* The procurement planning process must consider what products and services are available in the marketplace, from whom, and under what terms and conditions.

.5 *Other planning outputs.* To the extent that other planning outputs are available, they must be considered during procurement planning. Other planning outputs that must often be considered include preliminary cost and schedule estimates, quality management plans, cash-flow projections, the work breakdown structure, identified risks, and planned staffing.

.6 *Constraints.* Constraints are factors that limit the buyer's options. One of the most common constraints for many projects is funds availability.

.7 *Assumptions.* Assumptions are factors that, for planning purposes, will be considered to be true, real, or certain.

12.1.2 Tools and Techniques for Procurement Planning

.1 *Make-or-buy analysis.* This is a general management technique and a part of the initial scope definition process that can be used to determine whether a particular product can be produced cost effectively by the performing organization. Analysis should include both indirect as well as direct costs. For example, the "buy" side of the analysis should include both the actual out-of-pocket cost to purchase the product as well as the indirect costs of managing the purchasing process.

A make-or-buy analysis must also reflect the perspective of the performing organization, as well as the immediate needs of the project. For example, purchasing a capital item (anything from a construction crane to a personal computer) rather than renting or leasing it may or may not be cost effective. However, if the performing organization has an ongoing need for the item, the portion of the purchase cost allocated to the project may be less than the cost of the rental.

.2 *Expert judgment.* Expert technical judgment will often be required to assess the inputs to this process. Such expertise may be provided by any group or individual with specialized knowledge or training and is available from many sources, including:

■ Other units within the performing organization.
■ Consultants.
■ Professional and technical associations.
■ Industry groups.

.3 *Contract type selection.* Different types of contracts are more or less appropriate for different types of purchases. Contracts generally fall into one of three broad categories:

- Fixed-price or lump-sum contracts—this category of contract involves a fixed total price for a well-defined product. To the extent that the product is not well defined, both the buyer and seller are at risk—the buyer may not receive the desired product or the seller may need to incur additional costs to provide it. Fixed-price contracts may also include incentives for meeting or exceeding selected project objectives, such as schedule targets.

- Cost-reimbursable contracts—this category of contract involves payment (reimbursement) to the seller for its actual costs, plus typically a fee representing seller profit. Costs are usually classified as *direct costs* or *indirect costs*. Direct costs are costs incurred for the exclusive benefit of the project (e.g., salaries of full-time project staff). Indirect costs, also called overhead costs, are costs allocated to the project by the performing organization as a cost of doing business (e.g., salaries of corporate executives). Indirect costs are usually calculated as a percentage of direct costs. Cost-reimbursable contracts often include incentives for meeting or exceeding selected project objectives, such as schedule targets or total cost.

- Time and Material (T&M) contracts—T&M contracts are a hybrid type of contractual arrangement that contains aspects of both cost-reimbursable and fixed-price-type arrangements. T&M contracts resemble cost-type arrangements in that they are open ended, because the full value of the arrangement is not defined at the time of the award. Thus, T&M contracts can grow in contract value as if they were cost-reimbursable-type arrangements. Conversely, T&M arrangements can also resemble fixed-unit arrangements when, for example, the unit rates are preset by the buyer and seller, as when both parties agree on the rates for the category of "senior engineers."

12.1.3 Outputs from Procurement Planning

.1 *Procurement management plan.* The procurement management plan should describe how the remaining procurement processes (from solicitation planning through contract closeout) will be managed. For example:

- What types of contracts will be used?
- If independent estimates will be needed as evaluation criteria, who will prepare them and when?
- If the performing organization has a procurement department, what actions can the project management team take on its own?
- If standardized procurement documents are needed, where can they be found?
- How will multiple providers be managed?
- How will procurement be coordinated with other project aspects, such as scheduling and performance reporting?

   A procurement management plan may be formal or informal, highly detailed or broadly framed, based on the needs of the project. It is a subsidiary element of the project plan described in Section 4.1, Project Plan Development.

.2 *Statement(s) of work.* The statement of work (SOW) describes the procurement item in sufficient detail to allow prospective sellers to determine if they are capable of providing the item. "Sufficient detail" may vary, based on the nature of the item, the needs of the buyer, or the expected contract form.

Some application areas recognize different types of SOW. For example, in some government jurisdictions, the term *SOW* is reserved for a procurement item that is a clearly specified product or service, and the term *Statement of Objectives* (SOO) is used for a procurement item that is presented as a problem to be solved.

The statement of work may be revised and refined as it moves through the procurement process. For example, a prospective seller may suggest a more efficient approach or a less costly product than that originally specified. Each individual procurement item requires a separate statement of work. However, multiple products or services may be grouped as one procurement item with a single SOW.

The statement of work should be as clear, as complete, and as concise as possible. It should include a description of any collateral services required, such as performance reporting or postproject operational support for the procured item. In some application areas, there are specific content and format requirements for a SOW.

12.2 SOLICITATION PLANNING

Solicitation planning involves preparing the documents needed to support solicitation (the solicitation process is described in Section 12.3).

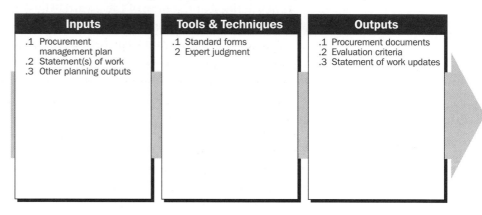

Inputs	Tools & Techniques	Outputs
.1 Procurement management plan .2 Statement(s) of work .3 Other planning outputs	.1 Standard forms 2 Expert judgment	.1 Procurement documents .2 Evaluation criteria .3 Statement of work updates

12.2.1 Inputs to Solicitation Planning

.1 *Procurement management plan.* The procurement management plan is described in Section 12.1.3.1.

.2 *Statement(s) of work.* The statement of work is described in Section 12.1.3.2.

.3 *Other planning outputs.* Other planning outputs (see Section 12.1.1.5), which may have been modified from when they were considered as part of procurement planning, should be reviewed again as part of solicitation. In particular, solicitation planning should be closely aligned with the project schedule.

12.2.2 Tools and Techniques for Solicitation Planning

.1 *Standard forms.* Standard forms may include standard contracts, standard descriptions of procurement items, or standardized versions of all or part of the needed bid documents (see Section 12.2.3.1). Organizations that do substantial amounts of procurement should have many of these documents standardized.

.2 *Expert judgment.* Expert judgment is described in Section 12.1.2.2.

A Guide to the Project Management Body of Knowledge (PMBOK® Guide) 2000 Edition
©2000 Project Management Institute, Four Campus Boulevard, Newtown Square, PA 19073-3299 USA

12.2.3 Outputs from Solicitation Planning

.1 *Procurement documents.* Procurement documents are used to solicit proposals from prospective sellers. The terms *bid* and *quotation* are generally used when the source selection decision will be based on price (as when buying commercial or standard items), while the term *proposal* is generally used when other considerations, such as technical skills or technical approach, are paramount. However, the terms are often used interchangeably, and care should be taken not to make unwarranted assumptions about the implications of the term used. Common names for different types of procurement documents include: Invitation for Bid (IFB), Request for Proposal (RFP), Request for Quotation (RFQ), Invitation for Negotiation, and Contractor Initial Response.

Procurement documents should be structured to facilitate accurate and complete responses from prospective sellers. They should always include the relevant SOW, a description of the desired form of the response, and any required contractual provisions (e.g., a copy of a model contract, nondisclosure provisions). With government contracting, some or all of the content and structure of procurement documents may be defined by regulation.

Procurement documents should be rigorous enough to ensure consistent, comparable responses, but flexible enough to allow consideration of seller suggestions for better ways to satisfy the requirements.

.2 *Evaluation criteria.* Evaluation criteria are used to rate or score proposals. They may be objective (e.g., "The proposed project manager must be a certified Project Management Professional, PMP®.") or subjective (e.g., "The proposed project manager must have documented, previous experience with similar projects."). Evaluation criteria are often included as part of the procurement documents.

Evaluation criteria may be limited to purchase price if the procurement item is readily available from a number of acceptable sources (*purchase price* in this context includes both the cost of the item and ancillary expenses such as delivery). When this is not the case, other selection criteria must be identified and documented to support an assessment. For example:

■ Understanding of need—as demonstrated by the seller's proposal.

■ Overall or life-cycle cost—will the selected seller produce the lowest total cost (purchase cost plus operating cost)?

■ Technical capability—does the seller have, or can the seller be reasonably expected to acquire, the technical skills and knowledge needed?

■ Management approach—does the seller have, or can the seller be reasonably expected to develop, management processes and procedures to ensure a successful project?

■ Financial capacity—does the seller have, or can the seller reasonably be expected to obtain, the necessary financial resources?

.3 *Statement of work updates.* The statement of work is described in Section 12.1.3.2. Modifications to one or more statements of work may be identified during solicitation planning.

12.3 SOLICITATION

Solicitation involves obtaining responses (bids and proposals) from prospective sellers on how project needs can be met. Most of the actual effort in this process is expended by the prospective sellers, normally at no cost to the project.

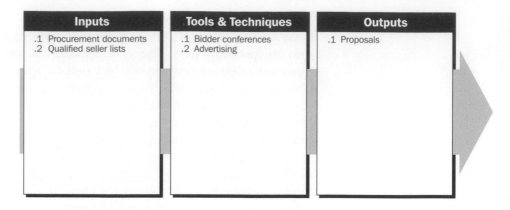

12.3.1 Inputs to Solicitation

.1 Procurement documents. Procurement documents are described in Section 12.2.3.1.

.2 Qualified seller lists. Some organizations maintain lists or files with information on prospective sellers. These lists will generally have information on relevant past experience and other characteristics of the prospective sellers.

If such lists are not readily available, then the project team will have to develop its own sources. General information is widely available through the Internet, library directories, relevant local associations, trade catalogs, and similar sources. Detailed information on specific sources may require more extensive effort, such as site visits or contact with previous customers.

Procurement documents may be sent to some or all of the prospective sellers.

12.3.2 Tools and Techniques for Solicitation

.1 Bidder conferences. Bidder conferences (also called *contractor conferences, vendor conferences,* and *pre-bid conferences*) are meetings with prospective sellers prior to preparation of a proposal. They are used to ensure that all prospective sellers have a clear, common understanding of the procurement (technical requirements, contract requirements, etc.). Responses to questions may be incorporated into the procurement documents as amendments. All potential sellers must remain on equal standing during this process.

.2 Advertising. Existing lists of potential sellers can often be expanded by placing advertisements in general circulation publications such as newspapers or in specialty publications such as professional journals. Some government jurisdictions require public advertising of certain types of procurement items; most government jurisdictions require public advertising of subcontracts on a government contract.

12.3.3 Outputs from Solicitation

.1 Proposals. Proposals (see also discussion of bids, quotations, and proposals in Section 12.2.3.1) are seller-prepared documents that describe the seller's ability and willingness to provide the requested product. They are prepared in accordance with the requirements of the relevant procurement documents. Proposals may be supplemented with an oral presentation.

A Guide to the Project Management Body of Knowledge (PMBOK® Guide) 2000 Edition
©2000 Project Management Institute, Four Campus Boulevard, Newtown Square, PA 19073-3299 USA

12.4 SOURCE SELECTION

Source selection involves the receipt of bids or proposals and the application of the evaluation criteria to select a provider. Many factors aside from cost or price may need to be evaluated in the source selection decision process.

- Price may be the primary determinant for an off-the-shelf item, but the lowest proposed *price* may not be the lowest *cost* if the seller proves unable to deliver the product in a timely manner.
- Proposals are often separated into technical (approach) and commercial (price) sections with each evaluated separately.
- Multiple sources may be required for critical products.

The tools and techniques described here may be used singly or in combination. For example, a weighting system may be used to:

- Select a single source who will be asked to sign a standard contract.
- Rank order all proposals to establish a negotiating sequence.

On major procurement items, this process may be repeated. A short list of qualified sellers may be selected based on a preliminary proposal, and then a more detailed evaluation will be conducted based on a more detailed and comprehensive proposal.

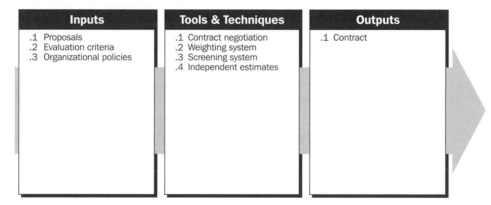

Inputs	Tools & Techniques	Outputs
.1 Proposals .2 Evaluation criteria .3 Organizational policies	.1 Contract negotiation .2 Weighting system .3 Screening system .4 Independent estimates	.1 Contract

12.4.1 Inputs to Source Selection

- *.1 Proposals.* Proposals are described in Section 12.3.3.1.
- *.2 Evaluation criteria.* Evaluation criteria may include samples of the suppliers previously produced products/services for the purpose of providing a way to evaluate their capabilities and quality of products. They also may include a review of the supplier's history with the contracting organization. Evaluation criteria are described in Section 12.2.3.2.
- *.3 Organizational policies.* Organizations involved in project procurement typically have formal policies that affect the evaluation of proposals.

12.4.2 Tools and Techniques for Source Selection

- *.1 Contract negotiation.* Contract negotiation involves clarification and mutual agreement on the structure and requirements of the contract prior to the signing of the contract. To the extent possible, final contract language should reflect all agreements reached. Subjects covered generally include, but are not limited to, responsibilities and authorities, applicable terms and law, technical and business management approaches, contract financing, and price.

For complex procurement items, contract negotiation may be an independent process with inputs (e.g., an issues or open items list) and outputs (e.g., memorandum of understanding) of its own.

.2 *Weighting system.* A weighting system is a method for quantifying qualitative data to minimize the effect of personal prejudice on source selection. Most such systems involve 1) assigning a numerical weight to each of the evaluation criteria, 2) rating the prospective sellers on each criterion, 3) multiplying the weight by the rating, and 4) totaling the resultant products to compute an overall score.

.3 *Screening system.* A screening system involves establishing minimum requirements of performance for one or more of the evaluation criteria. For example, a prospective seller might be required to propose a project manager who has specific qualifications—for example, a PMP®—before the remainder of the proposal would be considered.

.4 *Independent estimates.* For many procurement items, the procuring organization may prepare its own independent estimates as a check on proposed pricing. Significant differences from these estimates may be an indication that the SOW was not adequate, or that the prospective seller either misunderstood or failed to respond fully to the SOW. Independent estimates are often referred to as *should cost* estimates.

12.4.3 Outputs from Source Selection

.1 *Contract.* A contract is a mutually binding agreement that obligates the seller to provide the specified product and obligates the buyer to pay for it. *A contract is a legal relationship subject to remedy in the courts.* The agreement may be simple or complex, usually (but not always) reflecting the simplicity or complexity of the product. Contracts may be called, among other names, a *contract*, an *agreement*, a *subcontract*, a *purchase order*, or a *memorandum of understanding*. Most organizations have documented policies and procedures specifically defining who can sign such agreements on behalf of the organization, typically called a *delegation of procurement authority*.

Although all project documents are subject to some form of review and approval, the legally binding nature of a contract usually means that it will be subjected to a more extensive approval process. In all cases, a primary focus of the review and approval process should be to ensure that the contract language describes a product or service that will satisfy the identified need. In the case of major projects undertaken by public agencies, the review process may even include public review of the agreement.

12.5 CONTRACT ADMINISTRATION

Contract administration is the process of ensuring that the seller's performance meets contractual requirements. On larger projects with multiple product and service providers, a key aspect of contract administration is managing the interfaces among the various providers. *The legal nature of the contractual relationship makes it imperative that the project team be acutely aware of the legal implications of actions taken when administering the contract.*

A Guide to the Project Management Body of Knowledge (PMBOK® Guide) 2000 Edition
©2000 Project Management Institute, Four Campus Boulevard, Newtown Square, PA 19073-3299 USA

Contract administration includes application of the appropriate project management processes to the contractual relationship(s) and integration of the outputs from these processes into the overall management of the project. This integration and coordination will often occur at multiple levels when there are multiple sellers and multiple products involved. The project management processes that must be applied include:

- Project plan execution, described in Section 4.2, to authorize the contractor's work at the appropriate time.
- Performance reporting, described in Section 10.3, to monitor contractor cost, schedule, and technical performance.
- Quality control, described in Section 8.3, to inspect and verify the adequacy of the contractor's product.
- Change control, described in Section 4.3, to ensure that changes are properly approved and that all those with a need to know are aware of such changes.

Contract administration also has a financial management component. Payment terms should be defined within the contract and must involve a specific linkage between seller progress made and seller compensation paid.

Inputs	Tools & Techniques	Outputs
.1 Contract .2 Work results .3 Change requests .4 Seller invoices	.1 Contract change control system .2 Performance reporting .3 Payment system	.1 Correspondence .2 Contract changes .3 Payment requests

12.5.1 Inputs to Contract Administration

.1 Contract. Contracts are described in Section 12.4.3.1.

.2 Work results. The seller's work results—which deliverables have been completed and which have not, to what extent are quality standards being met, what costs have been incurred or committed, etc.—are collected as part of project plan execution. (Section 4.2 provides more detail on project plan execution.)

.3 Change requests. Change requests may include modifications to the terms of the contract or to the description of the product or service to be provided. If the seller's work is unsatisfactory, then a decision to terminate the contract would also be handled as a change request. Contested changes, those where the seller and the project management team cannot agree on compensation for the change, are variously called *claims*, *disputes*, or *appeals*.

.4 Seller invoices. The seller must submit invoices from time to time to request payment for work performed. Invoicing requirements, including necessary supporting documentation, are defined within the contract.

12.5.2 Tools and Techniques for Contract Administration

.1 *Contract change control system.* A contract change control system defines the process by which the contract may be modified. It includes the paperwork, tracking systems, dispute resolution procedures, and approval levels necessary for authorizing changes. The contract change control system should be integrated with the integrated change control system. (Section 4.3 describes the integrated change control system.)

.2 *Performance reporting.* Performance reporting provides management with information about how effectively the seller is achieving the contractual objectives. Contract performance reporting should be integrated with the integrated project performance reporting, described in Section 10.3.

.3 *Payment system.* Payments to the seller are usually handled by the accounts payable system of the performing organization. On larger projects with many or complex procurement requirements, the project may develop its own system. In either case, the payment system must include appropriate reviews and approvals by the project management team.

12.5.3 Outputs from Contract Administration

.1 *Correspondence.* Contract terms and conditions often require written documentation of certain aspects of buyer/seller communications, such as warnings of unsatisfactory performance and contract changes or clarifications.

.2 *Contract changes.* Changes (approved and unapproved) are fed back through the appropriate project planning and project procurement processes, and the project plan or other relevant documentation is updated as appropriate.

.3 *Payment requests.* This assumes that the project is using an external payment system. If the project has its own internal system, the output here would simply be "payments."

12.6 CONTRACT CLOSEOUT

Contract closeout is similar to administrative closure (described in Section 10.4) in that it involves both product verification (Was all work completed correctly and satisfactorily?) and administrative closeout (updating of records to reflect final results and archiving of such information for future use). The contract terms and conditions may prescribe specific procedures for contract closeout. Early termination of a contract is a special case of contract closeout.

Inputs	Tools & Techniques	Outputs
.1 Contract documentation	.1 Procurement audits	.1 Contract file .2 Formal acceptance and closure

A Guide to the Project Management Body of Knowledge (PMBOK® Guide) 2000 Edition
©2000 Project Management Institute, Four Campus Boulevard, Newtown Square, PA 19073-3299 USA

12.6.1 Inputs to Contract Closeout

.1 Contract documentation. Contract documentation includes, but is not limited to, the contract itself along with all supporting schedules, requested and approved contract changes, any seller-developed technical documentation, seller performance reports, financial documents such as invoices and payment records, and the results of any contract-related inspections.

12.6.2 Tools and Techniques for Contract Closeout

.1 Procurement audits. A procurement audit is a structured review of the procurement process from procurement planning through contract administration. The objective of a procurement audit is to identify successes and failures that warrant transfer to other procurement items on this project or to other projects within the performing organization.

12.6.3 Outputs from Contract Closeout

.1 Contract file. A complete set of indexed records should be prepared for inclusion with the final project records (see Section 10.4 for a more detailed discussion of administrative closure and project archives).

.2 Formal acceptance and closure. The person or organization responsible for contract administration should provide the seller with formal written notice that the contract has been completed. Requirements for formal acceptance and closure are usually defined in the contract.

SECTION III

APPENDICES

Appendix A

The Project Management Institute Standards-Setting Process

The Project Management Institute (PMI) Standards-Setting Process was established initially as Institute policy by a vote of the PMI Board of Directors at its October 1993 meeting. In March 1998, the PMI Board of Directors approved modifications to the process. Then in March 1999, it was modified again to make it consistent with the concurrent change in PMI governance procedures.

A.1 PMI STANDARDS DOCUMENTS

PMI Standards Documents are those developed or published by PMI that describe generally accepted practices of project management, specifically:
- *A Guide to the Project Management Body of Knowledge (PMBOK® Guide)*.
- Project Management Body of Knowledge Handbooks.

Additional documents may be added to this list by the PMI Standards Manager, subject to the advice and consent of the PMI Project Management Standards Program Member Advisory Group and the PMI Executive Director. Standards Documents may be original works published by PMI, or they may be publications by other organizations or individuals.

Standards Documents will be developed in accordance with the Code of Good Practice for Standardization developed by the International Organization for Standardization (ISO) and the standards development guidelines established by the American National Standards Institute (ANSI).

A.2 DEVELOPMENT OF ORIGINAL WORKS

Standards Documents that are original works developed by PMI, or revisions of such documents, will be handled as follows:
- Prospective developer(s) will submit a proposal to the PMI Standards Manager. The Manager may also request such proposals. The Manager will submit all received proposals to the PMI Standards Program Member Advisory Group who, with the Manager, will decide whether to accept or reject each proposal.

- The Manager will inform the prospective developer(s) as to the decision and the rationale for the decision. If an approved proposal requires funding in excess of that budgeted for standards development, the Manager will submit the proposal to the PMI Executive Director for funding.
- For all approved and funded proposals, the Manager will support the developer's efforts so as to maximize the probability that the end product will be accepted. Developer(s) will be required to sign the PMI Volunteer Assignment of Copyright.
- When the proposed material has been completed to the satisfaction of the developer(s), the developer(s) will submit the material to the PMI Standards Manager. The PMI Standards Program Member Advisory Group, with the Manager, will review the proposed material and decide whether to initiate further review by knowledgeable individuals or request additional work by the developer(s).
- The Manager will appoint, subject to review and approval by the PMI Standards Program Member Advisory Group, at least three knowledgeable individuals to review and comment on the material. Based on comments received, the Member Advisory Group will decide whether to accept the material as an *Exposure Draft*.
- The PMI Standards Manager will develop a plan for obtaining appropriate public review for each *Exposure Draft*. The plan will include a) a review period of not less than one month and not more than six months, b) announcement of the availability of the *Exposure Draft* for review in *PM Network*® (and/or any other similarly appropriate publication media), and c) cost of review copies. The PMI Standards Program Member Advisory Group must approve the Manager's plan for public review. Each *Exposure Draft* will include a notice asking for comments to be sent to the PMI Standards Manager at the PMI Headquarters and noting the length of and expiration date for the review period.
- *Exposure Drafts* will be published under the aegis of the PMI Publishing Division and must meet the standards of that group regarding typography and style.
- During the review period, the Manager will solicit the formal input of the Managers of other PMI Programs (e.g., Certification, Education, Components, and Publishing) that may be affected by the future publication of the material as a PMI Standard.
- At the conclusion of the review period, the PMI Standards Manager will review comments received with the PMI Standards Program Member Advisory Group and will work with the developer(s) and others as needed to incorporate appropriate comments. If the comments are major, the PMI Standards Program Member Advisory Group may elect to repeat the *Exposure Draft* review process.
- When the PMI Standards Manager and the PMI Standards Program Member Advisory Group have approved a proposed PMI Standards Document, the Manager will promptly submit the document to the PMI Executive Director for final review and approval. The PMI Executive Director will verify compliance with procedures and ensure that member input was sufficient. PMI Executive Director will a) approve the document as submitted; b) reject the document; or c) request additional review, and will provide explanatory comments in support of the chosen option.

A Guide to the Project Management Body of Knowledge (PMBOK® Guide) 2000 Edition
©2000 Project Management Institute, Four Campus Boulevard, Newtown Square, PA 19073-3299 USA

A.3 ADOPTION OF NONORIGINAL WORKS AS STANDARDS

Standards Documents that are the work of other organizations or individuals will be handled as follows:

■ Any person or organization may submit a request to the PMI Standards Manager to consider a non-PMI publication as a PMI Standard. The Manager will submit all proposals received to the PMI Standards Program Member Advisory Group who, with the Manager, will decide whether to accept or reject each proposal. If accepted, the Manager will appoint, subject to review and approval by the PMI Standards Program Member Advisory Group, at least three knowledgeable individuals to review and comment on the material.

■ During the review period, the Manager will solicit the formal input of the Managers of other PMI Programs (e.g., Certification, Education, Components, and Publishing) that may be affected by the future publication of the material as a PMI Standard.

■ Based on comments received, the Member Advisory Group, with the Manager, will decide whether to a) accept the proposal as written as a PMI Standard, b) accept the proposal with modifications and/or an addendum as a PMI Standard, c) seek further review and comment on the proposal (that is, additional reviewers and/or issuance as an *Exposure Draft*), or d) reject the proposal. The Manager will inform the submitter as to the decision and the rationale for the decision.

■ When the PMI Standards Manager and the PMI Standards Program Member Advisory Group have approved a proposed PMI Standards Document, the Manager will promptly submit the document to the PMI Executive Director for final review and approval. The Manager will prepare a proposal for the PMI Executive Director for consideration of a prospective relationship with the owner(s) of the material.

■ The PMI Executive Director will verify compliance with procedures and will ensure that member input was sufficient. The PMI Executive Director will a) approve the document as submitted; b) reject the document; or c) request additional review, and will provide explanatory comments in support of the chosen option.

Appendix B

Evolution of PMI's *A Guide to the Project Management Body of Knowledge*

B.1 INITIAL DEVELOPMENT

The Project Management Institute (PMI) was founded in 1969 on the premise that there were many management practices that were common to projects in application areas as diverse as construction and pharmaceuticals. By the time of the PMI Montreal Seminars/Symposium in 1976, the idea that such common practices might be documented as *standards* began to be widely discussed. This led in turn to consideration of project management as a distinct profession.

It was not until 1981, however, that the PMI Board of Directors approved a project to develop the procedures and concepts necessary to support the profession of project management. The project proposal suggested three areas of focus:
- The distinguishing characteristics of a practicing professional (ethics).
- The content and structure of the profession's body of knowledge (standards).
- Recognition of professional attainment (accreditation).

The project team thus came to be known as the Ethics, Standards, and Accreditation (ESA) Management Group. The ESA Management Group consisted of the following individuals:

Matthew H. Parry, Chair	David C. Aird
Frederick R. Fisher	David Haeney
Harvey Kolodney	Charles E. Oliver
William H. Robinson	Douglas J. Ronson
Paul Sims	Eric W. Smythe

More than twenty-five volunteers in several local chapters assisted this group. The Ethics statement was developed and submitted by a committee in Washington, D.C., chaired by Lew Ireland. The Time Management statement was developed through extensive meetings of a group in Southern Ontario, including

Dave MacDonald, Dave Norman, Bob Spence, Bob Hall, and Matt Parry. The Cost Management statement was developed through extensive meetings within the cost department of Stelco under the direction of Dave Haeney and Larry Harrison. Other statements were developed by the ESA Management Group. Accreditation was taken up by John Adams and his group at Western Carolina University, which resulted in the development of accreditation guidelines and a program for the certification of Project Management Professionals (PMPs) under the guidance of Dean Martin.

The results of the ESA Project were published in a Special Report in the *Project Management Journal* in August 1983. The report included:

■ A Code of Ethics, plus a procedure for code enforcement.

■ A standards baseline consisting of six major knowledge areas: Scope Management, Cost Management, Time Management, Quality Management, Human Resources Management, and Communications Management.

■ Guidelines for both accreditation (recognition of the quality of programs provided by educational institutions) and certification (recognition of the professional qualifications of individuals).

This report subsequently served as the basis for PMI's initial Accreditation and Certification programs. Western Carolina University's Master's Degree in Project Management was accredited in 1983, and the first PMPs were certified in 1984.

B.2 1986–87 UPDATE

Publication of the ESA Baseline Report gave rise to much discussion within PMI about the adequacy of the standards. In 1984, the PMI Board of Directors approved a second standards-related project "to capture the knowledge applied to project management … within the existing ESA framework." Six committees were then recruited to address each of the six identified knowledge areas. In addition, a workshop was scheduled as part of the PMI 1985 Annual Seminars/Symposium.

As a result of these efforts, a revised document was approved in principle by the PMI Board of Directors and published for comment in the *Project Management Journal* in August 1986. The primary contributors to this version of the document were:

R. Max Wideman, Chair (during development)	John R. Adams, Chair (when issued)
Joseph R. Beck	Peter Bibbes
Jim Blethen	Richard Cockfield
Peggy Day	William Dixon
Peter C. Georgas	Shirl Holingsworth
William Kane	Colin Morris
Joe Muhlberger	Philip Nunn
Pat Patrick	David Pym
Linn C. Stuckenbruck	George Vallance
Larry C. Woolslager	Shakir Zuberi

In addition to expanding and restructuring the original material, the revised document included three new sections:

■ Project Management Framework was added to cover the relationships between the project and its external environment, and between project management and general management.

■ Risk Management was added as a separate knowledge area in order to provide better coverage of this subject.

■ Contract/Procurement Management was added as a separate knowledge area in order to provide better coverage of this subject.

Subsequently, a variety of editorial changes and corrections were incorporated into the material, and the PMI Board of Directors approved it in March 1987. The final manuscript was published in August 1987 as a stand-alone document titled, *The Project Management Body of Knowledge*.

B.3 1996 UPDATE

Discussion about the proper form, content, and structure of PMI's key standards document continued after publication of the 1987 version. In August 1991, PMI's Director of Standards Alan Stretton initiated a project to update the document based on comments received from the membership. The revised document was developed over several years through a series of widely circulated working drafts and through workshops at the PMI Seminars/Symposia in Dallas, Pittsburgh, and San Diego.

In August 1994, the PMI Standards Committee issued an *Exposure Draft* of the document that was distributed for comment to all 10,000 PMI members and to more than twenty other professional and technical associations.

The publication of *A Guide to the Project Management Body of Knowledge (PMBOK® Guide)* in 1996 represented the completion of the project initiated in 1991. Contributors and reviewers are listed later in this section. A summary of the differences between the 1987 document and the 1996 document, which was included in the Preface of the 1996 edition, also is listed later in this section.

The document superseded PMI's *Project Management Body of Knowledge (PMBOK®)* document that was published in 1987. To assist users of the 1996 document, who may have been familiar with its predecessor, we have summarized the major differences here.

1. *We changed the title to emphasize that this document is not the project management body of knowledge.* The 1987 document defined the project management body of knowledge as "all those topics, subject areas and intellectual processes which are involved in the application of sound management principles to … projects." Clearly, one document will never contain the entire project management body of knowledge.

2. *We completely rewrote the Framework section.* The new section consists of three chapters:

■ Introduction, which sets out the purpose of the document and defines at length the terms *project* and *project management*.

■ The Project Management Context, which covers the context in which projects operate—the project life cycle, stakeholder perspectives, external influences, and key general management skills.

■ Project Management Processes, which describes how the various elements of project management interrelate.

3. *We developed a revised definition of* project. We wanted a definition that was both inclusive (It should not be possible to identify any undertaking generally thought of as a project that does not fit the definition.) and exclusive (It should not be possible to describe any undertaking that satisfies the definition and is not generally thought of as a project.). We reviewed many of the definitions of project in the existing literature and found all of them unsatisfactory in some way. The new definition is driven by the unique characteristics of a project: *a project is a temporary endeavor undertaken to create a unique product or service.*

4. *We developed a revised view of the project life cycle.* The 1987 document defined project phases as subdivisions of the project life cycle. We have reordered this relationship and defined *project life cycle* as a collection of phases whose number and names are determined by the control needs of the performing organization.

5. *We changed the name of the major sections from function to knowledge area.* The term *function* had been frequently misunderstood to mean an element of a functional organization. The name change should eliminate this misunderstanding.

6. *We formally recognized the existence of a ninth knowledge area.* There has been widespread consensus for some time that project management is an integrative process. Chapter 4, Project Integration Management, recognizes the importance of this subject.

7. *We added the word* project *to the title of each knowledge area.* Although this may seem redundant, it helps to clarify the scope of the document. For example, Project Human Resource Management covers only those aspects of managing human resources that are unique or nearly unique to the project context.

8. *We chose to describe the knowledge areas in terms of their component processes.* The search for a consistent method of presentation led us to completely restructure the 1987 document into thirty-seven *project management processes*. Each process is described in terms of its inputs, outputs, and tools and techniques. Inputs and outputs are documents (e.g., a scope statement) or documentable items (e.g., activity dependencies). Tools and techniques are the mechanisms applied to the inputs to create the outputs. In addition to its fundamental simplicity, this approach offers several other benefits:

- It emphasizes the interactions among the knowledge areas. Outputs from one process become inputs to another.
- The structure is flexible and robust. Changes in knowledge and practice can be accommodated by adding a new process, by resequencing processes, by subdividing processes, or by adding descriptive material within a process.
- Processes are at the core of other standards. For example, the International Organization for Standardization's quality standards (the ISO 9000 series) are based on identification of business processes.

9. *We added some illustrations.* When it comes to work breakdown structures, network diagrams, and S-curves, a picture is worth a thousand words.

10. *We significantly reorganized the document.* The following table provides a comparison of the major headings of the 1987 document and the 1996 one:

1987 Number and Name	1996 Number and Name
0. PMBOK® Standards	B. Evolution of PMI's *A Guide to the Project Management Body of Knowledge*
1. Framework: The Rationale	1. Introduction (basic definitions)
	2. The Project Context (life cycles)
2. Framework: An Overview	1. Various portions
	2. Various portions
	3. Various portions
3. Framework: An Integrative Model	3. Project Management Processes
	4. Project Integration Management
4. Glossary of General Terms	IV. Glossary
A. Scope Management	5. Project Scope Management
B. Quality Management	8. Project Quality Management
C. Time Management	6. Project Time Management
D. Cost Management	7. Project Cost Management
E. Risk Management	11. Project Risk Management
F. Human Resource Management	9. Project Human Resource Management
G. Contract/Procurement Management	12. Project Procurement Management
H. Communications Management	10. Project Communications Management

11. *We removed "to classify" from the list of purposes.* Both the 1996 document and the 1987 version provide a structure for organizing project management knowledge, but neither is particularly effective as a classification tool. First, the topics included are not comprehensive—they do not include innovative or unusual practices. Second, many elements have relevance in more than one knowledge area or process, such that the categories are not unique.

The following individuals, as listed in Appendix C of the 1996 document, contributed in many different ways to various drafts of the 1996 document. PMI is indebted to them for their support.

Standards Committee

The following individuals served as members of the PMI Standards Committee during development of the 1996 update of the PMBOK® document:

- William R. Duncan, Duncan • Nevison, PMI Director of Standards
- Frederick Ayer, Defense Systems Management College
- Cynthia Berg, Medtronic Micro-Rel
- Mark Burgess, KnowledgeWorks
- Helen Cooke, Cooke & Cooke
- Judy Doll, Searle
- Drew Fetters, PECO Energy Company
- Brian Fletcher, ABRINN Project Management Services
- Earl Glenwright, A.S.S.I.S.T.
- Eric Jenett, Consultant
- Deborah O'Bray, Manitoba Telephone System
- Diane Quinn, Eastman Kodak Co.
- Anthony Rizzotto, Miles Diagnostics
- Alan Stretton, University of Technology, Sydney
- Douglas E. Tryloff, TASC

Contributors

In addition to the members of the Standards Committee, the following individuals provided original text or key concepts for one or more sections in the chapters indicated:

- John Adams, Western Carolina University (Chapter 3, Project Management Processes)
- Keely Brunner, Ball Aerospace (Chapter 7, Project Cost Management)
- Louis J. Cabano, Pathfinder, Inc. (Chapter 5, Project Scope Management)
- David Curling, Loday Systems (Chapter 12, Project Procurement Management)
- Douglas Gordon, Special Projects Coordinations (Chapter 7, Project Cost Management)
- David T. Hulett, D. T. Hulett & Associates (Chapter 11, Project Risk Management)
- Edward Ionata, Bechtel/Parsons Brinckerhoff (Chapter 10, Project Communications Management)
- John M. Nevison, Duncan•Nevison (Chapter 9, Project Human Resource Management)
- Hadley Reynolds, Reynolds Associates (Chapter 2, The Project Management Context)
- Agnes Salvo, CUNA Mutual Insurance (Chapter 11, Project Risk Management)
- W. Stephen Sawle, Consultants to Management, Inc. (Chapter 5, Project Scope Management)
- Leonard Stolba, Parsons, Brinckerhoff, Douglas & Quade (Chapter 8, Project Quality Management)
- Ahmet Taspinar, MBP Network (Chapter 6, Project Time Management)
- Francis M. Webster Jr. (Chapter 1, definition of project)

Reviewers

In addition to the Standards Committee and the contributors, the following individuals provided comments on various drafts of the 1996 document:

- Edward L. Averill, Edward Averill & Associates
- A. C. "Fred" Baker, Baker, Barnes Associates, Inc.
- F. J. "Bud" Baker, Wright State University
- Tom Belanger, The Sterling Planning Group
- John A. Bing, Coastline Community College
- Brian Bock, Ziff Desktop Information
- Paul Bosakowski, Fluor Daniel
- Dorothy J. Burton, Management Systems Associates, Ltd.
- Cohort '93, University of Technology, Sydney
- Cohort '94, University of Technology, Sydney
- Kim Colenso, Applied Business Technologies
- Samuel K. Collier, Mead Corporation
- Karen Condos-Alfonsi, PMI Executive Office
- E. J. Coyle, VDO Yazaki
- Darlene Crane, Crane Consulting
- Russ Darnall, Fluor Daniel
- Maureen Dougherty, GPS Technologies
- John J. Downing, Digital Equipment Corporation
- Daniel D. Dudek, Optimum Technologies, Inc.
- Lawrence East, Westinghouse

- Quentin W. Fleming, Primavera Systems, Inc.
- Rick Fletcher, Acres
- Greg Githens, Maxicomm Project Services, Inc.
- Leo Giulianeti, Keane Inc.
- Martha D. Hammonds, AMEX TSG Systems
- Abdulrazak Hajibrahim, Bombardier
- G. Alan Hellawell, Eastman Kodak
- Paul Hinkley, Meta Consultants
- Wayne L. Hinthorn, PMI Orange Co.
- Mark E. Hodson, Eli Lilly & Company
- Lew Ireland, L. R. Ireland Associates
- Elvin Isgrig, North Dakota State University
- Murray Janzen, Procter & Gamble
- Frank Jenes
- Walter Karpowski, Management Assoc.
- William F. Kerrigan, Bechtel International, Inc.
- Harold Kerzner, Baldwin-Wallace College
- Robert L. Kimmons, Kimmons-Asaro Group Ltd., Inc.
- Richard King, AT&T
- J. D. "Kaay" Koch, Koch Associates
- Lauri Koskela, VTT Building Technology
- Richard E. Little, Project Performance Management
- Lyle W. Lockwood, Universal Technology Inc.
- Lawrence Mack, PMI Pittsburgh
- Christopher Madigan, Sandia National Laboratories
- Michael L. McCauley, Integrated Project Systems
- Hugh McLaughlin, Broadstar Inc.
- Frank McNeely, National Contract Management Association
- Pierre Menard, University of Quebec at Montreal
- Rick Michaels
- Raymond Miller, AT&T
- Alan Minson, A&R Minson
- Colin Morris, Delcan Hatch
- R. Bruce Morris
- David J. Mueller, Westinghouse
- Gary Nelson, Athena Consulting Inc.
- John P. Nolan, AACE International
- Louise C. Novakowski, Cominco Engineering Services, Ltd.
- James O'Brien, O'Brien-Kreitzberg
- JoAnn C. Osmer, Arbella Mutual Insurance Co.
- Jon V. Palmquist, Allstate Insurance
- Matthew Parry, Target Consultants
- John G. Phippen, JGP Quality Services
- Hans E. Picard, P&A Consultants Corporation
- Serge Y. Piotte, Cartier Group
- PMI, Houston Chapter
- PMI, Manitoba Chapter
- PMI, New Zealand Chapter
- Charles J. Pospisil, Procon, Inc.
- Janice Y. Preston, Pacifica Companies
- Mark T. Price, GE Nuclear Energy

- Christopher Quaife, Symmetric Resources
- Peter E. Quinn, Canadian Air Force
- Steven F. Ritter, Mead Corporation
- William S. Ruggles, Ruggles & Associates
- Ralph B. Sackman, Levi Strauss & Co.
- Alice Sapienza, Simmons College
- Darryl M. Selleck
- Melvin Silverman, Atrium Associates, Inc.
- Roy Smith, Decision Planning Corp.
- Craig T. Stone, Management Counseling Corp.
- Hiroshi Tanaka, JGC Corporation
- Robert Templeton, MW Kellogg
- Dick Thiel, King County (WA) DPW
- Saul Thomashow, Andersen Consulting
- J. Tidhar, Oranatech Management Systems, Ltd.
- Vijay K. Verma, TRIUMF
- Janet Toepfer, Business Office Systems
- Alex Walton, Harris Corporation
- Jack Way, Simetra, Inc.
- R. Max Wideman, AEW Services
- Rebecca Winston, EG&G Idaho Inc.
- Hugh M. Woodward, Proctor & Gamble
- Robert Youker, Management Planning & Control Systems
- Shakir H. Zuberi, ICF Kaiser Engineers Hanford
- Dirk Zwart, Computer Sciences Corp.

Production Staff

Special mention is due to the following employees of PMI Communications:
- Jeannette M. Cabanis, Editor, Book Division
- Misty N. Dillard, Administrative Assistant
- Linda V. Gillman, Office Administrator
- Bobby R. Hensley, Publications Coordinator
- Jonathan Hicks, Systems Administrator
- Sandy Jenkins, Associate Editor
- Mark S. Parker, Production Coordinator
- Dewey L. Messer, Managing Editor
- Danell Moses, Marketing Promotion Coordinator
- Shirley B. Parker, Business/Marketing Manager
- Melissa Pendergast, Information Services Coordinator
- James S. Pennypacker, Publisher/Editor-In-Chief
- Michelle Triggs, Graphic Designer
- Lisa Woodring, Administrative Assistant

Appendix C

Contributors and Reviewers of *PMBOK® Guide* 2000 Edition

The following individuals contributed in many different ways to various drafts of this document. The Project Management Institute (PMI) is indebted to them for their support and acknowledges their contributions.

C.1 PMI PROJECT MANAGEMENT STANDARDS PROGRAM MEMBER ADVISORY GROUP

The following individuals served as members of the PMI Standards Program Member Advisory Group during development of this edition of *A Guide to the Project Management Body of Knowledge (PMBOK® Guide)* document:

■ George Belev, KAPL, Inc. - A Lockheed Martin Company
■ Cynthia A. Berg, PMP, Medtronic Microelectronics Center
■ Sergio Coronado Arrechedera, MicroStrategy
■ Judith A. Doll, PMP, Monsanto
■ J. Brian Hobbs, PMP, University of Quebec at Montreal
■ David Hotchkiss, PMP, Nexgenix

C.2 *PMBOK® GUIDE* UPDATE PROJECT TEAM

The following individuals served as members of the project team for this 2000 Edition of the *PMBOK® Guide*, under the leadership of Cynthia A. Berg, PMP, as Project Manager:

■ Cynthia A. Berg, PMP, Medtronic Microelectronics Center
■ Judith A. Doll, PMP, Monsanto
■ Daniel Dudek, PMP, PlanView, Inc.
■ Quentin Fleming, Primavera Systems, Inc.
■ Earl Glenwright, ASSIST
■ David T. Hulett, Ph.D., International Institute for Learning Inc.
■ Gregory J. Skulmoski, University of Calgary
■ Greg Githens, PMP, Catalyst Management Consulting

C.3 CONTRIBUTORS

In addition to the members of the PMI Standards Program Member Advisory Group and the *PMBOK® Guide* Project Team, the following individuals provided original text or key concepts for one or more sections in the chapters indicated. Also, the PMI Risk Management Specific Interest Group provided leadership for the rewrite of Chapter 11, Project Risk Management.

- Quentin Fleming (Chapter 4, Project Integration Management, and Chapter 12, Project Procurement Management)
- David Shuster (Chapter 8, Project Quality Management)
- David Hulett (Chapter 11, Project Risk Management)
- Sam Lane (Chapter 11, Project Risk Management)
- Ed Smith (Chapter 11, Project Risk Management)
- Alfredo del Caño (Chapter 11, Project Risk Management)
- Roger Graves (Chapter 11, Project Risk Management)
- David Hillson(Chapter 11, Project Risk Management)
- Stephen Reed (Chapter 11, Project Risk Management)
- Janice Preston (Chapter 11, Project Risk Management - editing)
- Mike Wakshull (Chapter 11, Project Risk Management - editing)
- Robert Youker (several sections throughout document)

C.4 REVIEWERS

In addition to the PMI Standards Program Member Advisory Group, the *PMBOK® Guide* Project Team, and the Contributors, the following individuals provided comments on the *Exposure Draft* of this document:

Muhamed Abdomerovic, PMP, D. Eng.
Fabrizio Agnesi, PMP
Jon D. Allen, PMP
Robert A. Andrejko, PMP
Paul C. Aspinwall
Edward Averill, PMP
William W. Bahnmaier, PMP
Carole J. Bass, PMP
Sally Bernstein, PMP
John Blatta
Chris Cartwright, PMP
Raymond C. Clark, PE
Elizabeth Clarke
Kim Colenso, PMP
Kenneth G. Cooper
Richard F. Cowan, PMP
Mario Damiani, PMP
David M. Drevinsky, PMP
Edward Fern, PMP
Scott D. Freauf, PMP
Ichiro Fujita, PMP
Serge Garon, PEng, PMP
Eric Glover
Michael Goodman, PMP
Alexander Grassi Sr., PMP

Yassir Afaneh
Frank Allen, PMP
MaryGrace Allenchey, PMP
Ichizo Aoki
Ronald Auffrédou, PMP
Frederick L. Ayer, PMP
A. C. "Fred" Baker, PMP
Berndt Bellman
Nigel Blampied, PE, PMP
Patrick Brown, PMP
Bruce C. Chadbourne, PMP
Michael T. Clark, PMP
David Coates, PMP
Edmund H. Conrow, PMP
John Cornman, PMP
Kevin Daly, PMP
Thomas Diethelm, PMP
Frank D. Einhorn, PMP
Christian Frankenberg, PMP
Jean-Luc Frere, PMP
Chikako Futamura, PMP
Brian L. Garrison, PMP
Peter Bryan Goldsbury
Jean Gouix, PMP
Franz X. Hake

Peter Heffron
Dr. David Hillson, PMP, FAPM
Marion Diane Holbrook
Bill Hubbard
Thomas P. Hurley, PMP
Angyan P. Jagathnarayanan
Sada Joshi, PMP
Subramaniam Kandaswamy, Ph.D., PMP
Robert Dohn Kissinger, Ph.D, PMP
Jan Kristrom
Lawrence P. Leach
Gábor Lipi
J. W. Lowthian, PMP
James Martin (on behalf of INCOSE)
Glen Maxfield
Rob McCormack, PMP
David Michaud
Oscar A. Mignone
Roy E. Morgan, PMP
Bert Mosterd, PMP
John D. Nelson, PMP
Cathy Oest, PMP
Kazuhiko Okubo, PE, PMP
Jerry Partridge, PMP
Francisco Perez-Polo, PMP
Crispin (Kik) Piney, PMP
David L. Prater, PMP
Samuel L. Raisch, PMP
G. Ramachandran, PMP
William Simon Vaughan Robinson
Wolfgang Theodore Roesch
Linda Rust, PMP
James N. Salapatas, PMP
Bradford N. Scales
John R. Schuyler, PMP
Shoukat Sheikh, MBA, PMP
Larry Sieck
Melvin Silverman, Ph.D., P.E.
Loren J. Simer Jr.
Greg Skulmoski
Barry Smythe, PMP
Joe Soto Sr., PMP
Charlene Spoede, PMP
Emmett Stine, PMP
Jim Szpakowski
John A. Thoren Jr., PMP
Juan Luis Valero, PMP
Ricardo Viana Vargas, PMP
Stephen E. Wall, PMP
Tammo T. Wilkens, PE, PMP
Rebecca A. Winston

Chris Herbert, PMP
J. Brian Hobbs, PMP
Robin Hornby
Charles L. Hunt
George Jackelen
Elden F. Jones II, PMP, CMII
Lewis Kana, PMP
Ronald L. Kempf, PMP
Kurt V. Kloecker
Blase Kwok, PMP
Philip A. Lindeman
Lyle W. Lockwood, PMP
Arif Mahmood, PMP
Stephen S. Mattingly
Peter McCarthy
Krik D. McManus
Mary F. Miekoski, PMP
Gordon R. Miller, PMP
Jim Morris, PMP
William A. Moylan, PMP
Wolfgang Obermeier
Masato Ohori, PMP
Edward Oliver
Fernando Romero Peñailillo
James M. Phillips, PMP
George Pitagorsky, PMP
Bradford S. Price, PMP
Naga Rajan
Bill Righter, PMP
Bernice L. Rocque, PMP
Jon Rude
Fabian Sagristani, PMP
Seymour Samuels
H. Peter Schiller
Maria Scott, PMP
Kazuo Shimizu, PMP
(on behalf of the PMI Tokyo,
Japan, Chapter)
Keith Skilling, P.E., PMP
Kenneth F. Smith, PMP
Paul J. Solomon
Christopher Wessley Sours, PMP
Joyce Statz, PMP
Thangavel Subbu
Ahmet N. Taspinar, PMP
Alan D. Uren, PMP
S. Rao Vallabhaneni
Ana Isabel Vazquez Urbina
William W. Wassel, PMP
Robert Williford, PMP
Jean A. Yager

C.5 CONTRIBUTIONS TO PREDECESSOR DOCUMENTS

Portions of the 1996 edition and other predecessor documents are included in this edition. PMI wishes to acknowledge the following volunteers as substantial contributors to this document:

- John R. Adams
- William R. Duncan
- Matthew H. Parry
- Alan Stretton
- R. Max Wideman

PMI also wishes to acknowledge the contributions of the other volunteers listed in Appendix B.

C.6 PRODUCTION STAFF

Special mention is due to the following employees of PMI:

- Steven L. Fahrenkrog, Standards Manager
- Lisa Fisher, Assistant Editor
- Lewis M. Gedansky, Research Manager
- Linda V. Gillman, Advertising Coordinator/*PMBOK® Guide* Copyright Permissions Coordinator
- Eva T. Goldman, Technical Research & Standards Associate
- Paul Grace, Certification Manager
- Sandy Jenkins, Managing Editor
- Toni D. Knott, Book Editor
- Mark S. Parker, Production Coordinator
- Dewey L. Messer, Design and Production Manager
- John McHugh, Interim Publisher
- Michelle Triggs Owen, Graphic Designer
- Shirley B. Parker, Business/Book Publishing Manager
- Iesha D. Turner-Brown, Standards Administrator

A Guide to the Project Management Body of Knowledge (PMBOK® Guide) 2000 Edition
©2000 Project Management Institute, Four Campus Boulevard, Newtown Square, PA 19073-3299 USA

Appendix D

Notes

CHAPTER 1. INTRODUCTION

    1. *The American Heritage Dictionary of the English Language*, 3d ed. 1992. Boston, Mass.: Houghton Mifflin Company.

    2. Turner, J. Rodney. 1992. *The Handbook of Project-Based Management*. New York: McGraw-Hill.

CHAPTER 2. THE PROJECT MANAGEMENT CONTEXT

    1. Morris, Peter W. G. 1988. Managing Project Interfaces: Key Points for Project Success. In Cleland and King, *Project Management Handbook*, 2d ed. Englewood Cliffs, N.J.: Prentice-Hall.

    2. Murphy, Patrice L. 1989. Pharmaceutical Project Management: Is It Different? *Project Management Journal* (September).

    3. Muench, Dean, et al. 1994. *The Sybase Development Framework*. Oakland, Calif.: Sybase Inc.

    4. Kotter, John P. 1990. *A Force for Change: How Leadership Differs from Management*. New York: The Free Press.

    5. Pfeffer, Jeffrey. 1992. *Managing with Power: Politics and Influence in Organizations*. HBS Press. Quoted in Eccles et al., *Beyond the Hype*.

    6. Eccles, Robert, et al. 1992. *Beyond the Hype*. Cambridge, Mass.: Harvard University Press.

    7. International Organization for Standardization. 1994. *Code of Good Practice for Standardization (Draft International Standard)*. Geneva, Switzerland: ISO Press.

    8. *The American Heritage Dictionary of the English Language*, 3d ed.

CHAPTER 3. PROJECT MANAGEMENT PROCESSES

    1. *The American Heritage Dictionary of the English Language*, 3d ed.

CHAPTER 4. PROJECT INTEGRATION MANAGEMENT

    No notes for this chapter.

CHAPTER 5.   PROJECT SCOPE MANAGEMENT

1. Turner, J. Rodney. 1992. *The Handbook of Project-Based Management*.

2. İyigün, M. Güven. 1993. A Decision Support System for R&D Project Selection and Resource Allocation Under Uncertainty. *Project Management Journal* 3 (December).

3. Scope Definition and Control, Publication 6-2. 1986 (July). Austin, Tex.: Construction Industry Institute, p. 45.

CHAPTER 6.   PROJECT TIME MANAGEMENT

No notes for this chapter.

CHAPTER 7.   PROJECT COST MANAGEMENT

No notes for this chapter.

CHAPTER 8.   PROJECT QUALITY MANAGEMENT

1. International Organization for Standardization. ISO 8402. 1994. *Quality Management and Quality Assurance*. Geneva, Switzerland: ISO Press.

2. Ibid.

3. Ibid.

4. Ibid.

5. Ibid.

6. Ibid.

CHAPTER 9.   PROJECT HUMAN RESOURCE MANAGEMENT

No notes for this chapter.

CHAPTER 10.   PROJECT COMMUNICATIONS MANAGEMENT

No notes for this chapter.

CHAPTER 11.   PROJECT RISK MANAGEMENT

No notes for this chapter.

CHAPTER 12.   PROJECT PROCUREMENT MANAGEMENT

No notes for this chapter.

Appendix E

Application Area Extensions

E.1 NEED FOR APPLICATION AREA EXTENSIONS

Application area extensions are necessary when there are generally accepted knowledge and practices for a category of projects in one application area that are not generally accepted across the full range of project types in most application areas. Application area extensions reflect:

■ Unique or unusual aspects of the project environment of which the project management team must be aware in order to manage the project efficiently and effectively.

■ Common knowledge and practices that, if followed, will improve the efficiency and effectiveness of the project (e.g., standard work breakdown structures).

Application area-specific knowledge and practices can arise as a result of many factors, including, but not limited to, differences in cultural norms, technical terminology, societal impact, or project life cycles. For example:

■ In construction, where virtually all work is accomplished under contract, there are common knowledge and practices related to procurement that do not apply to all categories of projects.

■ In bioscience, there are common knowledge and practices driven by the regulatory environment that do not apply to all categories of projects.

■ In government contracting, there are common knowledge and practices driven by government acquisition regulations that do not apply to all categories of projects.

■ In consulting, there are common knowledge and practices created by the project manager's sales and marketing responsibilities that do not apply to all categories of projects.

Application area extensions are:

■ *Additions* to the core material of Chapters 1 through 12, *not substitutes* for it.

■ Organized in a fashion similar to this document—that is, by identifying and describing the project management processes unique to that application area.

- Unique additions to the core material such as:
  - ◆ Identifying new or modified processes.
  - ◆ Subdividing existing processes.
  - ◆ Describing different sequences or interactions of processes.
  - ◆ Increasing elements or modifying the common process definitions.
  - ◆ Defining special inputs, tools and techniques, and/or outputs for the existing processes.

  Application area extensions are *not*:

- "How-to" documents or "practice guidelines"—such documents may be issued as PMI Standards, but they are not what are intended as extensions.
- A lower level of detail than is addressed in this document—such details may be addressed in handbooks or guidebooks that may be issued as PMI Standards, but they are not what is intended as extensions.

E.2 CRITERIA FOR DEVELOPMENT OF APPLICATION AREA EXTENSIONS

Extensions will be developed under the following criteria:

- There is a substantial body of knowledge that is both project oriented and unique or nearly unique to that application area.
- There is an identifiable PMI component (e.g., a PMI Specific Interest Group, College, or Chapter) or an identifiable external organization willing and able to commit the necessary resources to subscribe to and support the PMI Standards Program with the development and maintenance of a specific PMI Standard. Or, the extension may be developed by PMI itself.
- The proposed extension is able to pass the same level of rigorous PMI Project Management Standard-Setting Process as any other PMI Standard.

E.3 PUBLISHING AND FORMAT OF APPLICATION AREA EXTENSIONS

Application area extensions are developed and/or published by PMI, or they are developed and/or published by either a PMI component or an external organization under a formal agreement with PMI.

- Extensions match this document in style and content. They use the paragraph and subparagraph numbers of this document for the material that has been extended.
- Sections and paragraphs of this document that are not extended are not repeated in extensions.
- Extensions contain a rationale/justification about the need for an extension and its material.
- Extensions are delimited in terms of what they are not intended to do.

E.4 PROCESS FOR DEVELOPMENT AND MAINTENANCE OF APPLICATION AREA EXTENSIONS

When approved in accord with the PMI Standards-Setting Process, application area extensions become PMI Standards. They will be developed and maintained in accordance with the process described below.

A Guide to the Project Management Body of Knowledge (PMBOK® Guide) 2000 Edition
©2000 Project Management Institute, Four Campus Boulevard, Newtown Square, PA 19073-3299 USA

■ An extension must be sponsored by PMI, a formally chartered PMI component (e.g., a Specific Interest Group, College, or Chapter), or another organization external to PMI, which has been approved by the PMI Standards Program Member Advisory Group and the PMI Standards Program Manager. Cosponsorship with PMI is the preferred arrangement. All approvals will be by formal written agreement between PMI and the sponsoring entity, which agreement will include, among other things, the parties' agreement as to intellectual property ownership rights and publications rights to the extension.

■ A project to develop, publish, and/or maintain an extension must be approved by the PMI Standards Program. Permission to initiate, develop, and maintain an extension must be received from PMI and will be the subject of an agreement between or among the organizations. If there is no other sponsoring organization, the PMI Standards Program may elect to proceed alone.

■ The sponsoring group will notify and solicit advice and support from the PMI Standards Program Member Advisory Group and PMI Standards Program Manager throughout the development and maintenance process. They will concur with the appropriateness of the sponsoring organization for the extension proposed and will review the extension during its development to identify any conflicts or overlaps with other similar projects that may be under way.

■ The sponsoring group will prepare a proposal to develop the extension. The proposal will include a justification for the project with a matrix of application-area-specific processes and the affected sections of this document. It will also contain the commitment of sufficient qualified drafters and reviewers; identification of funding requirements, including reproduction, postage, telephone costs, desktop publishing, etc.; commitment to the PMI procedures for PMI Standards extension development and maintenance; and a plan and schedule for extension development and maintenance.

■ Following acceptance of the proposal, the project team will prepare a project charter for approval by the sponsoring group and the PMI Standards Program Team. The charter will include sources of funding and any funding proposed to be provided by PMI. It will include a requirement for periodic review of the extension with reports to the PMI Standards Program Team and a "Sunset Clause" that specifies when, and under what conditions, the extension will be removed from active status as a PMI Standard.

■ The proposal will be submitted to the PMI Standards Manager in accordance with the PMI Standards-Setting Process. The PMI Standards Manager will determine if the proposal can be expected to result in a document that will meet the requirements for a PMI Standard and if adequate resources and sources of support have been identified. To help with this determination, the PMI Standards Manager will seek review and comment by the PMI Standards Program Member Advisory Group and, if appropriate, a panel of knowledgeable persons not involved with the extension.

■ The PMI Standards Manager, with the support of the PMI Standards Program Member Advisory Group, will monitor and support the development of the approved project.

■ The sponsoring organization will develop the extension according to the approved project charter, including coordinating with the PMI Standards Program Team for support, review, and comment.

■ When the extension has been completed to the satisfaction of the sponsoring organization, it will be submitted to the PMI Standards Manager, who will manage the final approval and publication processes in accordance with the PMI Standards-Setting Process. This final submittal will include listing of and commitment by the sponsoring organization to the PMI extension maintenance processes and efforts.

■ Following approval of the extension as a PMI Standard, the sponsoring organization will implement the extension maintenance process in accordance with the approved plan.

A Guide to the Project Management Body of Knowledge (PMBOK® Guide) 2000 Edition
©2000 Project Management Institute, Four Campus Boulevard, Newtown Square, PA 19073-3299 USA

Appendix F

Additional Sources of Information on Project Management

Project management is a growing, dynamic field; books and articles on the subject are published regularly. The entities listed below provide a variety of products and services that may be of use to those interested in project management.

F.1 PROFESSIONAL AND TECHNICAL ORGANIZATIONS

This document was developed and published by the Project Management Institute (PMI). PMI can be contacted at:

Project Management Institute
Four Campus Boulevard
Newtown Square, PA 19073-3299 USA
Phone: +610/356-4600
Fax: +610/356-4647
Email: pmihq@pmi.org
Internet: http://www.pmi.org

PMI currently has cooperative agreements with the following organizations:

■ Association for the Advancement of Cost Engineering (AACE International)
   Phone: +304/296-8444   Fax: +304/291-5728

■ Asociacion Espanola de Ingenieria de Proyectos (AEIPRO)
   Phone: +3476-976-761-910   Fax: +349-1447-3187

■ Australian Institute of Project Management (AIPM)
   Phone: +61-2-9960-0058   Fax: +61-2-9960-0052

■ Construction & Economy Research Institute of Korea (CERIK)
   Phone: +822-3441-0801   Fax: +822-544-6234

■ Defense Systems Management College Alumni Association (DSMCAA)
   Phone: +703/960-6802   Fax: +703/960-6807

■ Engineering Advancement Association of Japan (ENAA)
   Phone: +81-3-3502-4441   Fax: +81-3-3502-5500

■ Institute of Project Management (IPM-Ireland)
Phone: +353-1-661-4677   Fax: +353-1-661-3588

■ International Project Management Association (IPMA)
Phone: +44-1594-531-007   Fax: +44-1594-531-008

■ Korean Institute of Project Management & Technology (PROMAT)
Phone: +822-522-0360   Fax: +822-523-1680

■ National Contract Management Association (NCMA)
Phone: 703/448-9231   Fax: +703/448-0939

■ The NORDNET National Associations
(Denmark, Finland, Iceland, Norway, and Sweden)
Fax: +468-719-9316

■ Project Management Associates (PMA-India)
Phone: +91-11-852-6673   Fax: +91-11-646-4481

■ Project Management Institute South Africa
Phone/Fax: +2711-706-6813

■ Projekt Management Austria
Phone: +43-1-1313-52-215   Fax: +43-1-319-78-55

■ Russian Project Management Association (SOVNET)
Phone: +7-095-133-26-11   Fax: +7-095-133-24-41

■ Ukrainian Project Management Association
Phone: +38-044-272-9400 or +38-044-245-4857

■ Project Management Association of Slovakia (SPPR)
Phone: +421-805-599-1806   Fax: +421-805-599-1-818

■ Slovenian Project Management Association (ZPM)
Phone: +386-6117-667-134   Fax: +386-61217-431

In addition, there are numerous other organizations in related fields, which may be able to provide additional information about project management. For example:

■ Academy of Management
■ American Management Association International
■ American Society for Quality Control
■ Construction Industry Institute
■ Construction Management Association of America (CMAA)
■ Institute of Electrical and Electronics Engineers (IEEE)
■ Institute of Industrial Engineers (IIE)
■ International Council on Systems Engineering (INCOSE)
■ National Association for Purchasing Management
■ National Contract Management Association
■ Society for Human Resource Management
■ American Society of Civil Engineers

Current contact information for these and other professional and technical organizations worldwide can generally be found on the Internet.

F.2 COMMERCIAL PUBLISHERS

PMI is the largest publisher of books on project management. Many commercial publishers produce books on project management and related fields. Commercial publishers that regularly produce such materials include:

- Addison-Wesley
- AMACOM
- Gower Press
- John Wiley & Sons
- Marcel Dekker
- McGraw-Hill
- Prentice-Hall
- Probus
- Van Nostrand Reinhold

Most project management books from these publishers are available from PMI. Many of the books available from these sources include extensive bibliographies or lists of suggested readings.

F.3 PRODUCT AND SERVICE VENDORS

Companies that provide software, training, consulting, and other products and services to the project management profession often provide monographs or reprints.

The *PMI Registered Education Provider (R.E.P.) Program* facilitates the ongoing professional development of PMI Members, Project Management Professionals (PMPs), and other project management stakeholders by linking stakeholders and training coordinators with qualified educational providers and products. A listing of R.E.P.s and their associated educational offerings is found at http://www.pmi.org/education/rep.

F.4 EDUCATIONAL INSTITUTIONS

Many universities, colleges, and junior colleges offer continuing education programs in project management and related disciplines. Many of these institutions also offer graduate or undergraduate degree programs.

Appendix G

Summary of Project Management Knowledge Areas

PROJECT INTEGRATION MANAGEMENT

A subset of project management that includes the processes required to ensure that the various elements of the project are properly coordinated. It consists of:

- Project plan development—integrating and coordinating all project plans to create a consistent, coherent document.
- Project plan execution—carrying out the project plan by performing the activities included therein.
- Integrated change control—coordinating changes across the entire project.

PROJECT SCOPE MANAGEMENT

A subset of project management that includes the processes required to ensure that the project includes all the work required, and only the work required, to complete the project successfully. It consists of:

- Initiation—authorizing the project or phase.
- Scope planning—developing a written scope statement as the basis for future project decisions.
- Scope definition—subdividing the major project deliverables into smaller, more manageable components.
- Scope verification—formalizing acceptance of the project scope.
- Scope change control—controlling changes to project scope.

PROJECT TIME MANAGEMENT

A subset of project management that includes the processes required to ensure timely completion of the project. It consists of:

- Activity definition—identifying the specific activities that must be performed to produce the various project deliverables.
- Activity sequencing—identifying and documenting interactivity dependencies.
- Activity duration estimating—estimating the number of work periods that will be needed to complete individual activities.
- Schedule development—analyzing activity sequences, activity durations, and resource requirements to create the project schedule.
- Schedule control—controlling changes to the project schedule.

PROJECT COST MANAGEMENT

A subset of project management that includes the processes required to ensure that the project is completed within the approved budget. It consists of:

- Resource planning—determining what resources (people, equipment, materials) and what quantities of each should be used to perform project activities.
- Cost estimating—developing an approximation (estimate) of the costs of the resources needed to complete project activities.
- Cost budgeting—allocating the overall cost estimate to individual work activities.
- Cost control—controlling changes to the project budget.

PROJECT QUALITY MANAGEMENT

A subset of project management that includes the processes required to ensure that the project will satisfy the needs for which it was undertaken. It consists of:

- Quality planning—identifying which quality standards are relevant to the project and determining how to satisfy them.
- Quality assurance—evaluating overall project performance on a regular basis to provide confidence that the project will satisfy the relevant quality standards.
- Quality control—monitoring specific project results to determine if they comply with relevant quality standards and identifying ways to eliminate causes of unsatisfactory performance.

PROJECT HUMAN RESOURCE MANAGEMENT

A subset of project management that includes the processes required to make the most effective use of the people involved with the project. It consists of:

- Organizational planning—identifying, documenting, and assigning project roles, responsibilities, and reporting relationships.
- Staff acquisition—getting the needed human resources assigned to and working on the project.
- Team development—developing individual and group skills to enhance project performance.

A Guide to the Project Management Body of Knowledge (PMBOK® Guide) 2000 Edition
©2000 Project Management Institute, Four Campus Boulevard, Newtown Square, PA 19073-3299 USA

PROJECT COMMUNICATIONS MANAGEMENT

A subset of project management that includes the processes required to ensure timely and appropriate generation, collection, dissemination, storage, and ultimate disposition of project information. It consists of:

- Communications planning—determining the information and communications needs of the stakeholders: who needs what information, when they will need it, and how it will be given to them.
- Information distribution—making needed information available to project stakeholders in a timely manner.
- Performance reporting—collecting and disseminating performance information. This includes status reporting, progress measurement, and forecasting.
- Administrative closure—generating, gathering, and disseminating information to formalize phase or project completion.

PROJECT RISK MANAGEMENT

Risk management is the systematic process of identifying, analyzing, and responding to project risk. It includes maximizing the probability and consequences of positive events and minimizing the probability and consequences of adverse events to project objectives. It includes:

- Risk management planning—deciding how to approach and plan the risk management activities for a project.
- Risk identification—determining which risks might affect the project and documenting their characteristics.
- Qualitative risk analysis—performing a qualitative analysis of risks and conditions to prioritize their effects on project objectives.
- Quantitative risk analysis—measuring the probability and consequences of risks and estimating their implications for project objectives.
- Risk response planning—developing procedures and techniques to enhance opportunities and reduce threats from risk to the project's objectives.
- Risk monitoring and control—monitoring residual risks, identifying new risks, executing risk reduction plans, and evaluating their effectiveness throughout the project life cycle.

PROJECT PROCUREMENT MANAGEMENT

A subset of project management that includes the processes required to acquire goods and services to attain project scope from outside the performing organization. It consists of:

- Procurement planning—determining what to procure and when.
- Solicitation planning—documenting product requirements and identifying potential sources.
- Solicitation—obtaining quotations, bids, offers, or proposals, as appropriate.
- Source selection—choosing from among potential sellers.
- Contract administration—managing the relationship with the seller.
- Contract closeout—completion and settlement of the contract, including resolution of any open items.

SECTION IV

GLOSSARY AND INDEX

Glossary

Index

SECTION IV

Glossary

1. INCLUSIONS AND EXCLUSIONS

This glossary includes terms that are:

- Unique or nearly unique to project management (e.g., scope statement, work package, work breakdown structure, critical path method).
- Not unique to project management, but used differently or with a narrower meaning in project management than in general everyday usage (e.g., early start date, activity, task).

This glossary generally does not include:

- Application area-specific terms (e.g., project prospectus as a legal document—unique to real estate development).
- Terms whose use in project management do not differ in any material way from everyday use (e.g., calendar).
- Compound terms whose meaning are clear from the combined meanings of the component parts.
- Variants when the meaning of the variant is clear from the base term (e.g., exception report is included, exception reporting is not).

As a result of the above inclusions and exclusions, this glossary includes:

- A preponderance of terms related to Project Scope Management, Project Time Management, and Project Risk Management, since many of the terms used in these knowledge areas are unique or nearly unique to project management.
- Many terms from Project Quality Management, since these terms are used more narrowly than in their everyday usage.
- Relatively few terms related to Project Human Resource Management and Project Communications Management, since most of the terms used in these knowledge areas do not differ significantly from everyday usage.
- Relatively few terms related to Project Cost Management and Project Procurement Management, since many of the terms used in these knowledge areas have narrow meanings that are unique to a particular application area.

2. COMMON ABBREVIATIONS

AC	Actual Cost
ACWP	Actual Cost of Work Performed
ACWS	Actual Cost of Work Scheduled
AD	Activity Description
ADM	Arrow Diagramming Method
AF	Actual Finish date
AOA	Activity-on-Arrow
AON	Activity-on-Node
AS	Actual Start date
BAC	Budget at Completion
BCWP	Budgeted Cost of Work Performed
BCWS	Budgeted Cost of Work Scheduled
CAP	Control Account Plan (previously called Cost Account Plan)
CCB	Change Control Board
CPFF	Cost-Plus-Fixed-Fee
CPI	Cost Performance Index
CPIF	Cost-Plus-Incentive-Fee
CPM	Critical Path Method
CV	Cost Variance
DD	Data Date
DU	Duration
EAC	Estimate at Completion
EF	Early Finish date
ES	Early Start date
ETC	Estimate to Complete
EV	Earned Value
EVM	Earned Value Management
FF	Free Float or Finish-to-Finish
FFP	Firm Fixed-Price
FPIF	Fixed-Price-Incentive-Fee
FS	Finish-to-Start
GERT	Graphical Evaluation and Review Technique
IFB	Invitation for Bid
LF	Late Finish date
LOE	Level of Effort
LS	Late Start date
OBS	Organization(al) Breakdown Structure
PC	Percent Complete
PDM	Precedence Diagramming Method
PERT	Program Evaluation and Review Technique
PF	Planned Finish date
PM	Project Management or Project Manager
PMBOK®	Project Management Body of Knowledge
PMP®	Project Management Professional
PS	Planned Start date
PV	Planned Value
QA	Quality Assurance
QC	Quality Control
RAM	Responsibility Assignment Matrix

A Guide to the Project Management Body of Knowledge (PMBOK® Guide) 2000 Edition
©2000 Project Management Institute, Four Campus Boulevard, Newtown Square, PA 19073-3299 USA

RDU Remaining Duration
RFP Request for Proposal
RFQ Request for Quotation
SF Scheduled Finish date or Start-to-Finish
SOW Statement of Work
SPI Schedule Performance Index
SS Scheduled Start date or Start-to-Start
SV Schedule Variance
TC Target Completion date
TF Total Float or Target Finish date
TQM Total Quality Management
TS Target Start date
VE Value Engineering
WBS Work Breakdown Structure

3. DEFINITIONS

Many of the words defined here have broader, and in some cases different, dictionary definitions.

The definitions use the following conventions:

- Terms used as part of the definitions and that are defined in the glossary are shown in *italics*.
- When synonyms are included, no definition is given and the reader is directed to the preferred term (i.e., see *preferred term*).
- Related terms that are not synonyms are cross-referenced at the end of the definition (i.e., see also *related term*).

Accountability Matrix. See *responsibility assignment matrix*.

Activity. An element of work performed during the course of a *project*. An activity normally has an expected *duration*, an expected cost, and expected resource requirements. Activities can be subdivided into *tasks*.

Activity Definition. Identifying the specific *activities* that must be performed to produce the various project *deliverables*.

Activity Description (AD). A short phrase or label used in a *project network diagram*. The activity description normally describes the *scope* of work of the *activity*.

Activity Duration Estimating. Estimating the number of work periods that will be needed to complete individual *activities*.

Activity-on-Arrow (AOA). See *arrow diagramming method*.

Activity-on-Node (AON). See *precedence diagramming method*.

Activity Sequencing. Identifying and documenting interactivity logical relationships.

Actual Cost (AC). Total costs incurred that must relate to whatever cost was budgeted within the *planned value* and *earned value* (which can sometimes be direct labor hours alone, direct costs alone, or all costs including indirect costs) in accomplishing work during a given time period. See also *earned value*.

Actual Cost of Work Performed (ACWP). This term has been replaced with the term *actual cost*.

Actual Finish Date (AF). The point in time that work actually ended on an *activity*. (Note: In some *application areas*, the activity is considered "finished" when work is "substantially complete.")

Actual Start Date (AS). The point in time that work actually started on an *activity*.

Administrative Closure. Generating, gathering, and disseminating information to formalize *phase* or *project* completion.

Application Area. A category of projects that have common elements not present in all projects. Application areas are usually defined in terms of either the product of the *project* (i.e., by similar technologies or industry sectors) or the type of customer (e.g., internal versus external, government versus commercial). Application areas often overlap.

Arrow. The graphic presentation of an *activity*. See also *arrow diagramming method*.

Arrow Diagramming Method (ADM). A network diagramming technique in which activities are represented by arrows. The tail of the *arrow* represents the start, and the head represents the finish of the *activity* (the length of the arrow does not represent the expected *duration* of the activity). Activities are connected at points called *nodes* (usually drawn as small circles) to illustrate the sequence in which the activities are expected to be performed. See also *precedence diagramming method*.

As-of Date. See *data date*.

Assumptions. Assumptions are factors that, for planning purposes, are considered to be true, real, or certain. Assumptions affect all aspects of project planning, and are part of the progressive elaboration of the *project*. Project teams frequently identify, document, and validate assumptions as part of their planning process. Assumptions generally involve a degree of *risk*.

Assumptions Analysis. A technique that explores the assumptions' accuracy and identifies *risks* to the *project* from inaccuracy, inconsistency, or incompleteness of assumptions.

Backward Pass. The calculation of *late finish dates* and *late start dates* for the uncompleted portions of all network activities. Determined by working backwards through the *network logic* from the *project's* end date. The end date may be calculated in a *forward pass* or set by the customer or sponsor. See also *network analysis*.

Bar Chart. A graphic display of schedule-related information. In the typical bar chart, *activities* or other project elements are listed down the left side of the chart, dates are shown across the top, and activity *durations* are shown as date-placed horizontal bars. Also called a *Gantt chart*.

Baseline. The original approved plan (for a *project*, a *work package*, or an *activity*), plus or minus approved *scope* changes. Usually used with a modifier (e.g., cost *baseline*, schedule baseline, *performance measurement baseline*).

Baseline Finish Date. See *scheduled finish date*.

Baseline Start Date. See *scheduled start date*.

Brainstorming. A general creativity technique that can be used to identify *risks* using a group of team members or subject-matter experts. Typically, a brainstorming session is structured so that each participant's ideas are recorded for later analysis. A tool of the *risk identification process*.

Budget at Completion (BAC). The sum of the total budgets for a *project*.

Budget Estimate. See *estimate*.

Budgeted Cost of Work Performed (BCWP). This term has been replaced with the term *earned value*.

Budgeted Cost of Work Scheduled (BCWS). This term has been replaced with the term *planned value*.

Buffer. See *reserve*.

Calendar Unit. The smallest unit of time used in scheduling the *project*. Calendar units are generally in hours, days, or weeks, but can also be in shifts or even in minutes. Used primarily in relation to *project management software*.

Change Control Board (CCB). A formally constituted group of *stakeholders* responsible for approving or rejecting changes to the project *baselines*.

Chart of Accounts. Any numbering system used to monitor project costs by category (e.g., labor, supplies, materials, and equipment). The project chart of accounts is usually based upon the corporate chart of accounts of the primary performing organization. See also *code of accounts*.

Charter. See *project charter*.

Checklist. A listing of many possible risks that might occur on a *project*. It is used as a tool in the *risk identification process*. Checklists are comprehensive, listing several types of *risk* that have been encountered on prior projects.

A Guide to the Project Management Body of Knowledge (PMBOK® Guide) 2000 Edition
©2000 Project Management Institute, Four Campus Boulevard, Newtown Square, PA 19073-3299 USA

Code of Accounts. Any numbering system used to uniquely identify each element of the *work breakdown structure*. See also *chart of accounts*.

Communications Planning. Determining the information and communications needs of the project *stakeholders*: who needs what information, when they will need it, and how it will be given to them.

Component. A constituent part, an element.

Constraint. Applicable restriction that will affect the performance of the *project*. Any factor that affects when an *activity* can be scheduled.

Contingencies. See *reserve* and *contingency planning*.

Contingency Allowance. See *reserve*.

Contingency Planning. The development of a management plan that identifies alternative strategies to be used to ensure *project* success if specified *risk* events occur.

Contingency Reserve. The amount of money or time needed above the *estimate* to reduce the *risk* of overruns of *project* objectives to a level acceptable to the organization.

Contract. A contract is a mutually binding agreement that obligates the *seller* to provide the specified product and obligates the buyer to pay for it. Contracts generally fall into one of three broad categories:

- *Fixed-price* or lump-sum contracts—this category of contract involves a fixed total price for a well-defined product. Fixed-price contracts may also include incentives for meeting or exceeding selected project objectives, such as schedule targets.

- Cost-reimbursable contracts—this category of contract involves payment (reimbursement) to the contractor for its actual costs. Costs are usually classified as direct costs (costs incurred directly by the project, such as wages for members of the project team) and indirect costs (costs allocated to the project by the performing organization as a cost of doing business, such as salaries for corporate executives). Indirect costs are usually calculated as a percentage of direct costs. Cost-reimbursable contracts often include incentives for meeting or exceeding selected project objectives, such as schedule targets or total cost.

- Time and material contracts—time and material contracts are a hybrid type of contractual arrangement that contain aspects of both cost-reimbursable and fixed-price-type arrangements. Time and material contracts resemble cost-type arrangements in that they are open ended, because the full value of the arrangement is not defined at the time of the award. Thus, time and material contracts can grow in contract value as if they were cost-reimbursable-type arrangements. Conversely, time and material arrangements can also resemble fixed-unit arrangements when, for example, the unit rates are preset by the buyer and seller, as when both parties agree on the rates for the category of "senior engineers."

Contract Administration. Managing the relationship with the *seller*.

Contract Closeout. Completion and settlement of the *contract*, including resolution of any open items.

Control. The process of comparing actual performance with planned performance, analyzing variances, evaluating possible alternatives, and taking appropriate corrective action as needed.

Control Account Plan (CAP). Previously called a Cost Account Plan. The CAP is a management control point where the integration of *scope* and budget and schedule takes place, and where the measurement of performance will happen. CAPs are placed at selected management points of the *work breakdown structure*.

Control Charts. Control charts are a graphic display of the results, over time and against established control limits, of a process. They are used to determine if the process is "in control" or in need of adjustment.

Corrective Action. Changes made to bring expected future performance of the *project* in line with the plan.

Cost Budgeting. Allocating the overall cost estimates to individual work *activities*.

Cost Control. Controlling changes to the project budget.

Cost Estimating. Developing an approximation (*estimate*) of the cost of the resources needed to complete project *activities*.

Cost of Quality. The costs incurred to ensure quality. The cost of quality includes *quality planning, quality control, quality assurance,* and *rework.*

Cost Performance Index (CPI). The cost efficiency ratio of *earned value* to *actual costs.* CPI is often used to predict the magnitude of a possible cost overrun using the following formula: BAC/CPI = projected cost at completion. CPI = EV divided by AC.

Cost-Plus-Fixed-Fee (CPFF) Contract. A type of *contract* where the buyer reimburses the *seller* for the seller's allowable costs (allowable costs are defined by the contract) plus a fixed amount of profit (fee).

Cost-Plus-Incentive-Fee (CPIF) Contract. A type of *contract* where the buyer reimburses the *seller* for the seller's allowable costs (allowable costs are defined by the contract), and the seller earns its profit if it meets defined performance criteria.

Cost Variance (CV). 1) Any difference between the budgeted cost of an *activity* and the *actual cost* of that activity. 2) In *earned value*, EV less AC = CV.

Crashing. Taking action to decrease the total project *duration* after analyzing a number of alternatives to determine how to get the maximum *duration compression* for the least cost.

Critical Activity. Any *activity* on a *critical path*. Most commonly determined by using the *critical path method*. Although some activities are "critical," in the dictionary sense, without being on the *critical path*, this meaning is seldom used in the project context.

Critical Path. The series of *activities* that determines the *duration* of the *project*. In a deterministic model, the critical path is usually defined as those activities with *float* less than or equal to a specified value, often zero. It is the longest path through the project. See *critical path method*.

Critical Path Method (CPM). A *network analysis* technique used to predict project *duration* by analyzing which sequence of *activities* (which path) has the least amount of scheduling flexibility (the least amount of *float*). Early dates are calculated by means of a *forward pass*, using a specified *start date*. Late dates are calculated by means of a *backward pass*, starting from a specified completion date (usually the forward pass' calculated project *early finish date*).

Current Finish Date. The current *estimate* of the point in time when an *activity* will be completed.

Current Start Date. The current *estimate* of the point in time when an *activity* will begin.

Data Date (DD). The date at which, or up to which, the project's reporting system has provided actual status and accomplishments. Also called *as-of date*.

Decision Tree Analysis. The decision tree is a diagram that describes a decision under consideration and the implications of choosing one or another of the available alternatives. It incorporates probabilities or *risks* and the costs or rewards of each logical path of events and future decisions.

Definitive Estimate. See *estimate*.

Deliverable. Any measurable, tangible, verifiable outcome, result, or item that must be produced to complete a *project* or part of a project. Often used more narrowly in reference to an external *deliverable*, which is a deliverable that is subject to approval by the project sponsor or customer.

Dependency. See *logical relationship*.

Dummy Activity. An *activity* of zero *duration* used to show a *logical relationship* in the *arrow diagramming method*. Dummy activities are used when logical relationships cannot be completely or correctly described with regular activity arrows. Dummies are shown graphically as a dashed line headed by an *arrow*.

Duration (DU). The number of work periods (not including holidays or other nonworking periods) required to complete an *activity* or other project element. Usually expressed as workdays or workweeks. Sometimes incorrectly equated with elapsed time. See also *effort*.

Duration Compression. Shortening the *project schedule* without reducing the *project scope*. Duration compression is not always possible and often requires an increase in project cost.

A Guide to the Project Management Body of Knowledge (PMBOK® Guide) 2000 Edition
©2000 Project Management Institute, Four Campus Boulevard, Newtown Square, PA 19073-3299 USA

Early Finish Date (EF). In the *critical path method*, the earliest possible point in time on which the uncompleted portions of an *activity* (or the *project*) can finish, based on the *network logic* and any schedule constraints. Early finish dates can change as the project progresses and changes are made to the *project plan*.

Early Start Date (ES). In the *critical path method*, the earliest possible point in time on which the uncompleted portions of an *activity* (or the *project*) can start, based on the *network logic* and any schedule constraints. Early start dates can change as the project progresses and changes are made to the *project plan*.

Earned Value (EV). The physical work accomplished plus the authorized budget for this work. The sum of the approved cost estimates (may include overhead allocation) for activities (or portions of activities) completed during a given period (usually project-to-date). Previously called the budgeted cost of work performed (BCWP) for an *activity* or group of activities.

Earned Value Management (EVM). A method for integrating *scope*, schedule, and resources, and for measuring project performance. It compares the amount of work that was planned with what was actually earned with what was actually spent to determine if cost and schedule performance are as planned.

Effort. The number of labor units required to complete an *activity* or other project element. Usually expressed as staff hours, staff days, or staff weeks. Should not be confused with *duration*.

Element. One of the parts, substances, or principles that make up a compound or complex whole.

Estimate. An assessment of the likely quantitative result. Usually applied to project costs and *durations* and should always include some indication of accuracy (e.g., ±x percent). Usually used with a modifier (e.g., preliminary, conceptual, feasibility). Some *application areas* have specific modifiers that imply particular accuracy ranges (e.g., *order-of-magnitude estimate*, budget estimate, and definitive estimate in engineering and construction projects).

Estimate at Completion (EAC). The expected total cost of an *activity*, a group of activities, or the *project* when the defined *scope* of work has been completed. Most techniques for forecasting EAC include some adjustment of the original cost estimate, based on actual project performance to date.

Estimate to Complete (ETC). The expected additional cost needed to complete an *activity*, a group of activities, or the *project*. Most techniques for forecasting ETC include some adjustment to the original *estimate*, based on project performance to date. Also called "estimated to complete." See also *earned value* and *estimate at completion*.

Event-on-Node. A network diagramming technique in which events are represented by boxes (or *nodes*) connected by *arrows* to show the sequence in which the events are to occur. Used in the original *program evaluation and review technique*.

Exception Report. Document that includes only major variations from plan (rather than all variations).

Fast Tracking. Compressing the *project schedule* by overlapping *activities* that would normally be done in sequence, such as design and construction.

Finish Date. A point in time associated with an *activity's* completion. Usually qualified by one of the following: actual, planned, estimated, scheduled, early, late, baseline, target, or current.

Finish-to-Finish (FF). See *logical relationship*.

Finish-to-Start (FS). See *logical relationship*.

Firm Fixed-Price (FFP) Contract. A type of *contract* where the buyer pays the *seller* a set amount (as defined by the contract), regardless of the seller's costs.

Fixed-Price Contract. See *firm fixed-price contract*.

Fixed-Price-Incentive-Fee (FPIF) Contract. A type of *contract* where the buyer pays the *seller* a set amount (as defined by the contract), and the seller can earn an additional amount if it meets defined performance criteria.

Float. The amount of time that an *activity* may be delayed from its *early start* without delaying the project *finish date*. Float is a mathematical calculation, and can change as the *project* progresses and changes are made to the *project plan*. Also called *slack*, total float, and path float. See also *free float*.

Forecast Final Cost. See *estimate at completion*.

Forward Pass. The calculation of the *early start* and *early finish dates* for the uncompleted portions of all network activities. See also *network analysis* and *backward pass*.

Fragnet. See *subnet*.

Free Float (FF). The amount of time that an *activity* can be delayed without delaying the *early start* of any immediately following activities. See also *float*.

Functional Manager. A manager responsible for *activities* in a specialized department or function (e.g., engineering, manufacturing, marketing).

Functional Organization. An organization structure in which staff are grouped hierarchically by specialty (e.g., production, marketing, engineering, and accounting at the top level; with engineering, further divided into mechanical, electrical, and others).

Gantt Chart. See *bar chart*.

Grade. A category or rank used to distinguish items that have the same functional use (e.g., "hammer"), but do not share the same requirements for quality (e.g., different hammers may need to withstand different amounts of force).

Graphical Evaluation and Review Technique (GERT). A *network analysis* technique that allows for conditional and probabilistic treatment of *logical relationships* (i.e., some *activities* may not be performed).

Hammock. An aggregate or summary *activity* (a group of related activities is shown as one and reported at a summary level). A hammock may or may not have an internal sequence. See also *subproject* and *subnet*.

Hanger. An unintended break in a *network path*. Hangers are usually caused by missing *activities* or missing *logical relationships*.

Information Distribution. Making needed information available to project *stakeholders* in a timely manner.

Initiation. Authorizing the *project* or phase.

Integrated Change Control. Coordinating changes across the entire *project*.

Integrated Cost/Schedule Reporting. See *earned value*.

Invitation for Bid (IFB). Generally, this term is equivalent to *request for proposal*. However, in some *application areas*, it may have a narrower or more specific meaning.

Key Event Schedule. See *master schedule*.

Lag. A modification of a *logical relationship* that directs a delay in the successor *task*. For example, in a finish-to-start dependency with a ten-day lag, the successor *activity* cannot start until ten days after the predecessor has finished. See also *lead*.

Late Finish Date (LF). In the *critical path method*, the latest possible point in time that an *activity* may be completed without delaying a specified *milestone* (usually the project *finish date*).

Late Start Date (LS). In the *critical path method*, the latest possible point in time that an *activity* may begin without delaying a specified *milestone* (usually the project *finish date*).

Lead. A modification of a *logical relationship* that allows an acceleration of the successor *task*. For example, in a finish-to-start dependency with a ten-day lead, the successor *activity* can start ten days before the predecessor has finished. See also *lag*.

Lessons Learned. The learning gained from the process of performing the *project*. Lessons learned may be identified at any point. Also considered a project record.

Level of Effort (LOE). Support-type *activity* (e.g., vendor or customer liaison) that does not readily lend itself to measurement of discrete accomplishment. It is generally characterized by a uniform rate of activity over a period of time determined by the activities it supports.

Leveling. See *resource leveling*.

A Guide to the Project Management Body of Knowledge (PMBOK® Guide) 2000 Edition
©2000 Project Management Institute, Four Campus Boulevard, Newtown Square, PA 19073-3299 USA

Life-Cycle Costing. The concept of including acquisition, operating, and disposal costs when evaluating various alternatives.

Line Manager. 1) The manager of any group that actually makes a product or performs a service. 2) A *functional manager*.

Link. See *logical relationship*.

Logic. See *network logic*.

Logic Diagram. See *project network diagram*.

Logical Relationship. A dependency between two project activities, or between a project *activity* and a *milestone*. See also *precedence relationship*. The four possible types of *logical relationships* are:

- Finish-to-start—the initiation of work of the successor depends upon the completion of work of the predecessor.
- Finish-to-finish—the completion of the work of the successor cannot finish until the completion of work of the predecessor.
- Start-to-start—the initiation of work of the successor depends upon the initiation of the work of the predecessor.
- Start-to-finish—the completion of the successor is dependent upon the initiation of the predecessor.

Loop. A *network path* that passes the same *node* twice. Loops cannot be analyzed using traditional *network analysis* techniques such as *critical path method* and *program evaluation and review technique*. Loops are allowed in *graphical evaluation and review technique*.

Master Schedule. A summary-level schedule that identifies the major *activities* and key *milestones*. See also *milestone schedule*.

Mathematical Analysis. See *network analysis*.

Matrix Organization. Any organizational structure in which the *project manager* shares responsibility with the *functional managers* for assigning priorities and for directing the work of individuals assigned to the *project*.

Milestone. A significant event in the *project*, usually completion of a major *deliverable*.

Milestone Schedule. A summary-level schedule that identifies the major *milestones*. See also *master schedule*.

Mitigation. See *risk mitigation*.

Monitoring. The capture, analysis, and reporting of project performance, usually as compared to plan.

Monte Carlo Analysis. A technique that performs a project simulation many times to calculate a distribution of likely results. See *simulation*.

Near-Critical Activity. An *activity* that has low total *float*.

Network. See *project network diagram*.

Network Analysis. The process of identifying *early* and *late start* and *finish dates* for the uncompleted portions of project *activities*. See also *critical path method*, *program evaluation and review technique*, and *graphical evaluation and review technique*.

Network Logic. The collection of *activity* dependencies that makes up a *project network diagram*.

Network Path. Any continuous series of connected *activities* in a *project network diagram*.

Node. One of the defining points of a network; a junction point joined to some or all of the other dependency lines. See also *arrow diagramming method* and *precedence diagramming method*.

Order-of-Magnitude Estimate. See *estimate*.

Organizational Breakdown Structure (OBS). A depiction of the project organization arranged so as to relate *work packages* to organizational units.

Organizational Planning. Identifying, documenting, and assigning project roles, responsibilities, and reporting relationships.

Overlap. See *lead*.

Parametric Estimating. An estimating technique that uses a statistical relationship between historical data and other variables (e.g., square footage in construction, lines of code in software development) to calculate an *estimate*.

Pareto Diagram. A histogram, ordered by frequency of occurrence, that shows how many results were generated by each identified cause.

Path. A set of sequentially connected *activities* in a *project network diagram*.

Path Convergence. The *node* in the schedule where parallel paths merge or join. At that node, delays or elongation of any converging path can delay the *project*. In *quantitative risk analysis* of a schedule, significant *risk* may occur at this point.

Path Float. See *float*.

Percent Complete (PC). An *estimate*, expressed as a percent, of the amount of work that has been completed on an *activity* or a group of activities.

Performance Measurement Baseline. An approved plan against which deviations are compared for management control.

Performance Reporting. Collecting and disseminating performance information. This includes status reporting, progress measurement, and forecasting.

Performing Organization. The enterprise whose employees are most directly involved in doing the work of the *project*.

PERT Chart. The term is commonly used to refer to a *project network diagram*. See *program evaluation and review technique* for the traditional definition of PERT.

Phase. See *project phase*.

Planned Finish Date (PF). See *scheduled finish date*.

Planned Start Date (PS). See *scheduled start date*.

Planned Value (PV). The physical work scheduled, plus the authorized budget to accomplish the scheduled work. Previously, this was called the budgeted costs of work scheduled (BCWS).

Precedence Diagramming Method (PDM). A network diagramming technique in which *activities* are represented by boxes (or *nodes*). Activities are linked by *precedence relationships* to show the sequence in which the activities are to be performed.

Precedence Relationship. The term used in the *precedence diagramming method* for a *logical relationship*. In current usage, however, precedence relationship, *logical relationship*, and dependency are widely used interchangeably, regardless of the diagramming method in use.

Predecessor Activity. 1) In the *arrow diagramming method*, the *activity* that enters a *node*. 2) In the *precedence diagramming method*, the "from" activity.

Probability and Impact Matrix. A common way to determine whether a *risk* is considered low, moderate, or high by combining the two dimensions of a risk: its probability of occurrence, and its impact on objectives if it occurs.

Procurement Planning. Determining what to procure and when.

Product Scope. The features and functions that characterize a product or service.

Program. A group of related *projects* managed in a coordinated way. Programs usually include an element of ongoing work.

Program Evaluation and Review Technique (PERT). An event-oriented *network analysis* technique used to estimate program *duration* when there is uncertainty in the individual *activity duration estimates*. PERT applies the *critical path method* using durations that are computed by a weighted average of optimistic, pessimistic, and most likely duration estimates. PERT computes the standard deviation of the completion date from those of the path's activity durations. Also known as the Method of Moments Analysis.

Project. A temporary endeavor undertaken to create a unique product, service, or result.

Project Charter. A document issued by senior management that formally authorizes the existence of a *project*. And it provides the *project manager* with the authority to apply organizational resources to project activities.

A Guide to the Project Management Body of Knowledge (PMBOK® Guide) 2000 Edition
©2000 Project Management Institute, Four Campus Boulevard, Newtown Square, PA 19073-3299 USA

Project Communications Management. A subset of *project management* that includes the processes required to ensure timely and appropriate generation, collection and dissemination, storage and ultimate disposition of project information. It consists of *communications planning, information distribution, performance reporting*, and *administrative closure*.

Project Cost Management. A subset of *project management* that includes the processes required to ensure that the *project* is completed within the approved budget. It consists of *resource planning, cost estimating, cost budgeting*, and *cost control*.

Project Human Resource Management. A subset of *project management* that includes the processes required to make the most effective use of the people involved with the *project*. It consists of *organizational planning, staff acquisition*, and *team development*.

Project Integration Management. A subset of *project management* that includes the processes required to ensure that the various elements of the *project* are properly coordinated. It consists of *project plan development, project plan execution*, and *integrated change control*.

Project Life Cycle. A collection of generally sequential *project phases* whose name and number are determined by the control needs of the organization or organizations involved in the *project*.

Project Management (PM). The application of knowledge, skills, tools, and techniques to project *activities* to meet the project requirements.

Project Management Body of Knowledge (PMBOK®). An inclusive term that describes the sum of knowledge within the profession of *project management*. As with other professions—such as law, medicine, and accounting—the body of knowledge rests with the practitioners and academics that apply and advance it. The PMBOK® includes proven, traditional practices that are widely applied, as well as innovative and advanced ones that have seen more limited use.

Project Management Professional (PMP®). An individual certified as such by the Project Management Institute (PMI®).

Project Management Software. A class of computer applications specifically designed to aid with planning and controlling project costs and schedules.

Project Management Team. The members of the project team who are directly involved in project management *activities*. On some smaller projects, the project management team may include virtually all of the *project team members*.

Project Manager (PM). The individual responsible for managing a *project*.

Project Network Diagram. Any schematic display of the *logical relationships* of project *activities*. Always drawn from left to right to reflect project chronology. Often referred to as a *PERT chart*.

Project Phase. A collection of logically related project *activities*, usually culminating in the completion of a major *deliverable*.

Project Plan. A formal, approved document used to guide both project execution and project control. The primary uses of the project plan are to document planning assumptions and decisions, facilitate communication among *stakeholders*, and document approved scope, cost, and schedule *baselines*. A project plan may be summary or detailed.

Project Plan Development. Integrating and coordinating all project plans to create a consistent, coherent document.

Project Plan Execution. Carrying out the *project plan* by performing the *activities* included therein.

Project Planning. The development and maintenance of the *project plan*.

Project Procurement Management. A subset of *project management* that includes the processes required to acquire goods and services to attain *project scope* from outside the performing organization. It consists of *procurement planning, solicitation planning, solicitation, source selection, contract administration*, and *contract closeout*.

Project Quality Management. A subset of *project management* that includes the processes required to ensure that the *project* will satisfy the needs for which it was undertaken. It consists of *quality planning, quality assurance*, and *quality control*.

Project Risk Management. Risk management is the systematic process of identifying, analyzing, and responding to project *risk*. It includes maximizing the probability and consequences of positive events and minimizing the probability and consequences of events adverse to project objectives. It includes the processes of *risk management planning*, *risk identification*, *qualitative risk analysis*, *quantitative risk analysis*, *risk response planning*, and *risk monitoring and control*.

Project Schedule. The planned dates for performing *activities* and the planned dates for meeting *milestones*.

Project Scope. The work that must be done to deliver a product with the specified features and functions.

Project Scope Management. A subset of *project management* that includes the processes required to ensure that the *project* includes all of the work required, and only the work required, to complete the project successfully. It consists of *initiation*, *scope planning*, *scope definition*, *scope verification*, and *scope change control*.

Project Team Members. The people who report either directly or indirectly to the *project manager*.

Project Time Management. A subset of *project management* that includes the processes required to ensure timely completion of the *project*. It consists of *activity definition*, *activity sequencing*, *activity duration estimating*, *schedule development*, and *schedule control*.

Projectized Organization. Any organizational structure in which the *project manager* has full authority to assign priorities and to direct the work of individuals assigned to the *project*.

Qualitative Risk Analysis. Performing a qualitative analysis of risks and conditions to prioritize their effects on project objectives. It involves assessing the probability and impact of project *risk*(s) and using methods such as the *probability and impact matrix* to classify risks into categories of high, moderate, and low for prioritized *risk response planning*.

Quality Assurance (QA). 1) The process of evaluating overall project performance on a regular basis to provide confidence that the *project* will satisfy the relevant quality standards. 2) The organizational unit that is assigned responsibility for quality assurance.

Quality Control (QC). 1) The process of monitoring specific *project* results to determine if they comply with relevant quality standards and identifying ways to eliminate causes of unsatisfactory performance. 2) The organizational unit that is assigned responsibility for quality control.

Quality Planning. Identifying which quality standards are relevant to the *project*, and determining how to satisfy them.

Quantitative Risk Analysis. Measuring the probability and consequences of risks and estimating their implications for project objectives. Risks are characterized by probability distributions of possible outcomes. This process uses quantitative techniques such as *simulation* and *decision tree analysis*.

Remaining Duration (RDU). The time needed to complete an *activity*.

Request for Proposal (RFP). A type of bid document used to solicit proposals from prospective *sellers* of products or services. In some *application areas*, it may have a narrower or more specific meaning.

Request for Quotation (RFQ). Generally, this term is equivalent to *request for proposal*. However, in some *application areas*, it may have a narrower or more specific meaning.

Reserve. A provision in the *project plan* to mitigate cost and/or schedule *risk*. Often used with a modifier (e.g., management reserve, *contingency reserve*) to provide further detail on what types of risk are meant to be mitigated. The specific meaning of the modified term varies by *application area*.

Residual Risk. A *risk* that remains after risk responses have been implemented.

Resource Leveling. Any form of *network analysis* in which scheduling decisions (*start* and *finish dates*) are driven by resource management concerns (e.g., limited resource availability or difficult-to-manage changes in resource levels).

A Guide to the Project Management Body of Knowledge (PMBOK® Guide) 2000 Edition
©2000 Project Management Institute, Four Campus Boulevard, Newtown Square, PA 19073-3299 USA

Resource Limited Schedule. A *project schedule* whose *start* and *finish dates* reflect expected resource availability. The final project schedule should always be resource limited.

Resource Planning. Determining what resources (people, equipment, materials) are needed in what quantities to perform project *activities*.

Responsibility Assignment Matrix (RAM). A structure that relates the project organization structure to the *work breakdown structure* to help ensure that each element of the project's *scope* of work is assigned to a responsible individual.

Responsibility Chart. See *responsibility assignment matrix*.

Responsibility Matrix. See *responsibility assignment matrix*.

Retainage. A portion of a *contract* payment that is held until contract completion to ensure full performance of the contract terms.

Rework. Action taken to bring a defective or nonconforming item into compliance with requirements or specifications.

Risk. An uncertain event or condition that, if it occurs, has a positive or negative effect on a project's objectives.

Risk Acceptance. This technique of the *risk response planning process* indicates that the project team has decided not to change the *project plan* to deal with a *risk*, or is unable to identify any other suitable response strategy.

Risk Avoidance. Risk avoidance is changing the *project plan* to eliminate the *risk* or to protect the project objectives from its impact. It is a tool of the *risk response planning process*.

Risk Category. A source of potential *risk* reflecting technical, project management, organizational, or external sources.

Risk Database. A repository that provides for collection, maintenance, and analysis of data gathered and used in the *risk management processes*. A *lessons-learned* program uses a risk database. This is an output of the *risk monitoring and control process*.

Risk Event. A discrete occurrence that may affect the project for better or worse.

Risk Identification. Determining which *risks* might affect the *project* and documenting their characteristics. Tools used include *brainstorming* and *checklists*.

Risk Management Plan. Documents how the *risk* processes will be carried out during the *project*. This is the output of *risk management planning*.

Risk Management Planning. Deciding how to approach and plan risk management activities for a *project*.

Risk Mitigation. Risk mitigation seeks to reduce the probability and/or impact of a *risk* to below an acceptable threshold.

Risk Monitoring and Control. Monitoring residual risks, identifying new risks, executing risk reduction plans, and evaluating their effectiveness throughout the *project life cycle*.

Risk Register. See *risk response plan*.

Risk Response Plan. A document detailing all identified *risks*, including description, cause, probability of occurring, impact(s) on objectives, proposed responses, owners, and current status. Also known as *risk register*.

Risk Response Planning. Developing procedures and techniques to enhance opportunities and reduce threats to the project's objectives. The tools include avoidance, mitigation, transference, and acceptance.

Risk Transference. Risk transference is seeking to shift the impact of a *risk* to a third party together with ownership of the response.

S-Curve. Graphic display of cumulative costs, labor hours, percentage of work, or other quantities, plotted against time. The name derives from the S-like shape of the curve (flatter at the beginning and end, steeper in the middle) produced on a *project* that starts slowly, accelerates, and then tails off. Also a term for the cumulative likelihood distribution that is a result of a *simulation*, a tool of *quantitative risk analysis*.

Schedule. See *project schedule*.

Schedule Analysis. See *network analysis*.

Schedule Compression. See *duration compression*.

Schedule Control. Controlling changes to the *project schedule*.

Schedule Development. Analyzing *activity* sequences, activity *durations*, and resource requirements to create the *project schedule*.

Schedule Performance Index (SPI). The schedule efficiency ratio of *earned value* accomplished against the *planned value*. The SPI describes what portion of the planned schedule was actually accomplished. The SPI = EV divided by PV.

Schedule Variance (SV). 1) Any difference between the scheduled completion of an *activity* and the actual completion of that activity. 2) In *earned value*, EV less PV = SV.

Scheduled Finish Date (SF). The point in time that work was scheduled to finish on an *activity*. The scheduled finish date is normally within the range of dates delimited by the *early finish date* and the *late finish date*. It may reflect leveling of scarce resources.

Scheduled Start Date (SS). The point in time that work was scheduled to start on an *activity*. The scheduled start date is normally within the range of dates delimited by the *early start date* and the *late start date*. It may reflect leveling of scarce resources.

Scope. The sum of the products and services to be provided as a *project*. See *project scope* and *product scope*.

Scope Baseline. See *baseline*.

Scope Change. Any change to the *project scope*. A scope change almost always requires an adjustment to the project cost or schedule.

Scope Change Control. Controlling changes to *project scope*.

Scope Definition. Subdividing the major *deliverables* into smaller, more manageable components to provide better control.

Scope Planning. The process of progressively elaborating the work of the *project*, which includes developing a written *scope statement* that includes the project justification, the major *deliverables*, and the project objectives.

Scope Statement. The scope statement provides a documented basis for making future project decisions and for confirming or developing common understanding of *project scope* among the *stakeholders*. As the *project* progresses, the scope statement may need to be revised or refined to reflect approved changes to the *scope* of the *project*.

Scope Verification. Formalizing acceptance of the *project scope*.

Secondary Risk. A *risk* that arises as a direct result of implementing a risk response.

Seller. The provider of goods or services to an organization.

Should-Cost Estimate. An *estimate* of the cost of a product or service used to provide an assessment of the reasonableness of a prospective contractor's proposed cost.

Simulation. A simulation uses a project model that translates the uncertainties specified at a detailed level into their potential impact on objectives that are expressed at the level of the total *project*. Project simulations use computer models and estimates of *risk* at a detailed level, and are typically performed using the *Monte Carlo* technique.

Slack. Term used in *arrow diagramming method* for *float*.

Solicitation. Obtaining quotations, bids, offers, or proposals as appropriate.

Solicitation Planning. Documenting product requirements and identifying potential sources.

Source Selection. Choosing from among potential *sellers*.

Staff Acquisition. Getting needed human resources assigned to and working on the *project*.

Stakeholder. Individuals and organizations that are actively involved in the *project,* or whose interests may be positively or negatively affected as a result of project execution or project completion. They may also exert influence over the *project* and its results.

Start Date. A point in time associated with an *activity's* start, usually qualified by one of the following: actual, planned, estimated, scheduled, early, late, target, baseline, or current.

Start-to-Finish (SF). See *logical relationship*.

Start-to-Start (SS). See *logical relationship*.

Statement of Work (SOW). A narrative description of products or services to be supplied under *contract*.

A Guide to the Project Management Body of Knowledge (PMBOK® Guide) 2000 Edition
©2000 Project Management Institute, Four Campus Boulevard, Newtown Square, PA 19073-3299 USA

Subnet. A subdivision of a *project network diagram*, usually representing some form of *subproject*.

Subnetwork. See *subnet*.

Subproject. A smaller portion of the overall *project*.

Successor Activity. 1) In the *arrow diagramming method*, the *activity* that departs a *node*. 2) In the *precedence diagramming method*, the "to" activity.

Target Completion Date (TC). An imposed date that constrains or otherwise modifies the *network analysis*.

Target Finish Date (TF). The date that work is planned (targeted) to finish on an *activity*.

Target Schedule. See *baseline*.

Target Start Date (TS). The date that work is planned (targeted) to start on an *activity*.

Task. A generic term for work that is not included in the *work breakdown structure*, but potentially could be a further decomposition of work by the individuals responsible for that work. Also, lowest *level of effort* on a *project*.

Team Development. Developing individual and group competencies to enhance *project* performance.

Team Members. See *project team members*.

Technical Performance Measurement. Technical performance measurement compares technical accomplishments during project execution to the project plan's schedule of technical achievement.

Time-Scaled Network Diagram. Any *project network* diagram drawn in such a way that the positioning and length of the *activity* represent its *duration*. Essentially, it is a *bar chart* that includes *network logic*.

Total Float (TF). See *float*.

Total Quality Management (TQM). A common approach to implementing a quality improvement program within an organization.

Transference. See *risk transference*.

Triggers. Triggers, sometimes called risk symptoms or warning signs, are indications that a *risk* has occurred or is about to occur. Triggers may be discovered in the *risk identification process* and watched in the *risk monitoring and control process*.

Value Engineering (VE). Value engineering is a creative approach used to optimize life-cycle costs, save time, increase profits, improve quality, expand market share, solve problems, and/or use resources more effectively.

Workaround. A response to a negative *risk* event. Distinguished from contingency plan in that a workaround is not planned in advance of the occurrence of the risk event.

Work Breakdown Structure (WBS). A *deliverable*-oriented grouping of project elements that organizes and defines the total work *scope* of the *project*. Each descending level represents an increasingly detailed definition of the project work.

Work Item. Term no longer in common usage. Synonymous with activity—see *activity*.

Work Package. A *deliverable* at the lowest level of the *work breakdown structure*, when that deliverable may be assigned to another *project manager* to plan and execute. This may be accomplished through the use of a *subproject* where the work package may be further decomposed into *activities*.

Index

A

AC *See* actual cost (AC)

AD *See* activity description (AD)

ACWP *See* actual cost of work performed (ACWP)

ADM *See* arrow diagramming method (ADM)

AF *See* actual finish date (AF)

AOA *See* activity-on-arrow (AOA)

AON *See* activity-on-node (AON)

AS *See* actual start date (AS)

activity 14, 36, 47, 68–69, 71–75, 77–78, 80–81, 87–88, 100–01, 103, 123, 170, 197–204, 206, 208–09

   critical 76, 80, 200

   definition 7, 34, 65, 67, 71, 190, 197, 206

   description (AD) 196–97

   dummy 200

   duration(s) 34, 65, 67, 72–73, 75, 190, 198, 204, 208

   predecessor 204

   successor 74, 202, 209

      estimate(s) 73–75, 80, 86–87, 204

      See also *estimate(s)*

      estimating 7, 34, 65, 71–73, 190, 197, 206

      See also *estimate(s)*

   list 60, 67–68, 71, 73

   sequencing 7, 34, 49, 65, 68–70, 190, 197, 206, 208

activity-on-arrow (AOA) 70, 196–97

activity-on-node (AON) 69, 196–97

actual cost (AC) 88, 92, 123, 196–97, 200

   of work performed (ACWP) 123, 196–97, 200

actual finish date (AF) 196–97

actual start date (AS) 196–97

administrative closure 8, 37, 117, 125, 158–59, 191, 197, 205

application area(s) 4, 13, 30, 43, 46, 51, 56, 62, 68–69, 78, 89, 98, 110–11, 125, 131, 147, 161, 181–82, 195, 198, 206

arrow 198, 200

   diagramming method (ADM) 70, 196–98, 200, 203–04, 208–09

as-of date 198, 200

B

BAC *See* budget at completion (BAC)

BCWP *See* budgeted cost of work performed (BCWP)

BCWS *See* budgeted cost of work scheduled (BCWS)

backward pass 198, 200, 202

bar chart 78, 124, 198, 202, 209

baseline 43, 45–49, 57, 63–64, 72, 122, 139, 145, 168, 198, 201, 208–09.

   See also finish date, scope baseline, start date, and target schedule

   cost 45, 89–92, 198

   performance measurement 44–47, 198, 204

   schedule 45, 79, 198, 205

budget at completion (BAC) 92, 196, 198, 200

budget estimate 198, 201

budgeted cost of work performed (BCWP) 92, 123, 196, 198, 201

budgeted cost of work scheduled (BCWS) 92, 123, 196, 198, 204, 208

C

CAP *See* control account plan (CAP)

CCB *See* change control board (CCB)

CPFF *See* contract, cost-plus-fixed-fee (CPFF)

CPI *See* cost performance index (CPI)

CPIF *See* contract, cost-plus-incentive-fee (CPIF)

CPM *See* critical path method (CPM)

CV *See* cost variance (CV)

calendar unit 198

change control board (CCB) 49, 196, 198

change control system 48–49, 80, 91, 158

   See also integrated change control and scope change control

chart of accounts 87, 198–99

charter *See* project charter

code of accounts 198–99

communications planning 8, 34, 109, 117, 119, 120, 191, 199, 205

contingencies 45, 199

A Guide to the Project Management Body of Knowledge (PMBOK® Guide) 2000 Edition
©2000 Project Management Institute, Four Campus Boulevard, Newtown Square, PA 19073-3299 USA

P

PC   See percent complete (PC)

PDM   See precedence diagramming method (PDM)

PERT   See program evaluation and review technique (PERT)

PERT chart   70, 204–05
> See also program evaluation and review technique (PERT)

PF   See planned finish date (PF)

PM   See project management (PM) and project manager (PM)

PMBOK®   See project management body of knowledge (PMBOK®)

PMBOK® Guide   9–10, 173, 179, 185

PMP®   See project management professional(s) (PMP®)

PS   See planned start date (PS)

PV   See planned value (PV)

parametric estimating   204

Pareto diagram   103, 204

path   139, 200, 204
> convergence   204
> float   202, 204

percent complete (PC)   122, 196, 204

performance measurement baseline   See baseline, performance measurement

performance reporting   8, 36, 47, 117, 122–25, 151–52, 157–58, 191, 204–05

performing organization   4, 8, 10–12, 16, 19, 25–26, 41, 44, 49, 53–54, 64, 81, 86–87, 93, 97–98, 101, 110, 113–16, 147, 149–51, 158–59, 170, 191, 198–99, 204–05

phase   10–14, 20, 30, 32–33, 37, 51, 53–54, 57, 62, 70, 87, 108, 117, 125, 189, 191, 197, 202, 204

planned finish date (PF)   196, 204

planned start date (PS)   196, 204

planned value (PV)   92, 123, 196–98, 204, 208

precedence diagramming method (PDM)   69–70, 139, 196–98, 203–04, 209

precedence relationship   69, 203–04

predecessor activity   See activity, predecessor

probability and impact matrix   204, 206

procurement planning   8, 35, 98, 147, 149–52, 159, 191, 204–05

product scope   6, 41, 47, 51, 63, 204, 208

program   10, 70, 74, 146, 168, 204, 207, 209

program evaluation and review technique (PERT)   70, 75, 196, 201, 203–04
> See also PERT chart

project charter   45, 54–55, 114, 129, 131, 183, 198, 204

project communications management   7, 24–25, 117, 149, 171–72, 191, 195, 205

project cost management   7, 83, 171–72, 190, 195, 205

project human resource management   7, 107, 149, 170–72, 190, 195, 205

project integration management   7, 41, 170–71, 189, 205

project life cycle   6, 11–14, 30, 51, 57–58, 127, 130, 145, 169–70, 181, 191, 205, 207

project management (PM)   3–4, 6–7, 9–12, 18, 21, 29, 32, 45–46, 55, 58, 96, 99, 102, 127, 132, 135, 147, 163, 167–71, 189–91, 195–96, 205
> body of knowledge (PMBOK®)   3, 13, 19, 163, 169, 179, 181, 196, 215
> processes   7, 30, 32, 38, 41–42, 44, 56, 68, 97, 103, 157, 169–70, 172, 181
> professional(s) (PMP®)   4, 153, 156, 168, 175, 196, 205
> software   42, 44, 68–69, 74, 76, 80, 86, 88, 92, 121, 198, 205
> team   3, 7, 11, 16, 18, 26–27, 37, 44, 46–47, 49, 67, 69, 74, 88, 92–93, 96–103, 107–10, 112–13, 115, 120, 123, 147, 149, 151, 157–58, 181, 205
> See also project team, project team member(s), team development, and team member(s)

project manager (PM)   4, 16, 19–21, 24, 46, 54–55, 60–61, 96, 107, 110, 114–15, 130, 136, 144, 153, 156, 181, 196, 203–06, 209

project network diagram   69–71, 74, 77, 197, 203–05, 209

project objectives   5, 29–30, 34, 36, 55–56, 63, 65, 67, 86, 98, 122, 127, 133–35, 137–39, 142–44, 151, 191, 199, 206–08

project phase   11–12, 32, 41, 51, 53–54, 62, 65, 77, 83, 95, 109, 117, 119, 170, 204–05

project plan   26, 30, 32–33, 35, 41–46, 48–49, 51, 57, 61–62, 64, 78–81, 89, 92, 99, 103, 111, 115, 121–23, 132, 134, 142–46, 151, 158, 189, 201–02, 205–07, 209
> development   7, 34, 41–44, 77, 99, 111, 151, 189, 205
> execution   7, 35, 41, 45–47, 55, 62, 123, 157, 189, 205

project planning   33, 34, 36, 43–45, 53, 55, 97, 131, 158, 198, 205

project procurement management   8, 114, 147, 171–72, 191, 195, 205

project quality management   7, 95–96, 98, 171–72, 190, 195, 205

project risk management   8, 26, 72–73, 171–72, 191, 195, 206

project schedule   34, 36, 44–45, 65, 73–75, 77–81, 90, 96, 103, 139, 152, 190, 200–01, 206–08

T

V

W

A Guide to the Project Management Body of Knowledge (PMBOK® Guide) 2000 Edition
©2000 Project Management Institute, Four Campus Boulevard, Newtown Square, PA 19073-3299 USA